STANLEY COMPLETE

Built-Ins,
Shelves & Bookcases

Meredith® Books
Des Moines, Iowa

Stanley Complete Built-Ins, Shelves & Bookcases
Editor: Larry Johnston
Photo Researcher: Harijs Priekulis
Copy Chief: Terri Fredrickson
Publishing Operations Manager: Karen Schirm
Edit and Design Production Coordinator: Mary Lee Gavin
Editorial and Design Assistants: Renee E. McAtee,
    Kairee Windsor
Marketing Product Managers: Aparna Pande, Isaac Petersen,
    Gina Rickert, Stephen Rogers, Brent Wiersma, Tyler Woods
Book Production Managers: Pam Kvitne,
    Marjorie J. Schenkelberg, Rick von Holdt, Mark Weaver
Contributing Copy Editor: Steve Hallam
Technical Proofreader: Griffin Wall
Contributing Proofreaders: Sara Henderson, Juliet Jacobs,
    Cheri Madison
Indexer: Barbara L. Klein

Abramowitz Design
Publishing Director/Designer: Tim Abramowitz
Designer: Joel Wires
Editor: Catherine M. Staub, Lexicon Consulting
Writer: David Schiff
Photography: Image Studios
    Account Executive: Lisa Egan
    Project Coordinators: Deb Jack, Karla Kaphaem,
    Vicki Sumwalt
    Director of Photography: Bill Rein
    Photographers: Will Croft, Dave Classon, Scott Ehlers,
    Glen Hartjes, Shane Van Boxel, John von Dorn
    Assistants: Mike Clines, Mike Croatt, Max Hermans,
    Bill Kapinski, Roger Wilmers

Meredith® Books
Executive Director, Editorial: Gregory H. Kayko
Executive Director, Design: Matt Strelecki
Executive Editor/Group Manager: Larry Erickson
Senior Associate Design Director: Tom Wegner

Publisher and Editor in Chief: James D. Blume
Editorial Director: Linda Raglan Cunningham
Executive Director, Marketing: Jeffrey B. Myers
Executive Director, New Business Development: Todd M. Davis
Executive Director, Sales: Ken Zagor
Director, Operations: George A. Susral
Director, Production: Douglas M. Johnston
Business Director: Jim Leonard

Vice President and General Manager: Douglas J. Guendel

Meredith Publishing Group
President: Jack Griffin
Senior Vice President: Bob Mate

Meredith Corporation
Chairman and Chief Executive Officer: William T. Kerr
President and Chief Operating Officer: Stephen M. Lacy

In Memoriam: E.T. Meredith III (1933-2003)

All of us at Meredith® Books are dedicated to providing you with the information and ideas you need to enhance your home and garden. We welcome your comments and suggestions about this book. Write to us at:
    Meredith Corporation
    Meredith Books
    1716 Locust St.
    Des Moines, IA 50309-3023

If you would like more information on other Stanley products, call 1-800-STANLEY or visit us at: www.stanleyworks.com Stanley® and the notched rectangle around the Stanley name are registered trademarks of The Stanley Works and subsidiaries.

If you would like to purchase any of our home improvement, cooking, crafts, gardening, or home decorating and design books, check wherever quality books are sold. Or visit us at: meredithbooks.com

CONTENTS

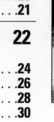

PROJECTS TO MEET YOUR NEEDS

Homes seldom come equipped with adequate display or storage space. That's why bookcases and shelves are at the top of almost every home furnishing list.

You can easily find ready-made pieces. The trouble is, if they're well-made, they're usually expensive. Or if they're low-cost, they're probably not sturdy and durable. Ready-to-assemble furniture is another option, but it's difficult to find a bookcase or shelf that exactly meets your needs, fits your space and your home style, and still fits your budget.

Building your own bookcase or shelving is usually the best solution. And it isn't difficult; if you've done home repairs or some remodeling, you've likely developed some of the woodworking skills to build your own pieces. You can easily develop the rest as you begin building. Along the way, you'll gain confidence and learn a new craft. Even more, you'll feel the satisfaction of doing the project yourself.

Before you get started, though, some planning is necessary.

Prime considerations

Here are some questions to consider about adding bookcases or shelves:
- What is the main purpose of the piece?
- What will best meet that purpose, a bookcase or simple shelving? A quick-to-build, low-cost utility piece or one of furniture quality?
- Where will it go?
- What size and style do you want?
- What material will work best?
- Should it be painted or naturally finished?

Other factors also influence your final decision on what to build.

Work space: With a basement, garage, or spare room available as a workshop, you can build large projects. A smaller space limits you to smaller projects or those that can be constructed as subassemblies or from precut parts.

Do-it-yourself skills: If you're new to woodworking, start with simpler projects, then move on to larger, more involved ones. All the skills you need to build the projects in this book are described with clear, step-by-step instructions. Stanley Pro Tips offer additional advice to help you work faster and easier. Use the right tool, in the right way, for the right job. And above all, work safely.

Budget: Buying tools adds to the project's cost, but the tools become an investment that can save time and money on future projects and repairs.

Time: It doesn't pay to rush. If you're pressed for time, build your projects in stages. The Prestart Checklist provided with each project gives you a clear idea of the time, as well as the skills and tools, needed to complete it. A complete bill of materials also accompanies each project.

CHAPTER PREVIEW

Learn new skills and have the satisfaction of doing it yourself as you add new storage space for your home.

Display your work
page 6

Create storage and seating
page 8

Build a sunny retreat
page 10

Build fireside bookcases
page 12

There's nothing as satisfying as building exactly what you need, exactly the way you want it to look. And shelves and bookcases, are not as difficult to make as you may think.

Craft custom storage pieces

Project gallery

Design standards

Customizing projects

DISPLAY YOUR WORK

Display shelves are a great first project for the novice woodworker. The basic construction is simple—you can either use brackets as shown in the project beginning on page 76, or you can make floating shelves like the project beginning on page 80.

Once you choose an attachment technique, you can get creative. Achieve the warm country look of simple pine shelves or the bold look of painted floating shelves; then, embellish the shelves with some fancy jigsaw work.

Each of these bold black display shelves is thicker than the one below— a nice design touch. The backs are hollow and fit snugly over full-length horizontal cleats that are firmly lag-bolted to the wall studs. Screws are driven through the top of the shelves into the cleats.

Your local home center has everything you need to achieve the custom country look of these cheery shelves. Choose wooden brackets and a molding you like for the pine shelves. Attach the shelves to the brackets, the brackets to the wall, and fit cleats between the brackets.

The square shelves are simply four boards glued and nailed together. This simple construction provides a place for creative jigsaw work. Draw and cut your design on one board, then use that board to lay out the design on the other three. The display shelf is a variation on the design you'll find on page 76.

Display shelves can be decorative and functional. This trio of shelves fits into a corner—a space that's often difficult to use—and shows off a dish collection. For more corner display space, you could add glazed doors to the corner linen cabinet on page 228 to create a corner china cabinet.

Shelving units can be mounted on the wall, providing handy storage over a desk as shown here or a bench as shown in the project beginning on page 110. Shelves like this require strong attachment. Use ¾-inch plywood for the back, or, if the back is ¼-inch plywood, reinforce it with a ¾-inch-thick cleat under the top shelf. Drive #8 flathead wood screws into the studs.

CREATE STORAGE AND SEATING

The only way to create bookcases that truly fit your space and décor is to build them yourself. Building your own can also help stretch your furniture budget further. Fortunately bookcases are easy to build, even for a novice woodworker, and you'll get a lot of satisfaction from constructing them yourself.

Ready for something a bit more challenging? Try your hand at crafting a kitchen bench. It's not a huge skill leap—there are just a few angled cuts added.

Here's the basic box in basic black. Build modular units as described beginning on page 190. You can make flat doors as in the modular project. Or make frame-and-panel doors like those shown here by adapting the door design from the corner linen closet project beginning on page 228.

Here's an example of how you can apply the modular idea to bookcases. Following the directions beginning on page 138, build as many bookcase units as you need, and then tie them together with molding at the top and bottom.

Your built-in storage units don't always have to match other elements in the room. Units that complement each other can be much more interesting, such as this low white CD shelving and natural wood, glass-front cabinet.

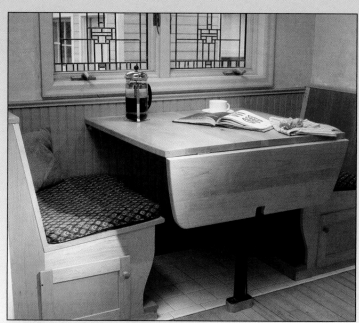

The kitchen bench project beginning on page 218 has a box built into its side for cookbooks. You can easily add a door as shown here. If you want to cut gracefully shaped side pieces, recess the front of the bench and cover the front edges of the side with edge banding veneer (page 44).

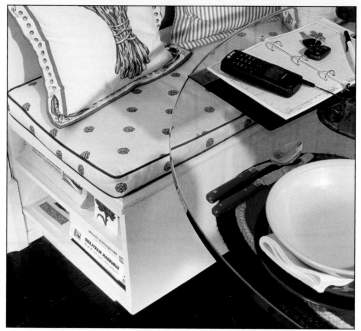

The open shelves in this banquette seat provide kitchen storage that's close at hand, with two shelves tucked snugly under the seat. Depending on the height of the seat you build, the space beneath could hold standing books or have a shelf as shown.

Even if your vision is beyond your skills, you can save money by doing some of the work yourself. For example, you could build the box for this banquette using techniques from the window bench project beginning on page 162. Order the doors to size at a cabinet shop or make simpler ones like those on the modular cabinets (page 190).

BUILD A SUNNY RETREAT

Window seats can be a cozy addition to a kitchen, bedroom, living room, dining room—almost any room in your home—or even a hallway at the top of the stairs.

Wherever there is a beautiful view, or a sunny window, consider a window seat. You may already have a nook with a window that cries out for a seat. Or if you are

surrounding a window with built-in bookcases, a window seat can be the perfect way to use the space under the window while tying together the bookcase units.

The window storage bench project beginning on page 162 shows how to build a window seat with a top that opens for storage. If there's a cast-iron radiator under the window, you can still build the seat by replacing the plywood panels with a radiator grill as shown here. The grill, available at hardware stores, is easy to cut and paint. The lid is still practical; it allows access to the radiator.

This decorative cover is another solution to building a window seat over a radiator. The legs recall classical architectural details. By changing the leg style, a similar bench could fit into any room design scheme. Add pillows to the cover to use it as a space to relax or, as pictured here, utilize it as additional shelving for ornamental plants and show pieces.

It's the little details that give your projects a truly professional built-in look. Notice how the lip at the top of this window seat continues around the bookcase, gracefully tying the two units together.

A window seat flanked by a recessed shelving unit are two built-in projects that naturally go together. You'll find plans for a window bench beginning on page 162 and a recessed shelving project beginning on page 176.

When designing built-ins, think about how the room is composed. In this room, the massive, handsome fireplace is the centerpiece. Notice how the white beaded board wainscoting around the window seat to the left of the fireplace complements the white cabinets to the right.

BUILD FIRESIDE BOOKCASES

In the days before central heating, bookshelves next to the fireplace were a common feature in the great rooms of the finest homes. Today this combination still evokes a traditional elegance. And while we can be warm anywhere in the house, there's still a lot of pleasure in curling up with a book by the fireplace on a cold winter's evening.

Fireplaces normally protrude into the room, so they often form a natural nook to each side. So all you'll need are shelves supported by cleats attached to the walls. Another fireside bookcase idea is shown in the project beginning on page 180.

Here's a variation on the fireside bookcase project you'll find beginning on page 180. This one carries the idea a step further, using the mantel and a matching long shelf above to tie together the flanking bookcases.

This fireside built-in shows how you can combine construction techniques to customize your project. The base cabinet has a plywood top edged with solid wood while the bookcase employs adjustable shelves supported by shelf pins—techniques you'll find in the adjustable-shelf bookcase beginning on page 130. The full overlay doors use European-style hinges like the modular built-ins beginning on page 190.

Sometimes little touches that add nothing to the cost or building time can really make a project distinctive. These fireside bookcases use beaded plywood instead of plain plywood for the backs, enhancing the cottage motif of this warm and sunny room.

Less can be more. The drama in this room comes from the soaring ceiling that's enhanced by the rustic vertical-board walls. The understated bookcases consist of simple shelves supported by cleats attached to side boards. There's no back to interrupt the vertical-board wall.

The mantel in this room needed repair, so the owners took the opportunity to integrate the mantel with flanking bookcases. The beautiful brickwork called for a simple mantel—just plywood faced with poplar. The bookcases use adjustable shelf pins like those in the project beginning on page 130.

CRAFT CUSTOM STORAGE PIECES

You simply can't have too many shelves. There's rough-and-ready utility shelving for the garage (page 96) or basement (page 170). There's elegant shelving in the living room and shelving designed to organize our closets. Appealing low shelves in children's rooms offer hope they may actually pick up their toys and books.

In addition to specific projects, you'll find lots of ideas and techniques throughout this book to help you design shelves to fit your needs. Be sure to check out the design tips on page 20.

Modern materials make elegant simplicity easy to achieve. These shelves consist of ¾-inch birch plywood assembled with dadoes and faced with birch veneer edge banding. (Birch has a smooth grain that takes paint well.) You'll see the same construction techniques used to build the shelves in the project beginning on page 200.

An attic's low ceiling creates the perfect child-scale play nook. The shelves, made of 5/4×6 pine (see page 34) are quite simple. Just screw cleats through the wall into studs and into uprights that will hold shelves. For lightweight items on 5/4 shelves, provide vertical support at least every 5 feet. Use a sliding bevel square to measure the roof angle, then transfer it to the shelf ends.

Your first inclination may be to build shelves all the way to the ceiling. But that's not a good idea if top shelves will become an out-of-reach space where dust and cobwebs will accumulate. Here the shelves meet a drywall-covered soffit that neatly frames the window.

The empty niches at both sides of this fireplace were perfect for this simple elegant shelving. The ³⁄₄-inch-thick birch plywood shelves are supported by ³⁄₄-inch-square cleats and faced with 1×2 poplar. Birch and poplar look great when painted.

Hiding the TV behind the doors of a built-in cabinet preserves the character of this room. A track allows the doors to roll back into the cabinet so they are concealed when the TV is in use.

Custom touches are a snap when you build it yourself. This fireplace shelving features two shadowboxes for displaying a clock collection. The dividers are two pieces of ¹⁄₂-inch-thick plywood. Each piece has a center slot cut halfway through its width so the two pieces interlock.

The beautiful, arching lines of this built-in provide a seamless integration with the design of the fireplace nearby. Careful planning went into this project resulting in a built-in with the perfect blend of display space and storage.

PROJECT GALLERY

To help you get started building your own projects, *Stanley Complete Built-Ins, Shelves, and Bookcases* features 21 projects, each with complete step-by-step instructions. Each project offers several options, so you can create a piece suited to your needs and style. For example, you'll find instructions on how to change the dimensions of a piece and how to add a decorative treatment. Remember, too, that you can use different woods and finishes.

"Easy, Great-Looking Shelves You Can Build," beginning on page 74, shows you how to build seven projects, including display shelves, expandable utility shelving, stackable modular boxes, and a multipurpose stand. The chapter on bookcase projects (page 122) shows how to build five styles of bookcases. "Built-In Storage," starting on page 160, has complete instructions for nine storage projects, ranging from a window seat to a corner linen cabinet.

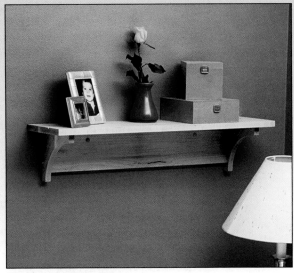

Display shelf (page 76).

Floating shelves (page 80).

Modular boxes (page 84).

Mission-style utility stand (page 88).

Utility shelves (page 96).

Desk hutch shelves (page 102).

Entry shelf and bench with shelves (page 110).

Fixed-shelf bookcase (page 124).

Adjustable-shelf bookcase (page 130).

Built-in bookcase (page 138).

Children's book rack (page 148).

Ladder bookcase (page 154).

Built-in window seat (page 162).

Basement under-stair storage shelves (page 170).

Recessed built-in shelves (page 176).

Built-in fireside bookcase (page 180).

Modular, contemporary built-ins (page 190).

Cabinets with cushions or shelves (page 200).

Closet organizer (page 212).

Built-in kitchen bench (page 218).

Corner linen cabinet (page 228).

DESIGN STANDARDS

The principal advantage to building something yourself is making it to best suit your needs or lifestyle. Few woodworkers can resist the temptation to alter the plan they begin with. However, shelves and bookcases need to be built according to a few basic design guidelines to ensure that your piece will be functional as well as good-looking.

If all books were the same size and shape, bookcase and shelf planning would be simple. But that's not the case. For attractiveness as well as stability, the size and spacing of shelves depend on what you'll put on them. Books vary greatly in size (see *below),* and if you want to have entertainment equipment in the same unit, you'll need shelves from 18 to 20 inches deep (for most systems) and spacing between shelves customized to fit your stereo, speakers, and accessories.

Shelving units that accommodate both books and audiovisual equipment are often built as modular components. A deeper unit holds the large equipment, and side or top units provide book or display storage.

Know the no-sag limits

You also must consider the shelving material's span limit—how far an unsupported shelf will span under load without sagging or breaking (page 39). Solid hardwood boards of ¾-inch thickness, for instance, span a greater distance than particleboard of the same thickness.

Keep it within reach

Design shelves with their users in mind. As shown *below,* men generally have a greater maximum reach than women, and teens can reach higher than children. While that may seem obvious, building shelves that no one can access is a waste of time and materials. Likewise, shelves shouldn't be too low to be used easily.

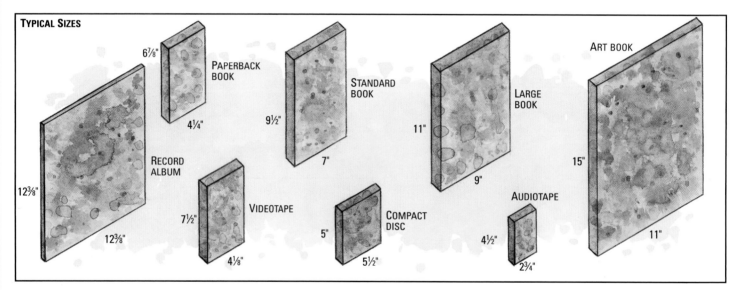

TYPICAL SIZES

- Record Album — 12⅜" × 12⅜"
- Paperback Book — 6⅞" × 4¼"
- Standard Book — 9½" × 7"
- Large Book — 11" × 9"
- Art Book — 15" × 11"
- Videotape — 7½" × 4⅛"
- Compact Disc — 5" × 5½"
- Audiotape — 4½" × 2¾"

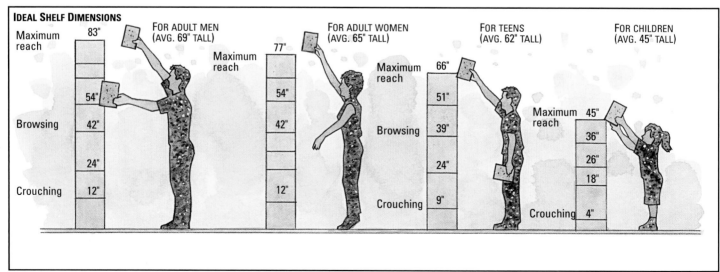

IDEAL SHELF DIMENSIONS

FOR ADULT MEN (AVG. 69" TALL) — Maximum reach 83", 54", Browsing 42", 24", Crouching 12"

FOR ADULT WOMEN (AVG. 65" TALL) — Maximum reach 77", 54", 42", 24", Crouching 12"

FOR TEENS (AVG. 62" TALL) — Maximum reach 66", 51", Browsing 39", 24", Crouching 9"

FOR CHILDREN (AVG. 45" TALL) — Maximum reach 45", 36", 26", 18", Crouching 4"

CUSTOMIZING PROJECTS

As you review the projects in this book, remember that you can change the dimensions of most of them. (The modular boxes, however, were designed to get the most from a 4×8 sheet of plywood.)

Changing the size of one component sometimes requires a change in another. For example, if you want to put deeper shelves in a bookcase, you will also have to widen the sides of the unit, so you'll have to buy wider stock.

You should be able to make changes in height easily unless the project plan includes a back. Then you'll need enough stock for the larger back. Carefully think through any changes and plan for them. Draw and label your plans carefully. If possible, have an experienced woodworker check your plans and dimensions. You will also find help at your local lumberyard or home center.

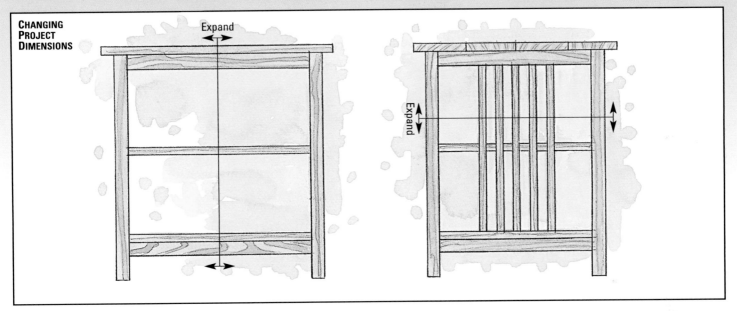

CHANGING PROJECT DIMENSIONS

Expand

Expand

Accessible to all

Special circumstances sometimes require altering or adapting standard dimensions. In a home designed for the elderly, for instance, the highest functional shelf should be lowered 3 inches from the standard 68 inches. The lowest drawer or shelf should be moved up 3 inches. A lower work surface or tabletop is also called for. It should be about 1½ inches lower than the normal 35 inches.

The physically disabled and those who work from a wheelchair also have special needs. For them, a tabletop or work surface should be no higher than 31 inches from the floor. To accommodate a wheelchair under a table, a free space 30 inches wide by 29½ inches deep must be provided. This allows for 24 inches of forward reach. Shelf height should also be taken into consideration so most frequently used items are within reach. For more information on space allowances and reach ranges, write to the U.S. Department of Justice, 950 Pennsylvania Ave. NW, Disability Rights Section—NYAVE, Washington, DC 20530; or go to the Americans with Disabilities Act (ADA) website at www.usdoj.gov/crt/ada/.

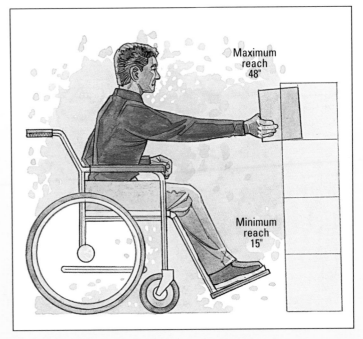

Maximum reach 48"

Minimum reach 15"

CHOOSING TOOLS

You don't need a workshop full of expensive tools to build top-quality bookcases and shelves. You can avoid the cost of some tools by having wood and sheet goods cut to size when you purchase them. Most lumberyards and home centers will cut or plane material for you. You'll pay extra for this service, but it's less expensive than buying a planer or tablesaw.

You probably already have some of the basic tools described on pages 24 and 25. Quality is important, though, so if you're starting your first serious woodworking project, you may need to upgrade. Each new project may call for the purchase of a specific tool. Budget that cost along with the materials and consider it an investment in future projects.

Shop smart
Many tool manufacturers produce two product lines: inexpensive homeowner tools and more costly, heavier-duty tools for professional use. Examine top-of-the-line tools and you'll quickly see the difference between them and the ones made cheaply. A good hammer, for instance, will have a drop-forged and heat-tempered steel head; the handle will be ash, hickory, or fiberglass; or it will be one-piece, all-steel construction.

The metal on all hand tools should be flawlessly machined; handles should be tight-fitting and hefty. When purchasing hand tools, buy the best you can afford, and consider the relatively few dollars more that you will pay to be an investment in your future satisfaction, safety, and productivity.

When shopping for power tools, on the other hand, don't buy more features than you need. Professional power tools can cost many times more than their hobbyist cousins. Capacity and durability are worth the money to professionals who use power tools all day, every day, but for most do-it-yourselfers, a 12-volt cordless drill is just as useful as an 18-volt one.

You can tell a lot about a tool's quality by how it is built. A well-made, precisely assembled housing usually suggests carefully made inner workings. Make sure steel or aluminum parts are smoothly finished, triggers and controls are user-friendly, and electrical cords are sturdy. Compare portable power tools by their amperage ratings rather than their horsepower; the more current (amperage) the tool uses, the more power it delivers.

Buy the best hand tools you can afford and power tools that meet your needs.

CHAPTER PREVIEW

Basic tools
page 24

Power tools
page 26

Stationary power tools
page 28

Accessories
page 30

You don't need a warehouse full of the latest, most expensive tools to build shelves and bookcases. A few high-quality power tools and their accessories will speed your work and ensure excellent results. Here, a layout square is being used as a guide to cut a shelf board at a precise 90-degree angle with a circular saw.

SAFETY FIRST

Always wear eye and ear protection when working with power tools.
  Use clamps to hold work materials securely to sawhorses, bench, or table.

BASIC TOOLS

The tools on these two pages are essential for most projects. You won't need all of them to begin woodworking, but you will find all of them useful by the time you've completed several projects.

Tools for cutting and shaping

A **crosscut saw** cuts wood across the grain (rip saws have special teeth to cut with the grain). A **backsaw** creates a finer, more accurate cut and is typically used with a **miter box** to cut accurate angles. The thin, narrow blade of a **coping saw** follows tight curves. Look for saws with solid wood handles, which are more comfortable and sturdy than hollow plastic ones. A **jack plane** smooths and squares the long sides of larger pieces of wood, while a **block plane** shaves their ends and angles. **Wood chisels** pare away material and cut recesses. A **rasp** and a **Surform plane** quickly remove wood. When buying these cutting tools, look for precision machining.

A **sanding block** holds sandpaper flat and firmly as you smooth wood. For trimming small pieces, a **utility knife** is handy.

Tools for joining wood pieces

A 7-ounce **finishing hammer** drives brads and small nails. A **nail set** pushes a nailhead below the wood's surface. Use a **dead-blow hammer** to tap wood pieces into place without marring. For screws, you'll need **phillips** and **standard screwdrivers** in several sizes.

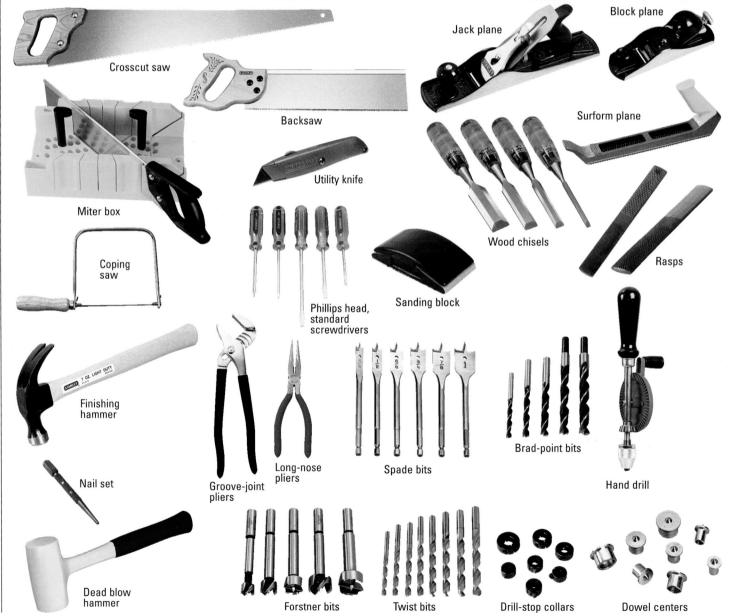

Crosscut saw

Backsaw

Jack plane

Block plane

Surform plane

Miter box

Utility knife

Wood chisels

Rasps

Coping saw

Phillips head, standard screwdrivers

Sanding block

Finishing hammer

Long-nose pliers

Spade bits

Brad-point bits

Hand drill

Nail set

Groove-joint pliers

Dead blow hammer

Forstner bits

Twist bits

Drill-stop collars

Dowel centers

Use a **hand drill** and **twist bits** or **brad-point bits** to make pilot holes for screws. Turn to **Forstner bits** for clean-sided, flat-bottomed holes or **spade bits** for rougher cut ones. **Drill-stop collars** control hole depth. **Dowel centers** help correctly align holes when making dowel joints.

C-clamps and adjustable **pipe clamps** or **bar clamps** hold work securely during gluing or machining. **Quick clamps** are easy to tighten with one hand. A **miter clamp** holds pieces at a precise 90-degree angle.

Tools for measuring and marking
A 12-foot **steel tape measure** is handy for making large measurements accurately and conveniently. The best ones have wide, tempered-steel blades with large high-visibility numbering. A **framing square** is handy for checking right angles and laying out 90-degree lines; choose one that has the gradations stamped into the metal, rather than simply painted on. A **layout square** quickly lays out angles up to 90 degrees.

A **combination square** lays out 45- and 90-degree angles, and its blade slides for adjustment. For checking 90-degree angles, use a **try square**. To measure odd angles and transfer them for duplication, use a **sliding bevel gauge**. Scribe lines parallel to an edge with or mark several pieces the same distance from an edge with a **marking gauge**. A **compass** draws circles. Mark layout lines with a **mechanical pencil**.

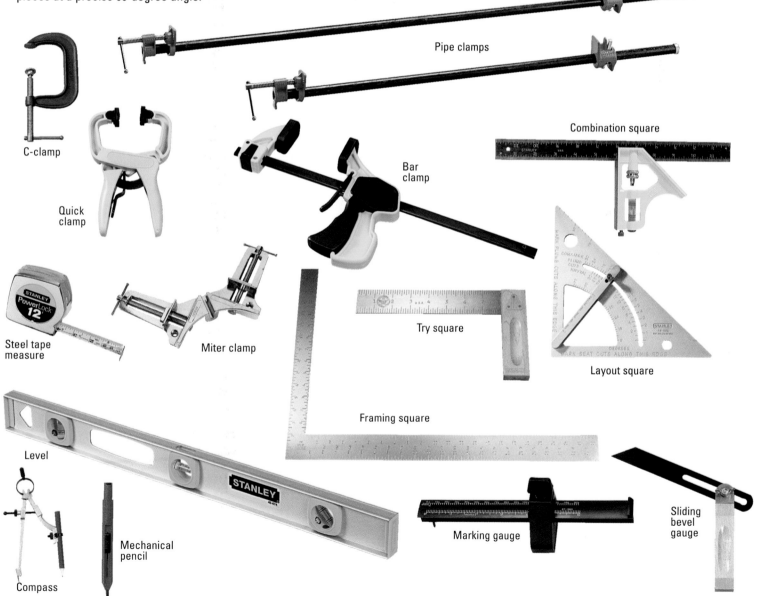

Pipe clamps

C-clamp

Quick clamp

Bar clamp

Combination square

Steel tape measure

Miter clamp

Try square

Layout square

Framing square

Level

Mechanical pencil

Compass

Marking gauge

Sliding bevel gauge

POWER TOOLS

Portable power tools do basically the same jobs as their hand-tool counterparts, but they do them faster and usually more accurately. For accuracy, power, and durability, buy a name-brand, high-quality model rather than a discount, hobbyist one.

Speedy sawing

One of the handiest tools you can own is a portable **circular saw,** which cuts lumber as well as plywood, with and across the grain. The gear-driven blades come in diameter sizes from 4 to 10 inches. The 7¼-inch size offers many blade options and is the most useful for do-it-yourself work. The better saws have ball bearings rather than sleeve bearings and an arbor lock that holds the blade while you loosen it.

A **jigsaw** (also called a saber saw) cuts circles and curves as well as straight lines. A variety of blade types allows you to cut materials other than wood, such as metal and plastic. Variable speed control adds versatility; an orbiting feature helps with complicated scrolling but is less steady when making straight cuts.

Smooth sanding

The **belt sander's** abrasive belt moves across a flat bed to remove wood quickly. Choose a sander with at least a 21-inch belt and a width you feel comfortable with—the wider the belt, the heavier the sander.

Orbital finishing sanders use an oscillating motion to move a piece of sandpaper in tiny circles over the wood. The ¼-sheet size, called a **palm sander,** is popular. A **detail sander** allows you to smooth hard-to-reach areas, such as inside corners. A **random-orbit sander** uses a round abrasive disk that moves in a random pattern to remove stock faster than hand sanding and minimize scratch marks. Models take 5- to 12-inch-diameter disks that attach with adhesive or

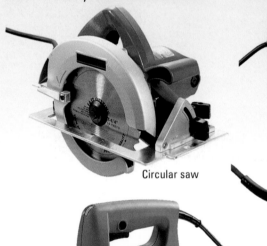
Circular saw

Belt sander

Palm sander

Detail sander

Random-orbit sander

Jigsaw

Keep these three blades handy

Portable circular saws usually come equipped with a general-purpose blade that works well for most crosscutting and limited ripping. Add a 150-tooth hollow-ground plywood blade for smooth cuts in plywood panels, and a 24- to 30-tooth rip blade for making efficient cuts with the grain, and you'll be well-equipped.

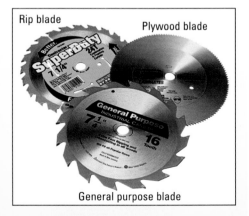
Rip blade
Plywood blade
General purpose blade

hook-and-loop fasteners. A good choice is a 5- or 6-inch-diameter model with a connection for dust collection.

Easy edging

A **router** uses various spinning bits to shape board edges, cut grooves and slots (called dadoes and rabbets), create profile moldings, and much more. Available in horsepower ratings from less than one to three, routers have either a fixed base or are the plunge type (the housing slides up and down for starting and stopping cuts in the middle of a board). Bits come with $\frac{1}{4}$- or $\frac{1}{2}$-inch-diameter shanks, the thicker being sturdier. Variable speed control isn't essential, but it can come in handy.

Versatile drilling

For drilling holes in wood and other materials, there's nothing handier than a **portable electric drill.** You'll find many types and styles, ranging from small cordless drill/screwdrivers to heavy-duty borers with a jackhammer action for tackling concrete. Most models can turn in reverse to withdraw screws, and many have torque control clutches that prevent the stripping of screw heads. Cordless models use rechargeable battery packs (up to 24 volts), which add to their convenience and versatility, but add weight.

Electric drills are sold in $\frac{1}{4}$-, $\frac{3}{8}$-, and $\frac{1}{2}$-inch chuck sizes. A $\frac{3}{8}$-inch variable speed reversing (VSR) cordless model with torque control is a workhorse tool for the home woodworker, combining high power with moderate price and weight.

Quick cleanup

The **shop vacuum** is indispensable for maintaining a tidy shop or work space. The largest ones hold about 28 gallons of debris; the smallest, under 5 gallons. Most vacuums handle both dry and wet material; most can connect to power tools to collect dust at the source. Look for a model with high suction, a large-diameter hose that resists clogging, and a low noise level—a noisy vacuum is not necessarily more powerful.

Portable drill

Router

Shop vacuum

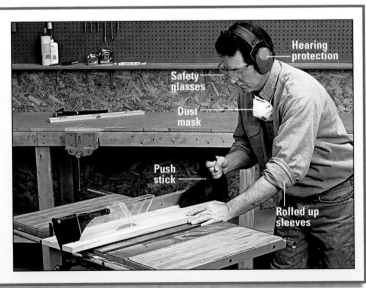

STATIONARY POWER TOOLS

Serious amateur woodworkers rely on stationary power tools for more complicated and larger projects. These tools allow you to work faster and more accurately, but they also cost more money and take up more room. A good compromise is high-quality, bench-top power tools. They perform nearly as well as full-size stationary models but take up less space when in use and can be stored out of the way when not in use.

A **10-inch tablesaw** (blade size) cuts more accurately and has more accessories than a portable circular saw. A contractor-style tablesaw (with open legs) is usually the first large power tool a woodworker purchases—and the one likely to be used most often. A **compound mitersaw** cuts angled pieces and makes crosscuts with precision. A mitersaw with a 10-inch blade has adequate cutting capacity for most jobs.

A **bandsaw** uses a thin loop blade to make curved cuts, such as circles and arcs. With a fence, it will also make straight cuts.

A **router table** provides a router with stability and versatility. **Drill presses** improve boring accuracy, and attachments are available for sanding and doing other tasks. A **planer** smooths the wide surfaces of rough-cut boards. A **jointer** straightens and smooths the edges of cut boards (especially useful when joining pieces) and will surface narrow boards.

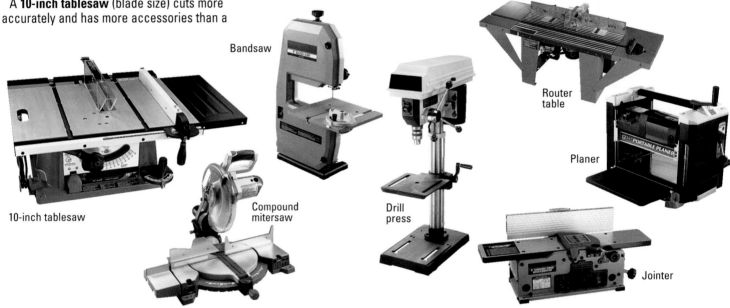

Bandsaw

Router table

Planer

10-inch tablesaw

Compound mitersaw

Drill press

Jointer

CLEAN CUTS
Choose the right blade for the job

The most important part of a tablesaw is its blade. Carbide-tipped blades are best, and they fall into four basic tooth configurations: flat top (FT), alternate top bevel (ATB), alternate top bevel and raker (ATB&R), and triple chip (TC). These types of carbide blades normally make a cut, called a kerf, about ⅛-inch wide. To minimize waste when sawing expensive woods, buy thin-kerf blades, which make a cut about half as wide. Their thinner teeth won't allow as many sharpenings as a regular blade, though, so don't use them for general sawing.

Flat-top blades with 24 teeth make fast, heavy-duty rip-cuts. ATB blades with 40 teeth give a smooth cut in plywood. ATB&R blades (called combination blades) cut with and across

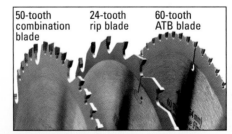

50-tooth combination blade   24-tooth rip blade   60-tooth ATB blade

the grain smoothly. Triple-chip blades tackle materials such as plastic laminate. With all blades, the more teeth, the smoother the cut.

The following three blades will cover most home woodworking tasks: a 50-tooth ATB&R or 40-tooth ATB; a 24-tooth FT rip blade; and a 60- to 80-tooth ATB blade.

Dado blades and **sets** allow you to make a

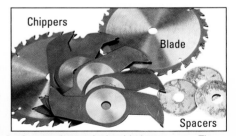

Chippers   Blade   Spacers

kerf up to about 1 inch wide in one pass. The sets include blades, which make the outside of the cut, and chippers, which remove material between the blades. Dado sets are expensive but leave a smoother kerf than a single adjustable dado blade, which wobbles at an angle to make a wide cut.

SET UP SHOP
Make the most of your workspace

No matter what the size and shape of your workspace, there are some planning points that you can follow to create a successful layout.

■ Divide the space into several machining areas. Identify all the steps you go through to make a project, then establish workstations near each power tool associated with them.

■ Plan for flexibility and mobility. Center a tablesaw at an angle in the shop to provide space for ripping long stock and sheet goods. Place it and other large tools on mobile bases so they can be easily moved as necessary.

■ Allow for moving materials and projects in and out. Don't block doorways with hard-to-move tools.

■ Leave adequate space between equipment. You'll need at least 30 inches between benches and stationary tools, and 20 inches for walkways.

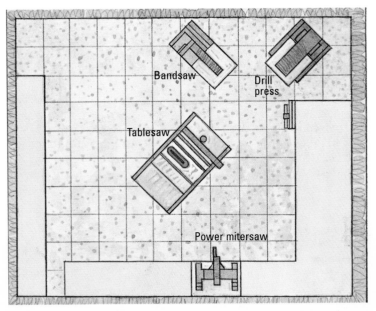

Typical basement plan: With mobile bases under the bandsaw, drill press, and tablesaw, you can move them as needed for work or storage.

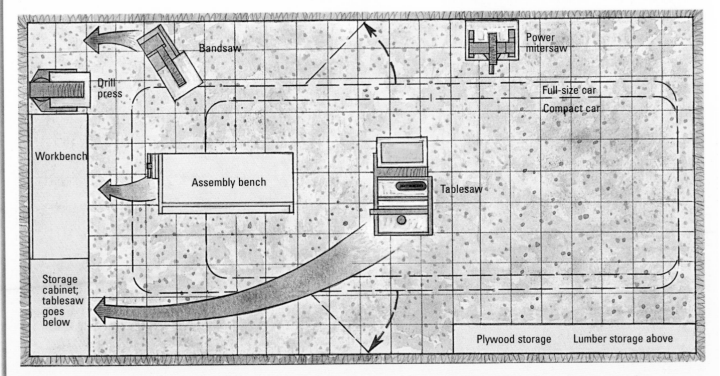

The garage shop: In either a single-car garage or half of a double one, you want to be able to roll out the machines when you need them and store them against the wall to make room for a car when they're not in use. Mobile bases make it possible.

ACCESSORIES

Power tools alone can do only so much—their accessories expand their capabilities and simplify specific tasks. That's especially true for portable power tools—match them with well-chosen accessories and they'll do many of the same tasks as stationary power tools. While you can buy many accessories at home centers, woodworking supply stores, or through mail-order, you can also make many of them yourself.

Home-built accessories that hold or guide a tool to perform specific jobs quickly or accurately are called jigs. See the example at the bottom of the *opposite page.*

One of the handiest accessories you can build is a reliable straightedge. Using the one shown at *right,* you'll be able to accurately rip large sheets of plywood with a portable circular saw. Make another straightedge to serve as a guide for cutting dadoes, grooves, and rabbets with your router. With straightedges like these, you can quickly saw or rout precise cuts.

Building a straightedge

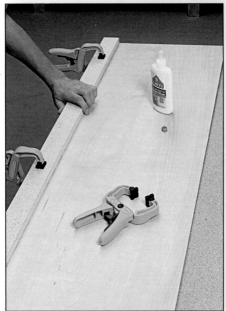

1 Glue and clamp a 2-inch-wide piece of ½-inch-thick stock to one edge of an equally long piece of ¼-inch plywood that's about 6 inches wider than your saw or router base. Both pieces should be a few inches longer than the longest cut you will make for your projects.

2 When the glue has dried, run the circular saw or the router with a straight-cutting bit along the ½-inch fence to rip the ¼-inch plywood to width. Using this jig guarantees a straight, accurate cut as long as you use the same blade or bit. Write the name of the tool and blade or bit on the jig.

Avoid underlit work, overloaded cords, and wobbly stock

It's difficult—and dangerous—to work in poorly lit areas. Portable, adjustable halogen work lights make sure you can see what you're doing.

To make sure your tools perform at peak power and to avoid dangerously overloaded extension cords, which can cause fires, use at least a 16-gauge extension cord with power tools that draw less than 10 amps, and a 14-gauge cord with ones that draw more current.

A pair of sawhorses become workhorses when working with plywood. You can buy the brackets and make them yourself. A roller stand supports long pieces of material.

Sawhorses

Roller stand

Portable work light

Extension cord

Crosscutting plywood

3 To use the straightedge for crosscutting or ripping stock, draw your cut line with a fine lead pencil. Place the straightedge on top of the good portion of the material and carefully align the edge opposite the fence with the cut line. Secure the straightedge with clamps tightened on top of the fence and the bottom of the piece to be cut (and not impeding the tool's path). Run the saw or router against the fence to make the cut.

To crosscut plywood, support the sheet underneath with a network of 2×4s to hold up the stock on both sides of the cut. Draw your cut line and align the side opposite the fence with it, with the jig over the good portion of the stock. Use clamps on top of the fence at both ends of the straightedge to hold it tightly in place on the plywood. After double-checking alignment and support placement, make the cut.

STANLEY PRO TIP

Build a crosscutting jig for your portable circular saw

This jig makes clean, accurate crosscuts possible. Build the base by screwing and gluing a pair of parallel 1×2s to the top of a piece of 12-inch × 4-foot ¾-inch particleboard. Attach aluminum angle bars at 90 degrees to the 1×2s to serve as saw guide bars. Space them to fit the width of the circular saw's base plate. Adjust the saw blade so it cuts through the 1×2s and makes a slight kerf (cut) in the base.

To use the jig, clamp it to your workbench, slip the board to be cut under the guide bars, hold or clamp it in place, and make the cut. Rub paraffin on the aluminum angle bars to help the saw slide more easily.

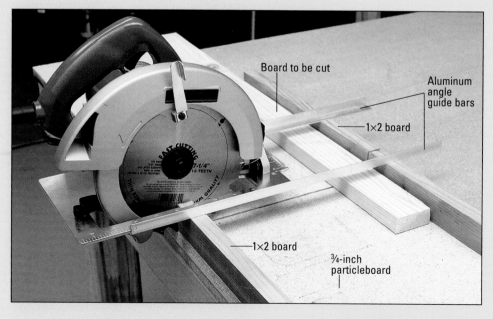

MATERIALS & HARDWARE

You put a lot of craftsmanship and time into your projects, so you want to use the right materials for the job. As with tools, always try to purchase the highest quality material and hardware your budget allows, as appropriate for your project's intended use. For instance, don't waste money buying a fine hardwood, such as cherry, for a utilitarian bookcase that's going to sit in a basement or workshop.

Know your stock
This chapter helps you decide the materials to choose for different purposes. You'll learn the differences between hardwoods and softwoods, when and where to use each type, and how to select them. You'll find out about the special properties of plywood, the many grades and types it comes in, and how to shop for it wisely. This chapter describes and compares other composite sheet goods, such as oriented strand board, particleboard, and fiberboard. It also includes pro tips for how best to use each type of material.

Understand the hardware
Walking the hardware aisles at a large home center can be overwhelming. This chapter will guide you through various types of fasteners.

And fasteners are just one category of hardware. No less puzzling is the variety of hinges, shelf brackets, and other products that help you assemble wood into functional pieces of case furniture and shelving. You'll learn to recognize these as well.

Finish off the project
Finally you'll discover the materials that experts use to give the finishing touches to bookcases and shelves—the magic, easy-to-use product that makes an inexpensive piece of plywood look like a costly solid board, for example. Or how to employ moldings to give simple boxes a degree of finish and flair that makes them a source of pride as well as practical functionality. Many cabinet- and furniture-making solutions are quite simple. This chapter will provide the material know-how you need to get the kinds of results you'll be proud to showcase in your home.

Materials for furniture-quality projects differ from those for carpentry.

CHAPTER PREVIEW

Lumber
page 34

Plywood
page 36

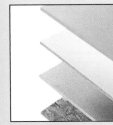

Composites
page 38

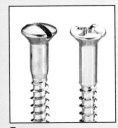

Fasteners
page 40

Selecting the wood and hardware from all that's available is a fun part of woodworking. But you have to prepare yourself to buy the right materials to make your project the best it can be. A little knowledge will help you appreciate and enjoy the craft.

Hardware
page 42

Edge banding
page 44

Molding
page 45

LUMBER

The lumber used to make furniture-quality projects differs in several ways from the dimensional lumber used in building construction. It's drier (less than 9 percent moisture content), has fewer defects (the number depends on the grade), and costs more. The first step to becoming a savvy lumber shopper is to learn the difference between softwoods and hardwoods.

Softwood

Commonly available lumber made from softwood species, such as those shown at *right,* is cut from coniferous evergreen trees, which do not drop their needles each year.

Of the many types of softwoods, the following are easiest to find:

■ **Western red cedar:** Attractive, aromatic, and naturally weather-resistant.
■ **White pine:** Clear boards can be naturally finished. Stains blotch.
■ **Redwood:** Attractive and naturally weather-resistant.
■ **Douglas fir:** Strong and hard.
■ **Spruce:** Inexpensive and paintable.
■ **Northern white cedar:** Light and naturally weather-resistant.

Softwoods are both lighter and softer than hardwoods, making them easier to work with. The best softwood lumber for furniture construction is listed in the chart at the bottom of the *opposite page.*

Redwood and western red cedar lumber are sold a bit differently from other softwoods. They're graded both by appearance and by the amount of decay-resistant heartwood the boards contain—the more, the better. Clear all-heart is the most costly; construction common, the least.

Softwood boards 1 inch thick—the type you'd use for bookcases and shelves—are sold in 2-inch-width increments, such as 1×2, 1×4, and so on up to 1×12. Home centers usually group softwood boards by width and length. The sizes shown are nominal, as explained in the Pro Tip box on the *opposite page.*

You won't want to use boards that display any of the major defects illustrated below,

especially ones that are warped. To check a board for warp, lay it on the floor and see if it lies flat. Also check for knots. Reject boards with loose ones—they'll have a visible dark line around them and will work loose and eventually drop out. Tight knots, on the other hand, are structurally sound but must be coated with a sealer before painting so they don't weep sap and discolor the paint.

Redwood

Northern white cedar

White pine

Douglas fir

Spruce

Western red cedar

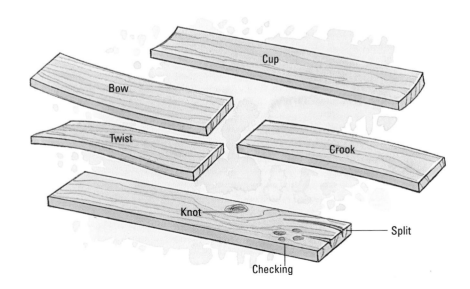

Bow

Cup

Twist

Crook

Knot

Split

Checking

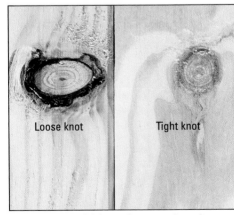

Avoid boards with loose knots such as the one above left. Loose knots often fall out as the wood dries, leaving a hole. Tight knots such as the one above right are acceptable but need sealing.

Hardwood

Produced by broad-leafed, deciduous trees that—in the world's temperate zone—lose their leaves each year, hardwoods are often used for cabinets and furniture because of their beauty, stability, strength, machining predictability, and resistance to abuse. Here are some woodworking favorites:

■ **Red oak:** A classic for furniture and cabinets, it is easy to work.
■ **White ash:** Strong and hard.
■ **Walnut:** Deep color, nice grain.
■ **Yellow poplar:** Fairly strong but plain. Best for painting; will stain to mimic cherry or walnut.
■ **Cherry:** Hard, strong, and beautiful.
■ **Philippine mahogany:** Imported and hard to find but easy to work and stain to imitate real mahogany.

Hardwood trees are not as abundant as softwood trees in North America, so their lumber is more valuable. That's also why hardwood logs are sawed to minimize waste, resulting in boards of varying quality. Because of that, hardwood boards are assigned grades, as listed in the chart *below*. The higher, costlier grades yield more defect-free (clear) material.

There's also a major difference in the way hardwoods are sold. You buy them by the board foot. That's a volume measurement of thickness, width, and length that equals 144 cubic inches. A board measuring 1×12×12 inches equals one board foot. You seldom have to do those calculations because most retail hardwood outlets, including home centers, have already done so before pricing their boards. Board footage is usually rounded up or down to the nearest one-half board foot.

Woodworkers usually refer to hardwood board thickness in ¼-inch increments. A 1-inch-thick board is 4/4 (four-quarter); a 1¼-inch-thick one, 5/4 (five-quarter); a 2-inch one, 8/4; and so on.

Hardwoods (and the best softwood grades) are also kiln-dried at a controlled temperature to reduce their moisture content to 6 to 9 percent, the ideal range for interior projects. Kiln-dried lumber won't readily reabsorb moisture when properly coated with a finish. That means it will remain stable in use and will be less likely to swell, shrink, crack, or warp over time.

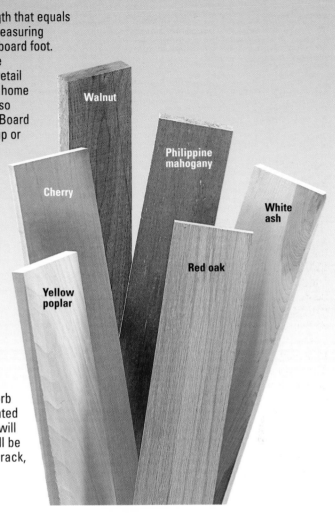

Walnut

Philippine mahogany

Cherry

White ash

Red oak

Yellow poplar

LUMBER GRADES

Here's what the grades of hardwood and softwood lumber mean:

HARDWOODS	
First and seconds (FAS)	Best grade. Boards yield 83⅓ percent clear wood.
Selects	One side FAS, other No. 1 common. Same yield as FAS on one side.
No. 1 common	Economical. Boards yield 66⅔ percent clear cuttings on one side.
SOFTWOODS	
C select & better	Minor imperfections.
D select	A few sound defects.
3rd clear	Well-placed knots allow for clear cuttings.
No. 1 shop	More knots and fewer clear cuts than 3rd clear.
No. 2, No. 3 common	Utility shelving grades. No. 2 has fewer and smaller knots.

Know what you're paying for

With hardwoods, you pay for a board's full thickness, but you actually get less because of planing. A rough board that's 1 inch thick measures ¹³⁄₁₆ inch after surfacing two sides (S2S).

Softwoods follow this measuring system as well. Keep in mind that due to milling, a nominal size 1×2 board is ¾×1½ inches in actual size; a 1×4 is ¾×3½ inches; a 1×6 equals ¾×5½ inches; and a 2×4 measures 1½×3½ inches.

PLYWOOD

G luing thin pieces of wood together to form a thicker one was used by ancient Egyptians, but plywood as we know it was born in the 20th century.

A 4×8-foot sheet of plywood is typically made up of an uneven number of thin wood layers, or plies, glued together with their grain running at right angles to one another. This cross-banded construction gives plywood great strength in all directions. It also results in extra dimensional stability— plywood doesn't swell or crack like solid sawed lumber. Plywood also has another big advantage: It's available in panels wider than natural boards and in thicknesses ranging from ⅛ to 1¼ inches in ⅛-inch increments.

Two types of **softwood plywood** are manufactured: interior, which is assembled with moisture-resistant glue; and exterior, which is made with 100 percent waterproof glue. All softwood plywood is sold by appearance grades using letter designations, with A being the highest quality. The two sides may carry different grades, such as A-C plywood.

Hardwood plywood differs from the softwood variety in that its face and back veneers are of a hardwood species such as red oak or maple. It is also assembled to best display grain (see chart, *opposite page*) and is strictly for interior use.

Softwood plywood

At a glance, you can tell the difference between the better grade A plywood panel at left and the less costly lower B grade at the right.

Get plywood edges smooth and paintable

Softwood plywood usually gets a coat of paint, but glued-up plies showing on the edges pose a problem because they're rough and often have gaps. You can apply wood putty as filler, but it requires heavy sanding. Exterior patching compound is cheaper, dries more quickly, sands easier, and works just as well.

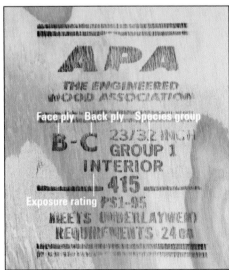

Face ply   Back ply   Species group

B-C   23/32 INCH
GROUP 1
INTERIOR
415

Exposure rating P51-95
MEETS UNDERLAYMENT
REQUIREMENTS 24 oc

Grade stamps on plywood tell you the quality of face and back plies (letters A through D) and its exposure rating.

Gaps in edge

Plug

The defects on softwood plywood include football-shaped plugs where knots were removed and filled and gaps between plies.

Hardwood plywood

Hardwood plywood graded A-Premium is the most costly and attractive. The sheet top left is oak veneer; the bottom right is birch veneer.

THE BEST HARDWOOD PLYWOOD GRADES

Grades differ by veneer quality and number and size of defects allowed.

Grade	Qualities
A-Premium	Sliced veneers matched for pleasing color and grain, one-piece rotary cut. Pin knots, small patches not allowed.
1-Good (cabinet grade)	Unmatched veneers OK. No sharp contrasts in color, grain, or figure. Burls, pin knots, and small patches allowed.
2-Sound	No figure, color, or grain match. Smooth patches, sound knots, and discoloration or varying color allowed.

Other designations may be dealer-applied.

JUDGING HARDWOOD PLYWOOD
Put the best face forward

You may not know which side to show on a project when using premium grades of hardwood plywood—AA, A, and A1. Both sides may appear identical, but there are subtle differences.

The best side has even color, consistent grain, no flaws, and the fewest visible splices. In the photos at *right,* the top panel has fewer splices and a better grain pattern than the other premium-grade panel.

COMPOSITES

Plywood isn't the only building material available in sheets. Today's forest products industry seeks to minimize waste by using every ounce of wood—from wood chips and flakes to sawdust—in the manufacture of sheet goods that are generally called composite wood products.

Oriented strand board (OSB) has bonded wood chips laid up in layers, each running in a different direction. Although nearly as strong as plywood, its rough surface texture generally limits its use to utility shelving.

Particleboard employs glued sawdust and tiny chips. It's hard and fairly smooth but sags under load, can fracture, and swells when wet.

Melamine-covered particleboard has a plastic-like coating that eliminates the need for finishing. Otherwise it has the same characteristics as uncoated particleboard.

Medium-density fiberboard (MDF) uses very fine wood fibers for an extremely smooth surface. It's stronger than particleboard and is moisture-resistant. However, it sometimes splits when nailed.

Medium-density fiberboard (MDF)

Melamine-covered particleboard

Particleboard

Oriented strand board (OSB)

STANLEY PRO TIP **Stand sheet goods to save space**

Sheet goods take up less space when stored on end. They're also easier to move in this position.

To slide them out easily, build an edged platform from plastic-laminate-covered stock (a piece of countertop works nicely). Hang a tilt-stop, made of 2×4 material, from the exposed overhead joists to catch the outside sheets when you pull out an inner one.

An easily constructed rack like this one simplifies storing and pulling sheet goods.

SAGLESS SPANS

Shelves that don't sag are the goal for any kind of shelving. Each material has a different span limit, the maximum distance it can span between supports without sagging or breaking under a load.

According to architect calculations, books represent an average load of 25 pounds per cubic foot. At right are the no-sag span limits under load for the most commonly used shelving materials.

Solid hardwood has the best no-sag rating; however, some species are stiffer than others. Birch, maple, and oak are the stiffest, followed by ash, cherry, and walnut.

You can increase the stiffness of a shelf by sinking screws into it through the solid back of the case. Or, as shown below, add more strength and maintain adjustability by attaching a cleat or molding to the front of the shelf. Aprons can also be added under the shelf.

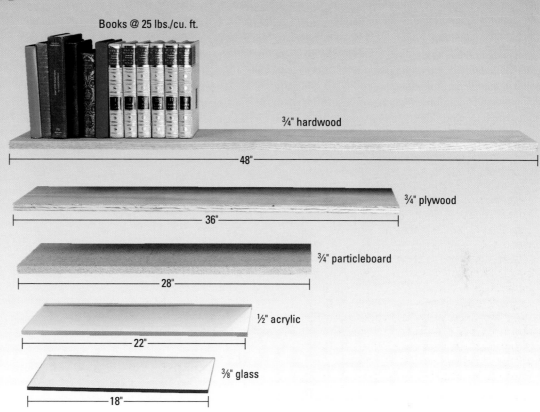

Books @ 25 lbs./cu. ft.

¾" hardwood — 48"

¾" plywood — 36"

¾" particleboard — 28"

½" acrylic — 22"

⅜" glass — 18"

STURDY SHELVES
Four ways to increase spans

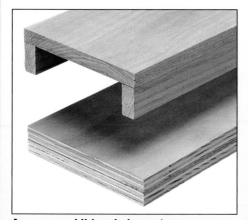

Aprons or additional pieces: Increase a wooden shelf's span limit by fastening wood-matched 1×2 aprons underneath *(top)* or simply by using two plywood pieces *(bottom)*.

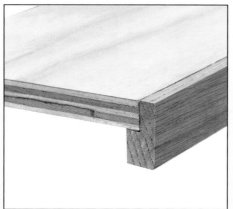

Railing: Cut a rabbet into a piece of solid molding and attach it as a rail that conceals the plywood edge and adds support.

Molding: Simply attach a 1×2 molding to the shelf's front edge. This method also hides the unsightly edge.

FASTENERS

Wood screws, brads, nails, and adhesives are some of the fasteners you'll become familiar with as you assemble your woodworking project.

Screws

Common wood screws are made of steel and normally have a rust-resistant zinc coating. Flathead wood screws (FHWS) are made to be driven flush with the surface. You also can counterbore them into a hole in the surface and cover the screw with either a wood plug or wood putty so the fastener is hidden. Oval-head and roundhead wood screws (RHWS) protrude above the surface for decorative effect or a finished look when

fastening metal hardware. You'll also choose from three common screw-head slot types: slotted, phillips, and square drive. These match different screwdriving tools.

Lag screws are heavy-duty fasteners that have a threaded shank like a wood screw. They have a hex-head like a machine bolt that allows you to use a wrench, rather than a screwdriver, to apply more torque when tightening them. Hanger screws have a wood-screw thread on one end and a machine-screw thread on the other. This allows you to screw one end into a wall stud, for example, and use a nut and bolt on the other. Both of these fasteners are useful when attaching heavy cabinets to a wall.

Case-hardened steel screws, often called drywall screws, have a skinny shank and a dull black finish. They're exceptionally tough and are most often used with a power drill-driver. Case-hardened screws come in two thread configurations. One-thread single-leads hold best in softwoods and particleboard. Double-leads have twin threads that bite into hardwoods better. A trim-head screw is a thin, case-hardened double-lead screw with a small head used in place of a finishing nail when fastening trim. Screw sizes are easy to understand. The gauge indicates the size of the shank diameter in a range from #0 (smallest) to #24 (largest). Gauge increases about 1/64 inch in

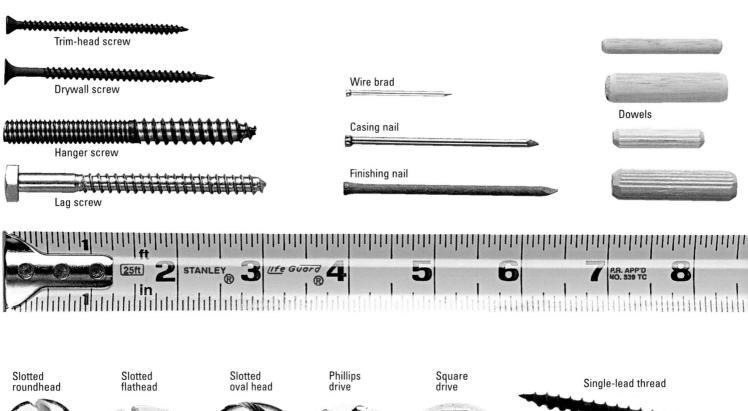

Trim-head screw

Drywall screw

Hanger screw

Lag screw

Wire brad

Casing nail

Finishing nail

Dowels

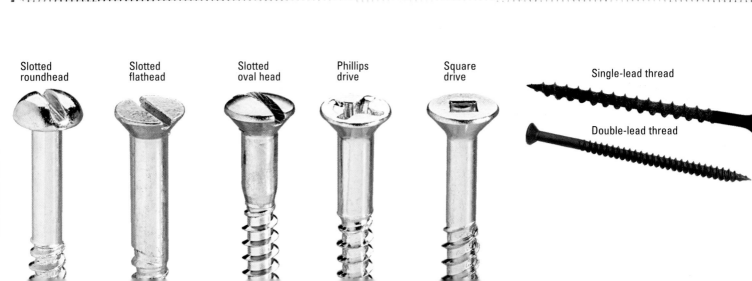

Slotted roundhead

Slotted flathead

Slotted oval head

Phillips drive

Square drive

Single-lead thread

Double-lead thread

each size increment. Lengths begin at ¼ inch and extend to 4 inches and longer. Each length comes in three or more gauges. The thinner the wood, the smaller gauge screw you need.

Other fasteners

Some joinery uses wooden **dowels,** coated with glue and inserted into holes, to join components together. You can buy them in various diameters and lengths.

Finishing nails are thin, small-headed nails used for fastening molding and other interior trim. The heads are usually countersunk below the wood surface. The resulting hole is then filled with wood filler. Use **casing nails** where the heads will be exposed to moisture. **Brads** have heads like finishing nails but are much smaller.

Used to reinforce joints, **mending plates** and **brackets** are screwed in places where they won't be seen.

Glues

Although many types of adhesives are on the market, including epoxies and instant-bondglues, the best all-purpose glue for most woodworking is aliphatic resin (AR) glue and modified formulas of it. Those glues are premixed, so you apply them from squeeze-bottle containers. They c⸺ white (PVA), yellow, and darker tin⸺ woods. They're strong, and they dr⸺ three hours. (The white variety dries more slowly, giving you extended time to work.) Newer formulas provide extended water resistance. Shelf life is about six months to a year if refrigerated (but not frozen) when not in use.

Polyurethane glue is gaining favor with some woodworkers because it performs much like epoxy without the mixing and the strong chemical odor. It's waterproof too. You'll pay more, however, for polyurethane than AR glue.

SHOP REFERENCE GUIDE FOR SCREWS

Typical uses	Attaching small hardware					General assembly			Heavy-duty assembly		
Gauge	2	3	4	5	6	7	8	9	10	12	14
Head bore size	11/64"	13/64"	15/64"	¼"	9/32"	5/16"	11/32"	23/64"	25/64"	7/16"	½"
Shank drill size	3/32"	7/64"	7/64"	⅛"	9/64"	5/32"	5/32"	11/64"	3/16"	7/32"	¼"
Pilot drill size	1/16"	1/16"	5/64"	5/64"	3/32"	7/64"	7/64"	⅛"	⅛"	9/64"	5/32"

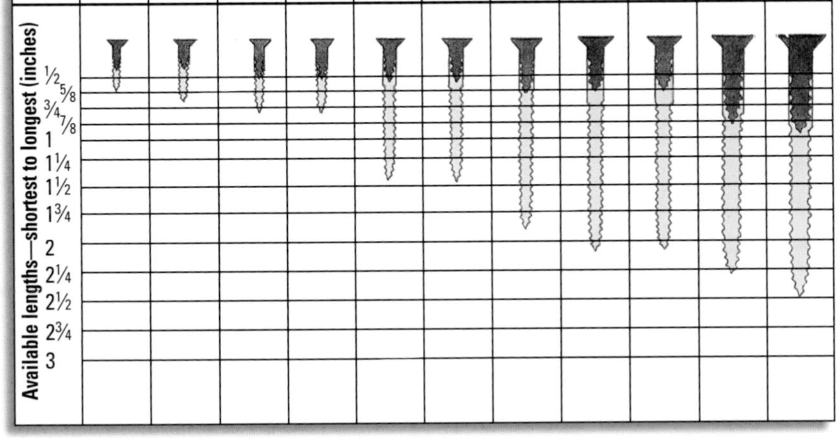

Available lengths—shortest to longest (inches): ½, ⅝, ¾, ⅞, 1, 1¼, 1½, 1¾, 2, 2¼, 2½, 2¾, 3

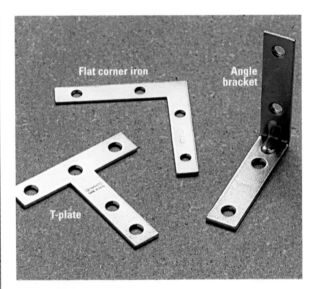

Flat corner iron
Angle bracket
T-plate

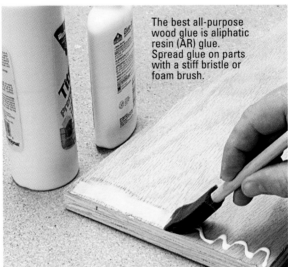

The best all-purpose wood glue is aliphatic resin (AR) glue. Spread glue on parts with a stiff bristle or foam brush.

HARDWARE

If you build adjustable shelves, you'll find a line of specialized hardware to pick from, depending on the type of shelving you're going to build.

Open shelving

Often called utility shelving because it plays an important storage role in a basement, garage, or laundry room, open shelving is attached directly to a wall rather than built into a case. But it can be dressed up for the den and living room too. Getting the look you want begins with **shelf standards.** These metal tracks are made in various styles and finishes. They're either fastened directly to the wall or mounted in wall-attached wood channels. To carry heavy loads, mount them to the wall studs with heavy screws or lag bolts. For lighter loads, you can use hollow-wall anchors or toggle bolts.

Some styles of standards only accept **metal shelf brackets.** Others are designed for decorative, wooden **corbel-type brackets.** Another type, usually used in cabinets, takes only **metal clips.** Dress your shelves up or down by selecting the appropriate design and finish.

Encased shelving

When building adjustable shelves inside a bookcase or cabinet, you can support the shelves where they meet the sides of the piece in one of three ways: using surface-mounted standards, standards flush-mounted in a groove, or **pin supports**.

Wood dowels can be used as pin supports, and there are dozens of metal and plastic varieties available as well. All pin supports require two rows of evenly spaced ¼-inch or 5 mm holes on each side of the cabinet or case.

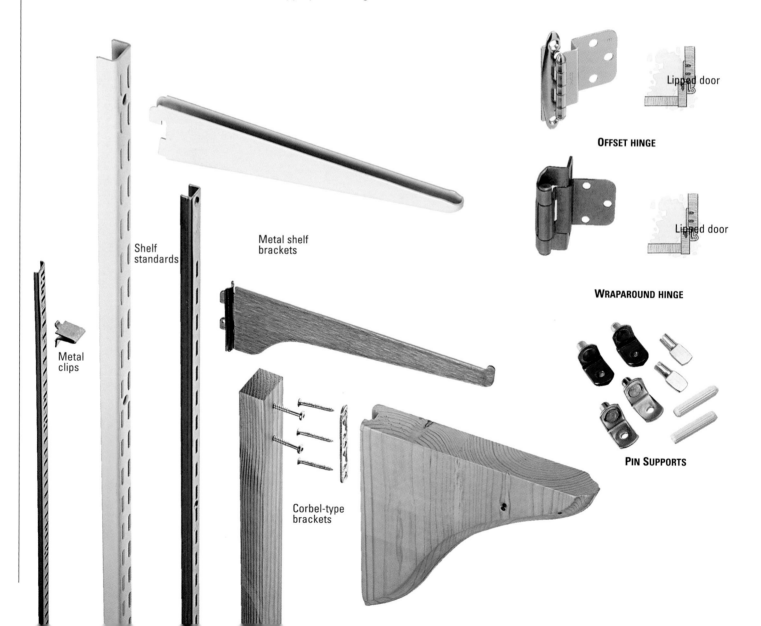

Metal clips

Shelf standards

Metal shelf brackets

Corbel-type brackets

Lipped door

OFFSET HINGE

Lipped door

WRAPAROUND HINGE

PIN SUPPORTS

If you plan to add doors and drawers to a bookcase, you'll have to get to know other types of hardware as well. Door catches, hinges, pulls, and drawer slides are so numerous in configuration, finish, and style that all the varieties fill catalogs. Start by learning the basic types.

Lipped doors—doors that partially cover the cabinet's frame—generally require one of two hinge types. The **offset hinge** fastens to the face frame and the back of the door. A **wraparound hinge** is attached to the back of the door and the inside edge of the face frame. They're used on doors that overlap the frame, too.

For doors without lips that either cover, partially cover, or fit flush with the cabinet face, you have several options.

A **cylinder-style hinge** mounts to the face frame and into a recess cut in the back of a door. **Pivot hinges,** attached to the back of an overlapped door and the face frame, are concealed. A **semi-concealed hinge** attaches the same way but to a partially overlapped door. For a flush door, use a **butt hinge** that folds between the door and face frame. Growing in popularity is the **Eurostyle hinge,** which fastens to the door back and cabinet side.

To open doors and to keep them closed, handles and catches are used. Handles come in many forms, colors, and finishes but fall into only two categories: **pulls** and **knobs.** Both require drilling through the door, then attaching the hardware with screws. Catches tightly hold doors closed and are available in several common styles including **friction** and **magnetic** catches.

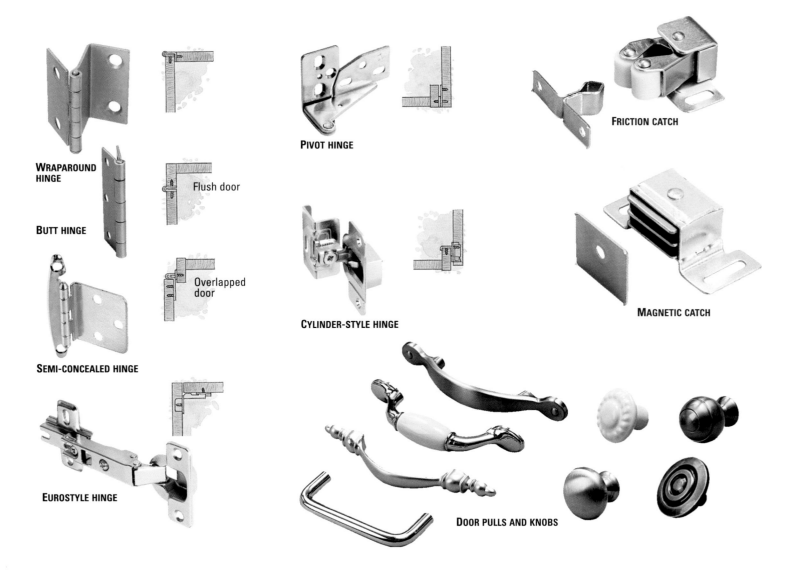

WRAPAROUND HINGE

BUTT HINGE

Flush door

SEMI-CONCEALED HINGE

Overlapped door

PIVOT HINGE

FRICTION CATCH

CYLINDER-STYLE HINGE

MAGNETIC CATCH

EUROSTYLE HINGE

DOOR PULLS AND KNOBS

EDGE BANDING

Before applying a finish to a bookcase or shelf project made from plywood or other sheet goods, you must decide what to do with the exposed edges. They're normally rough, and with plywood, the visible plies detract from the project's appearance.

For a plywood project that you plan to paint, fill and sand the exposed edge (page 68). When working with melamine-coated MDF, use preglued melamine edge banding. It's available in almond or white. Simply cut it to length and iron it in place.

For a bookcase or shelf made from furniture-quality hardwood plywood, cut and attach molding or thin strips of solid wood. A quicker method is to apply wood-veneer edge banding. Like the melamine variety, wood edge banding is preglued with hot-melt adhesive, making it easy to iron in place. Its ⅟₁₀₀-inch thickness makes it flexible, yet it won't crack because it's tenderized. You can buy the presanded, ¾-inch-wide material in a variety of hardwoods, including cherry, mahogany, maple, oak, and walnut.

(page 68)

APPLYING EDGE BANDING
Two quick and easy steps to great-looking edges

You'll be amazed at how easy it is to finish the edges of hardwood plywood shelves and cases. All you need are a roll of wood-veneer edge banding, a sharp utility knife, a ruler, and a household iron set on medium-low heat, no steam. (Use an old iron; you won't want to iron clothing with it after this.)

Measure the length of each edge that needs covering. Cut banding strips to rough length with the knife. Position on the edge, check that the glued side is down (the grain is less distinct on the glued side), and press evenly and firmly with the iron *(left)*.

If you have corners to cover, the job will look neater if you miter-cut them. Overlap the two pieces that will join. Hold them in place as you make a clean 45-degree cut through both pieces *(right)* to ensure the ends will match perfectly when you iron the strips in place.

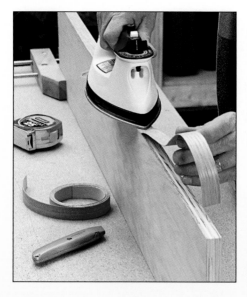

MOLDING

Molding not only conceals unsightly shelf edges, it adds a decorative touch. It's also a way to hide gaps and dress up built-ins and other projects when you don't have the power tools to shape the wood yourself.

Although most molding profiles were created for specific purposes, they come in dozens of styles that can be adapted for a variety of uses. Note that although oak moldings are shown here, you'll find them in other hardwoods and in less costly paintable and stainable composite materials as well. Here are some available styles:

■ **Baseboard molding** covers the gap between the floor and a built-in such as a bookcase. Select a profile that matches the baseboard in your home.

■ **Strips** conceal plywood edges and also can be used to add strength to shelves. Strips are usually available in 1-inch thickness up to 4 inches wide.

■ **Crown molding** is used to finish the top of a built-in and covers the gap between it and the ceiling.

■ **Cove molding** is a plainer version of crown molding.

■ **Door-edge molding** is used to give hardwood plywood doors and drawers the appearance of solid wood panel construction.

■ **Base cap molding** provides an appealing edge for shelves.

■ **Base shoe molding** conceals gaps on all sides of a built-in. It's flexible, so it conforms to irregular floors and walls.

■ **Ornamental moldings** have embossed faces for a handcrafted look.

Baseboard

Strip

Crown

Cove

Door-edge

Base cap

Base shoe

Ornamental

TRANSFORM WITH TRIM
Add moldings to increase visual appeal

The most common problem associated with moldings is deciding which ones to use. Crisp, clean profiles contribute to plain, contemporary lines, while ornate ones relate to antique and traditional styles. The contrast can be dramatic, as shown in the two self-edge treatments, *top.* So select moldings that complement your home's decor.

A colonial profile casing in oak, *middle,* becomes the cornice on an entertainment center. The unit's doors, *bottom,* were trimmed with door-edge molding.

Add smaller moldings by gluing and clamping. Larger moldings are best fastened with finishing nails. Sink the heads of finishing nails below the surface and fill the holes with wood filler.

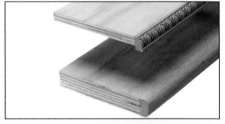

STANLEY PRO TIP

No long clamps?

If your clamps fall short of spanning the width of a plywood shelf to hold a trim piece while the glue dries, use masking tape. When the glue has dried and you remove the tape, wipe off the tape's adhesive residue with a little solvent, such as lacquer thinner.

MASTERING BASIC SKILLS

If you've done some home repair or even a bit of remodeling, you've already acquired many of the basic skills needed to build bookcases and shelves. This chapter will add to that knowledge. If you're just getting started as a do-it-yourselfer, this is essential basic information to increase your range of skills as you complete your first project, then another.

In previous chapters, you learned about hand and power tools and about the materials and hardware available. In this chapter, you'll learn the skills that will help you use the tools and materials to create beautiful, practical pieces of furniture that you and your family will enjoy for years to come. Read carefully, then practice the techniques on scrap wood. And always work with common sense and safety in mind.

Building skills

The first few pages tell you how to lay out, measure, and mark precisely. The old woodworking adage, "Measure twice, cut once," is a lesson that many learn only after wasting material.

Following that introduction, you learn how to make straight cuts with hand and power tools in both boards and sheet goods. You'll soon become familiar with some basic terminology, such as "rip" and "crosscut." Ripping simply means cutting wood with the grain; crosscutting, as the word implies, means cutting wood across the grain.

You'll also learn how to cut precise angles and smooth curves. Along the way, you'll read about a sliding bevel gauge, a tool for accurately duplicating angles when making cuts, and a miter box, an accessory that will help you make those cuts by hand with precision.

Drilling may seem boring (pun intended), but there are several kinds of tools and accessories that will help you create clean, smooth holes more easily and accurately than you could before.

Using a chisel, one of the oldest tools around, is almost a lost art these days. We'll show you how to properly use one to help make strong, tight-fitting, handcrafted joinery that sets your project apart from—and will probably make it outlast—much of the machine-made furniture found in stores.

It's not just tools that make the project— it's the skill with which they're used.

CHAPTER PREVIEW

Layout and marking
page 48

Straight cuts
page 50

Angled and curved cuts
page 52

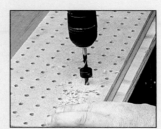

Drilling
page 54

Chiseling
page 55

Building adjustable shelves requires drilling precisely spaced holes of exactly the same depth. Here's a way to make that task easy, fast, and accurate: Clamp a piece of perforated hardboard squarely and securely to your work. Using the holes as a guide, drill the holes in your stock. A stop on the drill bit limits each hole's depth.

LAYOUT AND MARKING

Never take dimensions for granted when working with boards and sheet goods. That goes for squareness too.

Due to super-fast milling processes, shrinkage, and other factors, board ends may be out of square. Boards may also taper slightly along their length.

A 4×8-foot sheet of plywood usually has true edges, but check it for squareness and measure its thickness. A ¾-inch-thick sheet may be slightly off—a good reason to buy all the plywood you'll need from the same batch at the same time. If the sheets are not the precise thickness they're supposed to be, chances are they'll at least be uniform in thickness.

To measure accurately every time, use the same tape measure throughout the project. Furniture making requires precision; use a mechanical pencil, which makes a finer line. If you use a carpenter's pencil, mark with the narrow edge of the lead.

Check for square: Always check a board's end for squareness before measuring and marking other cuts. Put the handle of a try square against the edge of the board with its blade across the end. Light showing between them indicates the board is out of square. Mark the board and cut it square.

Measure for length: Use a steel tape to measure and mark for cuts to length. Make one measurement on each board edge, then join them by marking along a try square.

Can you trust your tape?

Tape measures become inaccurate if the rivet holes in the end get elongated. If that happens, line up the 1-inch mark with the squared end of the board, then subtract an inch from the tape reading when marking at the other end. Better yet, avoid confusion—replace the tape. And use the same tape on a project.

CUTTING THE LONG WAY
Use a marking gauge

Marking materials for ripping (cutting a board down its length with the grain or plywood in its long dimension) requires great accuracy.
If you have a straightedge that's long enough, use it. If you have a tablesaw, you don't need a guideline to follow. Simply set the fence away from the blade to the width of the cut, then feed the material through.

For cut lines in boards or narrow rip-cuts in plywood, many woodworkers use a marking gauge. Its thumbscrew-adjustable fence slides along one edge of the material while a sharp pin set in its post scribes the cut line. The post length determines maximum width.

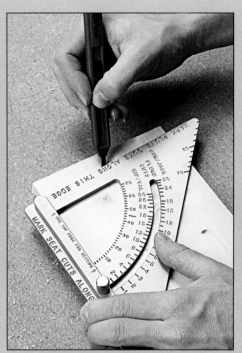

Mark with a V: Rather than making a simple straight-line pencil mark, make a V-shape mark with its point exactly on the tape measurement you want. This way, you're less likely to lose track of a mark.

Use a layout square: A try square works fine for marking crosscuts, but its blade sometimes gets out of square. Whenever possible, use a layout square so your marks will always be perpendicular to the edge.

Marking large sheets: To mark a sheet of plywood for a cut across its width, you'll need a straightedge at least 4 feet long (page 30). After measuring and marking each end of the cutoff line, clamp the straightedge in place at the marks. Then draw your line.

CUTTING DIAGRAMS
Make the most of materials

If your project has many parts, a cutting diagram will keep waste to a minimum. It also helps you maximize the use of grain for appearance because you'll be able to see how the grain runs on each part.

Select which side of the material you want to show (to choose the best side of plywood, see page 36. Then follow the Bill of Materials provided with your project plan and lay out parts directly on the wood. Draw light, erasable pencil lines. Write a part number on a masking tape label for each part and attach it to the wood. You can use a dark marker for greater visibility because you won't have to erase pencil marks later. When marking cuts, make an allowance for the kerf—the material removed by the blade as it cuts—so your pieces aren't too small.

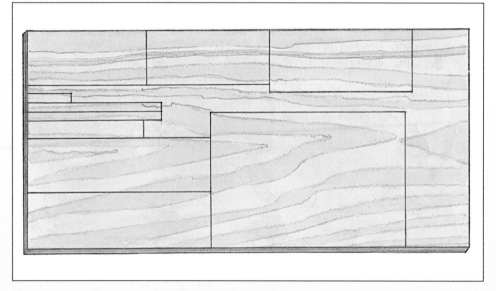

STRAIGHT CUTS

You'll reduce a lot of large pieces of wood to smaller ones when you build projects. The straight cuts you make are either rip-cuts or crosscuts.

A rip-cut reduces the width of a piece of stock. On a board, it's a cut along the length in the direction of the grain. On plywood and other sheet goods, it's a cut parallel to the sheet's long side, no matter the direction of the grain. Ripping stock to width is usually the first machining step in building a project.

After stock has been ripped to the width desired, it's cut to length with a crosscut. This is done across (perpendicular to) the board's grain or in the narrow dimension of plywood and other sheet goods. Parts of the same length should be sawed at the same time (especially with power saws) using a stop. A stop is a piece of wood clamped in place so the stock being cut won't move beyond the required length. Using a stop eliminates remeasuring.

STANLEY PRO TIP

Saving the face of plywood's thin veneers

Hardwood plywood faced with veneers of cherry, oak, maple, and walnut is expensive, so always use a specially made plywood rip blade when cutting it with circular saws. These blades usually have about 55 alternately beveled teeth and make the cleanest cuts.

Face veneers differ too. American-made hardwood veneers are from 1/28 inch to 1/32 inch thick. Asian veneers may only be 1/100. To reduce chipping, apply masking tape over the area to be sawed, then saw through the tape.

Ripping

A portable circular saw makes ripping boards fairly easy. Support the board with 2×4s underneath and clamp a guide in place. A kerf splitter behind the saw keeps the board from closing and binding the saw blade.

On a tablesaw, reduce the chance of kickback during ripping by using a feather board ahead of the blade. To keep your hands away from the blade, feed the board with a push stick. Never reach over the blade or between the blade and the fence.

A circular saw can rip-cut even a large sheet of plywood accurately if you use a long straightedge (page 30) securely clamped to the wood. Place supports under the sheet as shown.

Safely cutting large sheets of plywood on a tablesaw requires a second pair of hands. The helper *(left)* holds the sheet level without lifting or pulling as you feed the other end through the blade.

Crosscutting

With a portable circular saw: First support the wood on both sides of the cut. Then tightly clamp a piece of scrap wood to the workpiece along the cut line to act as a saw guide. Hold the board firmly as you make the cut.

On a tablesaw: Use the saw's miter gauge, which rides in a slot as it carries the board through the blade, not the rip fence. For even greater accuracy, lengthen the face of the miter gauge by fastening a piece of square, true scrap wood to its face.

With a handsaw: Clamp a piece of scrap wood on the cut line as a blade guide. For a smooth cut, use long, even strokes and gentle pressure. Short, fast, jerky strokes can leave you with a rough cut—or, even worse, a bent and ruined saw.

RIP RIGHT
Know which side is up

The tiny splinters, fractures, and rough edges caused by a blade exiting the wood is called tear-out. This is especially noticeable when ripping plywood with power saws.

To avoid tear-out when using a portable circular saw, place the best face of the workpiece *down* and away from the blade when ripping. Any tear-out will be on the bad side of the sheet, which will probably be hidden. For that reason, draw all cut lines on the bad face.

When ripping with a tablesaw, do just the opposite. Draw cut lines on the best face and place that side *up* on the table.

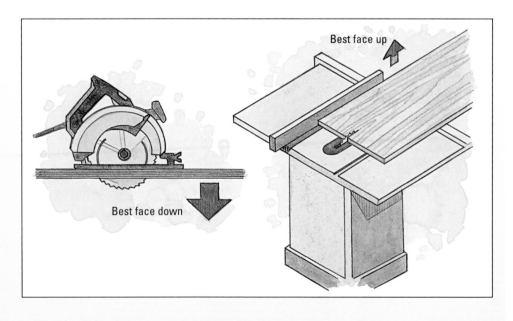

Best face up

Best face down

ANGLED AND CURVED CUTS

Rip-cuts and crosscuts separate materials. Angled cuts are used mostly in the early stages of making joints. Curved cuts shape wood decoratively.

A miter is probably the most common type of angle cut. They're usually made at 45 degrees in order to join two pieces of wood at a 90-degree angle (page 59), as in a picture frame. Cutting an accurate miter is more difficult than it looks because even the slightest movement of the wood or shifting of the cutting tool will throw it off.

Bevels are angle cuts along the edges or ends of boards, often for decorative purposes. Use a sliding bevel gauge to copy and transfer unusual angles.

Curved cuts in wood also add a decorative element.

Miter cuts

1 Use a miter box. Mark the cut line, place the workpiece in the box, and align the cut line with the corresponding notches. Clamp the piece flush with the edge of the miter box that's farthest from you as you saw.

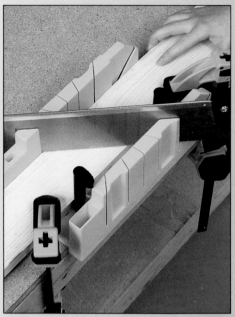

2 Make the cut with smooth, even strokes. Get the cut started with a couple of pull strokes, then use gentle, even pressure and cut on the forward stroke. Keep the saw level, especially when finishing the cut, or you'll saw through the floor of the miter box.

With a portable circular saw, clamp the workpiece in place, draw a cut line, then hold a saw guide next to the saw's bottom plate to steady the saw.

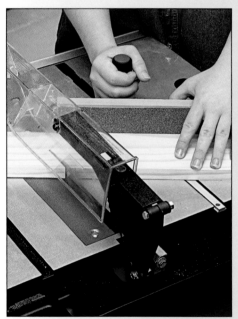

On a tablesaw, cut short miters with the help of the miter gauge. Set the gauge, place the wood against its fence, then feed the stock smoothly through the blade using the miter slot.

With a power mitersaw, set the degree angle of the saw, position the board, and make the cut. A compound mitersaw allows you to tilt the saw head as well as angle it.

Beveled cuts

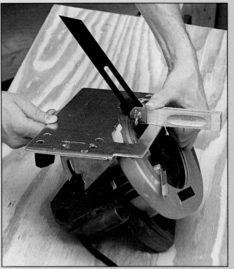

Record the angle: You sometimes have to cut a bevel on a workpiece to match an existing angle. Record the old angle with a sliding bevel gauge that adjusts and locks by turning a wing nut. You can use it to transfer both inside and outside angles.

Set the angle: To transfer a bevel angle to a portable circular saw, unplug the tool and turn it over. Loosen the foot plate, and with the gauge in place, tilt the foot plate to the desired angle, then retighten it. Set the blade depth to cut through the material.

On a tablesaw: Use a similar technique to transfer an angle with the sliding bevel gauge to a tablesaw. Loosen the arbor lock, place the bevel against the blade, and turn the tilt wheel until the angle of the blade aligns with the angle of the gauge.

Curved cuts

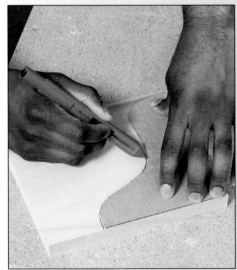

1 A jigsaw easily follows curved and rounded pattern lines for scrolling cuts. If you have a pattern to follow, trace it onto a piece of cardboard, then cut it out to make a template. Use the template to transfer the pattern to the wood by drawing a cut line with a pencil.

2 Clamp the workpiece securely to your workbench, making sure the saw's blade won't cut into supporting surfaces. You might need to make a partial cut, then reposition the workpiece and reclamp it before continuing to make the cut.

Need to cut a pair?

Cutting exact duplicates is fast and easy if you use masking tape to join the workpieces. Mark the cut on one piece, then apply the tape to tightly join the pieces in precise alignment. It doesn't matter where you place the tape—the saw will cut right through it—but don't hide the pattern line. You also can use double-faced carpet tape, which you apply between the two pieces.

DRILLING

You need two basic tools to make holes in wood: a bit to cut and a drill to turn it. If you want the hole to be of a precise depth or angle, you'll need some extra help, as shown at *right*.

Although you can use a hand-powered brace or a hand drill, a corded electric drill or a cordless drill/driver gives you better control and more power for little added cost. A drill guide increases accuracy.

There are many types of bits you can buy. Brad-point bits are better than standard twist drills for woodworking. The twist drill's point tends to wander when starting a hole. Brad-point bits have a sharp center point that keeps the hole where you want it.

Use special counterbore and countersink bits to make pilot and countersink holes for screws, as shown *below right*. A drill stop limits hole depth.

As you go through this book, you'll see other special drilling accessories described that will help make your work easier and more accurate.

Drilling repetitive holes, such as for a bookcase's adjustable shelves, can be accurately done by using a piece of perforated hardboard as a spacing template.

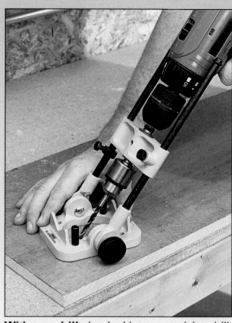

With your drill chucked into a precision drill guide, you can accurately drill at any angle between 45 and 90 degrees. The guide's built-in depth stop limits hole depth.

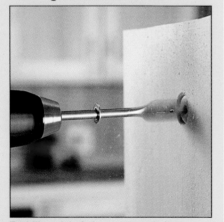

STANLEY PRO TIP

Drilling horizontal holes

To drill straight holes—not angled ones—horizontally, slip a metal washer over the bit as a guide. The washer should be a close fit on the shaft. If the drill is perpendicular when the bit is turning, the washer won't move along the bit.

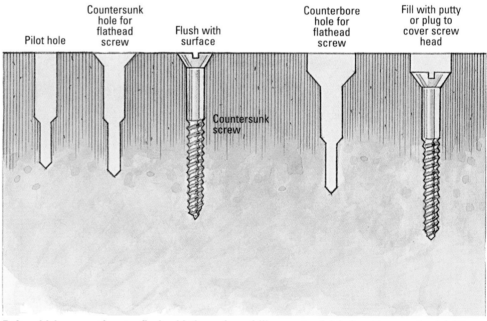

Pilot hole · Countersunk hole for flathead screw · Flush with surface · Countersunk screw · Counterbore hole for flathead screw · Fill with putty or plug to cover screw head

Before driving a wood screw flush with the surface, drill a countersink hole with a countersink bit. Use a combination bit to drill a countersink hole with a counterbore to recess the screw into. Conceal the screw head with a standard wood plug or one you make with a plug-cutting bit.

CHISELING

One of a woodworker's simplest tools is a chisel. For general use, a blade that's 3 to 5 inches long is useful. But you'll likely end up with several chisels of different lengths and widths. Buy chisels that have high-carbon steel blades and durable handles (plastic handles absorb shock and resist deformation when hit with a mallet). Use a dead blow hammer or wood mallet to drive a chisel.

Chisels are versatile tools. They perform many woodworking tasks well—if you keep them sharp and handle them carefully and properly. Don't use them to pry open paint cans or stuck windows, and they'll give you years of good service.

Choosing a chisel

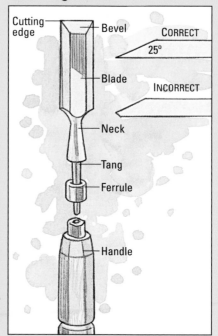

A good wood-handled chisel has a steel hoop at the top of the handle to keep it from mushrooming. Plastic handles absorb shock.

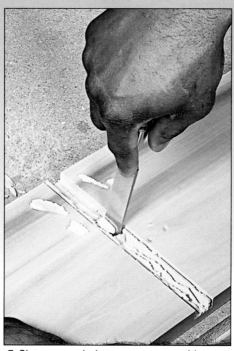

1 Clean out a dado or groove cut with a saw by turning the chisel bevel down to pare away the small ridges. Cut, don't pry.

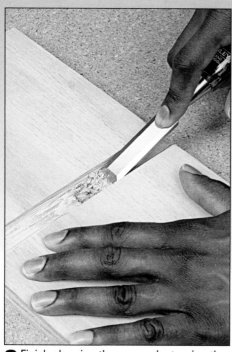

2 Finish cleaning the groove by turning the chisel bevel up and running it through the groove or dado to flatten and smooth the bottom.

KEEP THEM SHARP
How to hone a chisel on a flat stone

1 Start with the stone's coarser side up; apply a light coat of oil to the stone. With firm, even pressure, move the chisel's bevel side around the stone in a figure-eight pattern. Make sure both the heel and toe of the bevel remain in contact with stone.

2 A thin ridge of metal called a wire edge will form at the tip. To remove it, turn the chisel over, lay it flat on the stone, and give it a few light sideways strokes. Turn the stone over and repeat the steps on the finer-grained side.

PUTTING IT ALL TOGETHER

The process of assembling a project's wooden parts and subassemblies is called joinery. It's among the most complex aspects of woodworking and demands a thorough understanding of the properties of wood and precision craftsmanship. It is also among the most rewarding processes, turning a collection of what looks like miscellaneous pieces of wood into a sturdy and attractive piece of furniture. The stronger and more durable the joint, the more demanding the work will be. That's why woodworkers decide early on what joints they'll use. In this chapter, you'll learn how to make many traditional joints, as well as some new, faster, easier ways woodworkers have come up with to make strong joints. You'll find that even the more complex joints can be mastered if you work carefully and methodically and understand wood movement and grain direction.

Wood movement

Wood is a hygroscopic material: it can absorb moisture and swell, as well as lose moisture and shrink, even when covered with finish. That's why a drawer that slides easily in winter at low humidity may stick in summer when humidity is high. This tendency for wood to change dimension—even if just slightly—is called wood movement.

Joinery techniques take wood movement into consideration by withstanding it, allowing it, or arranging pieces so movement has little effect on the joint.

Grain direction

When you look at the end of a board, you see a pattern in the wood that's quite different from what's on its edge, face, or back. Softwoods have a series of rings representing the tree's growth layers. Hardwoods, depending on their density, may have a similar pattern, a series of minuscule pores, or a combination of both. It's all end grain, and it all wicks up moisture—as you'll notice when applying finish.

That's why it's best to avoid end-grain-to-end-grain joints. The glue disappears into the wood, leaving little or nothing to permanently bond the pieces together. Without additional strengthening, such as dowels, an end-grain-to-end-grain joint eventually comes apart.

Creating tight, strong joints is one of the most demanding, but rewarding, tasks in woodworking.

CHAPTER PREVIEW

Basic joints
page 58

Reinforced joints
page 63

Advanced joints
page 64

Clamping
page 65

Clamps and glue are used in the last stages of joinery. It's the careful planning and precision cutting and fitting preceding glue-up that ensures a sturdy and elegant piece. Here, C-clamps and bar clamps—carefully buffered with pieces of scrap wood to avoid marring the finished piece—aid in the final assembly of a mitered corner.

BASIC JOINTS

Edge joints create a panel from several narrow boards. The result is stronger and more resistant to splitting and warping than a single wide piece of wood.

A **butt joint** joins two pieces at 90 degrees in a corner or along their length. Reinforce these joints for strength.

Cutting away part of two pieces to be joined adds gluing surface and creates lap joints. For a **lap joint,** remove half the thickness of each piece. In a half-lap joint, material is removed only from one piece.

A **miter joint** requires an accurate angle cut on both pieces to be joined (45 degrees for a 90-degree corner). Strengthen these joints with glue blocks or screws.

Edge joint

1 With all edges perfectly square, lay the boards on equally spaced bar clamps. Adjust them for visual appeal, then mark with a pencil for later realignment.

2 Turn all but the first board on edge. Apply a thin, even coat of woodworking glue to one edge of each joint with a small brush. Be sure board edges are completely coated.

3 Align boards on the bottom clamps. Place scrap wood between the clamps and workpiece. Tighten clamps. Turn over the workpiece and clamp. Leave clamped until glue dries.

Half-lap joint

1 Hold the two boards together to mark the edges for cuts. Mark the width and depth of the cut. The depth of the cut is the thickness of the thinner piece.

2 With the help of a try or combination square, draw the width and depth cut lines onto the thicker piece.

3 Using a backsaw, make the first cut across the grain to the depth indicated by the mark. Hold the saw at 90 degrees to the wood as you cut.

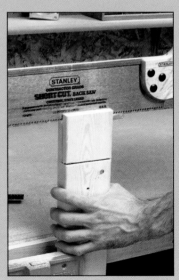

4 Make the final cut through the end grain to remove the waste. Either turn the wood on edge and saw vertically or stand the wood on end in a vise.

Butt joint

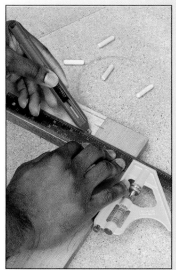   

1 Strengthen a butt joint with dowels. Begin by marking the location of each dowel's center, about 1½ inches apart, on one of the pieces to be joined.

2 Using a guide and a bit that's the same size as your dowels, drill holes slightly longer than one-half the dowel length into the center of one piece at the dowel markings.

3 Dowel centers mark the exact location of the dowel holes in the second piece. Insert one in each hole, then press the two pieces to be joined together to mark. Drill the holes.

4 Drop glue into each dowel hole. Spread glue around half the length of each dowel. Tap each halfway into its hole. Glue holes and exposed dowels, then draw together.

Miter joint

Shim

With a miter box: A power mitersaw provides great accuracy, but you can make miter cuts with a backsaw and miter box. With either, mark the 45-degree cut line, then hold or clamp the piece while sawing.

Corrections: After sawing both pieces to 45 degrees, fit them together to check the angle. If the cut was slightly off, correct it by placing a tiny shim against the fence or inside the miter box, then saw again.

Clamping: A miter clamp holds the two joined pieces together while the glue dries. It also keeps the pieces joined if you want to strengthen the joint with brads or finishing nails after the glue dries.

Dado joint

1 Dadoes are channels that run across the grain. They're often used in the sides of a bookcase to hold shelves. Use a carpenter's square and pencil to mark their location and widths on the wood. If the project uses plywood shelves, double-check their thickness. Don't assume ¾-inch plywood will always be ¾ inch thick. Dimensions vary with the manufacturer, and if the dadoes are not the exact width of the shelves' thickness, you'll have a bad fit.

2 Cutting a dado with a portable circular saw requires setting the blade to the depth you want the dado, usually one-third the wood's thickness. (Be sure the blade is perpendicular to the saw's foot plate.) Next, with a straightedge as a guide, saw kerfs in the wood to shape the dado edges. Then saw narrowly spaced kerfs in the wood remaining between the sides.

RABBET AND DADO JOINTS

Shoulder

Double rabbet

Rabbet

Through dado joint

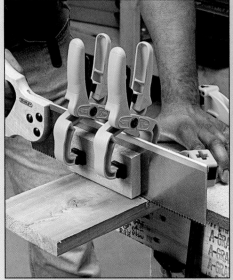

3 Short dadoes can be cut with a backsaw. Clamp a piece of wood with one true edge to the saw as a depth gauge. Then make several thinly spaced cuts to dado width.

4 To clean waste out of the dado, move a chisel from side to side with the bevel pointing down. Then run the chisel (bevel side up) down the dado's length to flatten and smooth the bottom of the dado.

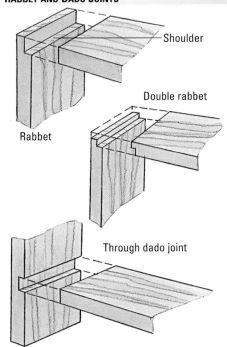

Rabbet joint

1 A rabbet is cut along an end or edge of a board or panel for another piece of wood to fit into. The rabbet cut may be as deep as the width of the mating piece and up to one-half the workpiece's depth. Use a depth gauge to mark the rabbet's width.

2 On a tablesaw, cut the rabbet's width (shoulder cut) with the workpiece flat on the table and against the rip fence. Set the blade to the desired depth, turn the board on edge and against the fence, and run it through the saw.

3 A router cuts small rabbets in one pass, larger and deeper ones in a few shallow passes. Chuck a piloted rabbeting bit of the correct size and set to the desired depth of cut. Securely clamp the workpiece to your bench top while routing the rabbet.

Groove joint

1 Grooves run with the grain and away from the edge. Use a straight-cutting bit and either the router's edge guide or a clamped straightedge as a guide. For deep grooves, make several shallow passes.

2 As with dadoes, you can cut grooves with a handsaw too. You'll need a longer straightedge that you'll have to move several times as you cut kerfs across the groove's width. Chisel out waste.

STANLEY PRO TIP

Labels help you avoid costly errors

When you're working with expensive hardwoods or hardwood plywood, mistakes can be costly. To prevent accidentally sawing a dado, rabbet, or groove in the wrong side of a workpiece, use masking tape to label where cuts will go. It's easily removed, and you can wipe off any remaining adhesive with a solvent.

Mortise-and-tenon joint

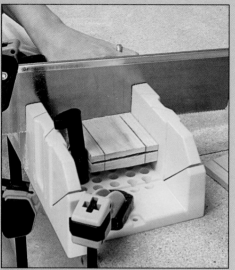

1 Measure and mark for a tenon's length and shoulders on the end and all four sides of the stock, using a combination or try square. Make the tenon from one-third to one-half the stock's thickness and about $\frac{1}{16}$ inch shorter than the mortise's depth. In a through mortise, the tenon should be $\frac{1}{8}$ inch longer than the stock thickness of the mortised piece.

2 Tightly clamp the marked tenon piece in a bench vise, using scrap wood to protect the sides of the workpiece from the clamp jaws. With a backsaw, carefully saw through the end grain to the shoulder line on either side of the tenon. Make sure you keep the saw perpendicular to the wood. For a four-shouldered tenon, make two more cuts down the narrow sides.

3 To complete the tenon, remove the workpiece from the vise and securely clamp it in your miter box with a waste side up. Use a backsaw guided by the miter box slots to free the waste from one of the tenon sides. With that cut complete, turn over the workpiece and repeat. If the tenon will have four shoulders, turn the workpiece on edge to make those cuts.

4 Use the tenon as a pattern to mark the outline of the mortise on the mating workpiece. Center the tenoned piece on the stock to be mortised. A blind mortise requires marking only one side. For a through mortise, carefully transfer position lines to the other side and mark.

5 You can cut a mortise with a mortising chisel, but an electric drill is faster. Using a bit about the same diameter as the mortise width and a drill stop, drill overlapping holes to remove most of the waste. For a through mortise, place scrap wood under the workpiece to prevent splintering.

6 After drilling, clean up the sides of the mortise with a sharp chisel. Keep the chisel's bevel facing into the mortise. Be particular about the mortise corners; they must be smooth and square. For a through mortise, turn over the workpiece and use the chisel to clean up the other side too.

REINFORCED JOINTS

Some of the simplest joints you can make need help when required to hold heavy loads. A glued miter joint (page 59) holds up well in a picture frame but isn't strong enough for the corner of a cabinet door or face frame without some reinforcement, such as wood **dowels.** Miter joints reinforced with dowels hold better than glue alone. In some instances, they add visual appeal.

Similar techniques can reinforce many simple joints used to build utility shelving or casework. Use metal **plates** and **brackets** from the home center or hardware store, or make your own **plywood gussets** and wooden **corner blocks.**

Even traditionally strong joints like the mortise-and-tenon can be strengthened with a peg that locks the parts together.

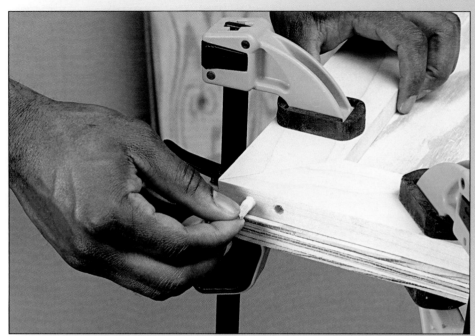

Add strength to a miter joint with dowels. Glue and clamp the joint first and let dry. Drill dowel holes deep enough to penetrate both the joined pieces. Apply glue to the dowels and insert them into the holes, tapping as necessary. Saw off any protruding dowels and sand them flush.

Wood and metal gusset and strap

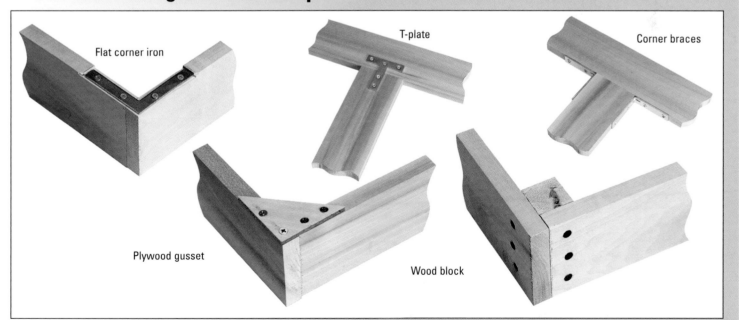

Flat corner iron

T-plate

Corner braces

Plywood gusset

Wood block

Metal and wood reinforcements for simple joints are normally placed where they're less visible—at the back of a bookcase or inside a cabinet, for instance. You might also consider these strengtheners to shore up old bookcases and other furniture. They take only minutes to install. Use brass or other decorative hardware when reinforcements can't be hidden.

ADVANCED JOINTS

Traditional joinery takes a lot of time to do right. That's why woodworkers seek quicker ways to accomplish the same result. During the past decade, two new joinery techniques have grown in popularity.

Pocket-hole joinery employs a small, fairly inexpensive jig; a special bit; and auger-point screws to cut project construction time in half. The technique is easy to learn and eliminates the need for a large number of clamps.

Biscuit joinery uses a biscuit or plate joiner machine to cut oval slots in the wood pieces. Compressed wood biscuits are inserted in the slots and glued. The glue makes the biscuits expand, creating a solid joint.

Pocket-hole joinery

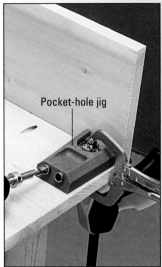

Pocket-hole jig

1 To make a joint, clamp the pocket-hole jig in place. Set the depth stop; then drill angled screw holes in one of the pieces.

2 After drilling the holes, remove the jig from the workpiece. Apply glue to the mating piece and butt the two together. Drive the screws.

Reinforcing block

3 Pocket-hole joinery, best used where it won't be visible, is an easy way to attach reinforcing corner blocks to a project.

Biscuit joinery

1 Use a speed square or combination square to mark biscuit locations in both boards. The boards must be machined as for edge joining (page 58).

2 Clamp the workpiece in place and center the biscuit joiner on a mark. Cut out the biscuit slot, then repeat for all slots in each board.

3 Insert biscuits, without glue, in the edge of one board and test fit. Make any needed adjustments. When you're satisfied with the fit, apply glue evenly inside the slots on both pieces and to all mating surfaces. Clamp and let dry.

CLAMPING

Clamping is as important to sound joinery as machining and gluing. Glue alone will hold two pieces of wood together, but a good bond requires pressure to force the glue into the wood's fibers. Clamping also holds a project's parts in proper position until the glue dries and anchors them.

Walk the tool aisle in a home center and you'll find dozens of clamp types and sizes. You won't need them all, but you should have the essentials shown here.

For large projects like bookcases and cabinets, use **bar clamps** or **pipe clamps**. A **band clamp** is versatile; it can even bind cylinders. **Spring clamps** are always useful for holding small assemblies together.

You can find many more types of specialty clamps. As with all tools beyond the basics, buy clamps only as you need them.

STANLEY PRO TIP

Checking for square

There's nothing more frustrating than finding that a case is out of square *after* the glue has dried. Check for square before the glue sets by measuring diagonally from corner to corner, first one way, then the other. If the measurements are equal, the case is square. If not, adjust and reset the clamps.

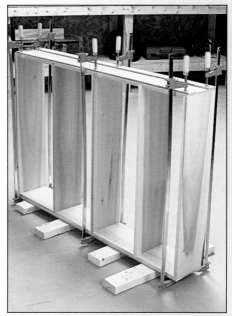

Pipe clamps hold together large assemblies, such as this bookcase, while glue dries. Note the cauls (wood strips) under the clamp jaws at the top and bottom to distribute clamp pressure.

Bar clamps do the same work as pipe clamps. Note how the clamps on this cabinet face frame are placed at the joints most likely to need support. Bar clamps can be laid flat on a surface.

A band clamp holds together boxes and odd-shaped projects while you reinforce joints or make repairs, such as to a shaky drawer. They are not meant for use with large projects.

Spring clamps work well in pairs or in a series for small joinery work. They are easier to adjust and tighten than the standard C-clamp, and they have a protective rubber coating that won't mar wood surfaces.

FINISHING TOUCHES

The project is finally built. You've chosen the perfect design, bought the best material and hardware, and put it all together with first-rate joinery. Now it's ready for finishing.

Or almost ready. Careful preparation is the difference between a ho-hum finish and one that invites compliments. This chapter describes how to properly prepare your project for finishing, select the right finish for the job, and apply it like a pro. Done with care, these final steps result in a finished project you'll be proud to show off.

Why to finish

Finishes primarily protect wood and wood products from absorbing or expelling moisture too fast, which can lead to warping, cracking, and loose joints. Finishes also add protection from dirt, oxidation, spills, and stains. You can wipe off dirt and moisture from a finished surface that would otherwise penetrate and permanently stain the wood.

Finishes make wood projects more beautiful, too. Clear finishes allow you to actually see the wood, making a rich grain sparkle. Stains can change a wood's color and bring out contrast in the grain patterns. Some stains make inexpensive wood look more like an exotic species. Paint can give your projects a colorful gloss or a rich glow. It also conceals plywood edges, fasteners, and puttied-over dings, dents, scratches, and other imperfections.

Where to finish

Because preparation creates dust and finishing produces odors, wear protective safety equipment (page 27), and set aside a special place for these tasks.

If you have a shop, you can do most of your finish preparation at your workbench, including dust-producing activities such as sanding. But it's a good idea to clean a special area just for finish application and drying, so dust and dirt won't mar your results. Or designate a room or part of the basement or garage. (Stay away from the furnace or water heater, as dust and finish fumes can be flammable or explosive.) Be sure you have good ventilation and bright lighting. Sometimes, weather permitting, finishing (especially preparation) is done outdoors.

A poor finish results from second-rate preparation. Take the time to do it right.

CHAPTER PREVIEW

Preparing wood
page 68

Paints, stains, and finishes
page 70

Applying finishes
page 72

Finishes do more than enhance the beauty of wood. They slow the wood's ability to absorb moisture and protect wood from scratches, stains, and dirt. Obtaining a beautiful finish requires some preparation; don't rush the process.

PREPARING WOOD

Make the wood as smooth and perfect as possible to ensure a great finish. Find and fill defects, conceal unsightly edges in plywood, and sand thoroughly.

Detecting defects

Natural defects in wood include tiny, solid knots; thin splits or cracks; and minuscule pest holes. Inspect your project carefully for these and note them. If you find them on hardwood that will be stained and clear finished, it's best to wait until after you've completed the finishing to take care of them. Then apply a colored putty that matches the final finish.

Or you can fill small gaps and other minor imperfections prior to adding a clear finish. One way to do this is to mix some of the wood's own sawdust with a bit of the finish and fill with that. Fine sanding dust is best; the dust-collecting bag or cup of a finishing sander, if yours is so equipped, is a great source. The other way is to simply buy a prepared filler in a matching color.

Use a commercial filler or exterior patching compound to smooth the rough edges of softwood plywood you plan to paint. Then sand the repair. For hardwood plywood, use iron-on veneer tape of the same wood species. In some cases, moldings (page 45) can conceal the edge and add style at the same time.

Sand smooth

Do all prefinish sanding with orange-colored, open-coat garnet sandpaper. Dust won't clog it as easily as closed-coat papers, so it lasts longer and works better. For hand-sanding, "A" weight paper works best. Wrap it around a sanding block so the surface you're working on remains flat as you smooth it.

The higher the grit number, the finer the grit. For most work, start with 100-grit, then use 150-, and end with 220- grit. Clean the surface of the wood between sandings with a vacuum, a tack cloth, or a paper towel lightly dampened with a solvent such as lacquer thinner.

Filling

1 Use a nail set and a hammer to drive the nailhead below the surface. Press filler into the hole, let it dry, then sand flush.

2 Softwood and softwood plywood often have blemishes that will show through a finish. To prevent this, apply a wood filler with a putty knife, then sand when dry.

Edges

Wood filler: Softwood plywood edges usually look rough. Before painting plywood edges, spread wood filler in the voids and sand smooth when dry. Exterior patching compound also works well.

Veneer tape: Easily applied, heat-activated veneer tape neatly covers hardwood plywood edges. Simply trim it with a crafts knife, and use an iron set on medium-low to adhere the tape.

Sanding

A belt sander quickly smooths large surfaces, such as plywood sheets. It is aggressive, however, so keep it moving. If held too long in one place, it can dig into the wood and cause a low spot.

Orbital finishing sanders do a fine job on hardwoods. They are lightweight and maneuverable and are handy for small areas and narrow parts.

A sanding block produces the best results when hand-sanding. Purchase one or make one from a piece of scrapwood. Change paper frequently.

The right abrasive

Select the correct grit for the woodworking job at hand.

Grit	Uses
36–80	Surfacing rough wood
60–100	Rough sanding saw marks
80–320	Sanding contours
120–320	Smooth sanding
240–600	Sanding between coats

Open-coat papers in garnet or aluminum oxide last longer and cut faster.

STANLEY PRO TIP **Dampen hardwood for final sanding**

Get a super-smooth surface on hardwoods by dampening them before the final sanding. Simply moisten a lint-free cloth and wipe down the wood. This raises the "hairs" in the grain so you can remove them with fine sandpaper for a silk-smooth surface.

PAINTS, STAINS, AND FINISHES

The chart on the next page tells you what to expect from several types of finishes. The photos above it show what some popular finishes look like when they're applied to commonly used materials. Here are comparisons of finish categories:

Paint completely obscures the material it covers and is the easiest to apply. Its colored pigments are suspended in either water (water-base/latex paint) or a petroleum product (oil-base paint). Water is the solvent for the first; paint thinner or mineral spirits is the solvent for the latter. Paint is available in several levels of sheen, including flat (little sheen), semigloss (medium sheen), and high-gloss (high sheen). Paint is often used to coat less expensive materials.

Stain colors wood too, but the thin pigment highlights and emphasizes grain features instead of hiding them. Both water-base and oil-base stains are simple to apply but must be followed by a clear top coat.

Clear finishes come in water-base and oil-base varieties, as different types of oils (penetrating), and in combinations. These finishes show the grain of the wood. Oil-base clear finishes add a slight, warm color. The hardest to apply without fault, they normally require several coats for the best appearance and protection.

What to have on hand

You won't need all the items shown *below* for each type of finish. Applicators, for instance, differ with the type of finish you select. The personnel in the finishing department at a home center or hardware store can advise you on your specific needs. **Brushes** are either foam, synthetic bristle, or natural bristle. Natural bristle works best when applying oil-base products. You can use a **roller** with either water- or oil-base coatings, but it will add texture. Lint-free **cheesecloth** is an optional applicator for stains and clear finishing oils.

Steel wool in the fine (#000) and finest (#0000) grades smooths a finish between coats. Don't use it with water-base finishes—any residue will rust. Woven **abrasive pads** perform like steel wool with all finishes.

Fill sticks repair minor surface imperfections, while **wood filler** handles larger ones (see page 68). **Putty knives** are useful for filling large surface defects.

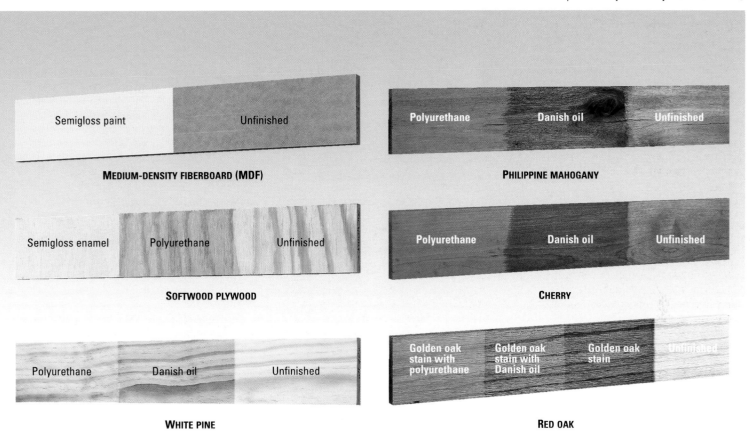

MEDIUM-DENSITY FIBERBOARD (MDF)

Semigloss paint | Unfinished

SOFTWOOD PLYWOOD

Semigloss enamel | Polyurethane | Unfinished

WHITE PINE

Polyurethane | Danish oil | Unfinished

PHILIPPINE MAHOGANY

Polyurethane | Danish oil | Unfinished

CHERRY

Polyurethane | Danish oil | Unfinished

RED OAK

Golden oak stain with polyurethane | Golden oak stain with Danish oil | Golden oak stain | Unfinished

FINISH FEATURES

Not all finishes perform or apply equally. Note the comments following each type to aid in your selection. Finishes described are normally available at home centers and hardware stores.

Type of finish	Description	Application	Comments
PAINT			
Water-base, latex	Easy to apply, simple cleanup	Synthetic brush, roller	Many colors, two coats, fast drying
Oil-base	Easy to apply, durable	Natural bristle brush, roller	Bad odor, flammable, slow drying
CLEAR SURFACE FINISHES			
Lacquer	Moderately durable, lustrous	Best sprayed	Many coats, flammable, bad odor, fast drying
Varnish	Durable, clear	Natural bristle brush	Flammable, bad odor, slow drying, yellows
Polyurethane varnish	High durability/protection	Natural/synthetic/foam brush	Flammable, bad odor, slow drying
Water-base varnish	Durable, no color, easy cleanup	Synthetic/foam brush, spray	Nonflammable, fast drying
Shellac	Easy to apply, difficult cleanup	Natural bristle brush	Low protection, needs wax, many coats, flammable
PENETRATING FINISHES			
Danish oil	Easy to apply, enhances grain	Natural bristle brush or cloth	Low protection, many coats, slow drying
Tung oil	Easy to apply, low luster	Natural bristle brush or cloth	Low protection, many coats, slow drying

APPLYING FINISHES

Apply stain with either a brush or a cloth, always in the direction of the grain. It may look muddy at first—that's why you wipe it off with a cloth before it dries. The remaining pigment soaks into the wood pores, giving it color. If it's too light, repeat the steps. For a lighter color, limit a stain's penetration by first sealing the wood with a prepared wood conditioner.

When you apply any clear finish to wood, start at one edge of the piece and work in the direction of the grain. Smooth out any ridges and pools in the finish with cross-grain strokes while it's still wet. Finishes such as shellac and water-base varnish dry quickly, so you have to work quickly.

For greater visual appeal and durability, apply several coats of clear finish, rubbing with #0000 steel wool or very fine abrasive between each coat.

Stain

1 Mix stain thoroughly before using. With either a brush or lint-free cloth, apply it in the direction of the grain. Overlap your strokes slightly so you don't miss any spots.

2 Before the stain begins to dry, wipe the entire wood surface to remove excess. This also forces the stain's pigment into the grain, enhancing contrast.

Penetrating oil

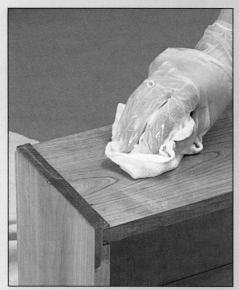

1 When using any type of penetrating oil finish, pour a liberal amount onto the wood, then spread it around with a lint-free cloth. For large areas, apply finish to a section at a time.

2 Let the oil soak in for about 10 minutes (read label directions). Wipe to remove excess oil. Allow the finish to dry 24 hours before applying a second coat. Reapply until the wood will not absorb any more oil.

3 For a satiny-smooth oil finish, rub the dry surface between coats with extra-fine (#0000) steel wool. Wipe off the entire surface after rubbing. When the oil has cured, apply paste wax for protection.

Clear surface finish

1 Stir, don't shake, the polyurethane. For the smoothest application, use a disposable foam brush and work across the grain to fill the pores.

2 For the second coat, brush with the grain so any ridges of finish won't be as visible. To avoid runs, don't load the brush when working near edges.

3 When the finish has thoroughly dried, go over it with #0000 steel wool or fine (320-grit) sandpaper. Repeat between coats.

4 Small flaws such as nicks and nail holes can be filled with a tinted filler stick of matching color after the finish has completely dried.

Paint

1 A first coat of sanding sealer, then a second of primer helps ensure a smooth final coat. Sand it lightly with fine abrasive.

2 Fill any defects that show up in the primer coat—even tiny flaws—with patching compound or wood filler.

3 After filling, go over the entire project with a finish sander and extra-fine abrasive. Grain direction doesn't matter.

4 Thoroughly clean off the sanding dust with a vacuum or tack cloth. Stir paint, then brush on evenly along the grain.

Easy, Great-Looking Shelves You Can Build

Shelves offer unsurpassed versatility. They can be simple or ornate. They can be quickly constructed of rough, unfinished materials or carefully built from fine hardwoods with a rich, lustrous finish. They can store or display, organize or catch clutter.

This chapter presents seven shelf designs, from a simple wall-mounted display shelf to a furniture-quality shelf stand in the popular Mission style. You'll find instructions for building expandable utility shelving for your basement or garage, dramatic display shelves that seem to float on the wall, stylish modular boxes that stack, and a bench with shelves. Each project is easy to build, with complete plans, a materials list, and step-by-step instructions.

A beginner can complete any of the projects using the tools and skills shown in the preceding chapters. The display shelf is the easiest to complete; the Mission-style stand is the most complex.

Material options

All the shelf designs are built with materials that are available at home centers or lumberyards. Most use nominal-size boards—such as 1×2 or 1×4—that only need to be cut to length before assembly.

The instructions for each project specify the type of material to use, but remember that you can build them with materials of your choice. For example, the floating shelves on page 80 are shown made from oak, with a stain and clear finish, but you may choose to construct them of pine and paint them. The modular boxes on page 84 could be made of medium-density fiberboard (MDF). It's less expensive than the birch plywood shown but doesn't take a finish as well.

There are plenty of trim options. For example, if colonial base molding is specified, but there's another molding profile that matches your decor or one that you simply like better, use that. Substituting another style won't alter the project's basic construction. And after all, customizing a project to your taste and decorative style is what's satisfying and fun about building something yourself. So when you're looking at a project, consider how you want it to appear in your home.

Shelves can add more than storage to your home.

Chapter Preview

Display shelf
page 76

Floating shelves
page 80

Modular boxes
page 84

Mission-style utility stand
page 88

Utility shelves
page 96

The floating display shelves (page 80) are made of ready-made molding pieces, adding style to their simple design. The project demands only basic woodworking skills: accurate measuring and cutting, drilling holes, hammering nails, and driving screws.
Read the preceding chapters on tools, materials, and skills before taking on any of the projects in the book.

DISPLAY SHELF

The clean lines of this simple shelf in your bedroom, bath, entryway, kitchen, or living room enhance whatever you choose to display on it. Those same lines tell you that this project is easy to build from readily available materials.

Size considerations
The shelf is 32 inches long, sized to span two wall studs spaced 16 inches on center, the traditional construction of a framed plaster or drywall-covered wall.
If you want to lengthen it, keep stud spacing in mind. Some homes are built using 24-inch stud spacing. If your walls are lath-and-plaster or brick, you'll need to use appropriate hangers.

Other treatments
Although this shelf is shown in naturally finished maple, it can easily be made of any species available. Finish options are as varied as the range of stains and paints available (pages 70–71). Keep in mind, though, that softwoods, such as pine, and some plain hardwoods, such as poplar, often look best when painted.

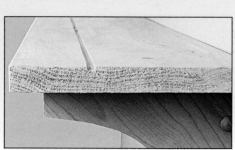

You can build one shelf or several in an afternoon or evening. Mounted directly to wall studs, it can display heavy objects.

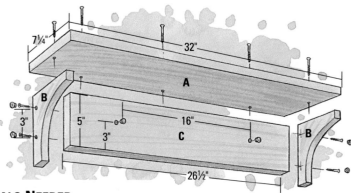

You can add ready-made maple Shaker pegs to hang hats and coats.

You also can cut a groove in the shelf top to display plates (see *opposite page*).

PRESTART CHECKLIST

☐ **TIME**
About two hours to construct, plus an hour to finish

☐ **TOOLS**
Tape measure, clamps, drill bits, counterbore, countersink, electric drill/driver, circular saw or tablesaw, jigsaw with hardwood cutting blade, combination square, level, stud finder

☐ **SKILLS**
Sawing, gluing, clamping, finishing

☐ **PREP**
Find and mark wall studs at shelf location

MATERIALS NEEDED

Part	Finished size			Mat.	Qty.
	T	W	L		
A top shelf	¾"	7¼"	32"	HM	1
B supports	¾"	6¼"	6"	HM	2
C support rail	¾"	5"	26½"	HM	1

Material key: HM–hard maple
Hardware: #8×1½", ×3" FHWS
Supplies: Glue, ⅜" maple mushroom screw hole plugs, ⅜" maple screw hole plugs, sandpaper, clear finish

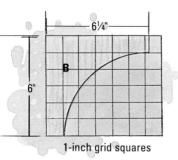

1-inch grid squares

A. Forming parts

1 Cut the top (A) to size and check the ends for square. Measure and mark the points where you'll drill the screws through the top to attach the support rail (C) and the side supports (B).

2 Copy the side support pattern grid *(opposite page)* onto heavy paper (each square = 1 inch). Make pencil dots where the pattern line crosses the grid lines. Connect the dots to form an arc.

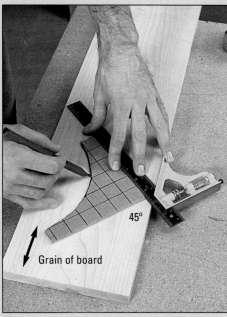

45°

Grain of board

3 Place the cutout pattern on a maple piece wide enough for the side supports. With a combination square, draw a line at a 45-degree angle to the direction of the grain. Align the pattern with the line and trace it onto the board. Repeat for a second piece (two are needed).

STANLEY PRO TIP

Break the edges

Sharp saw blades leave sharp edges on wood that can splinter and cut your hands. So it's always a good idea to break, or soften, the edges of project pieces before assembling them.

Use fine abrasive paper (120-grit) on a sanding block or a fine mesh sanding pad to go over all edges. You'll still finish-sand the entire assembly before applying a finish.

OPTIONS TO CONSIDER
Add a plate groove

If you want to display plates on the shelf, rout a groove to keep the plates from slipping off. Before you assemble the shelf, mount a 1/8-inch round-nose bit in a router. With a guide attached to the router, cut a 1/4-inch-deep plate groove in the top of the shelf (A), 2 1/4 inches from the back edge. If you don't have a router, you can cut a shallow groove using a straightedge, backsaw, and chisel (page 61), or you could use a tablesaw.

Forming parts *(continued)*

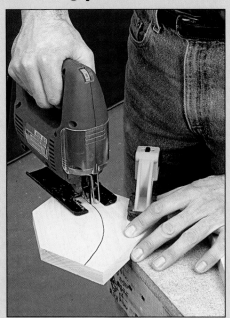

4 Make sure the side support profile aligns across the grain, as shown in the side support pattern drawing. Cut the straight edges. Use a jigsaw to make the curved cut along the pattern line. Repeat for the second piece. Sand edges smooth.

B. Assembling the parts

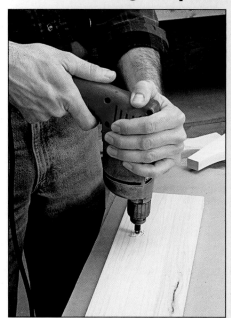

1 Cut the rear support rail (C) to size. Refer to the drawing on page 76 to lay out screw hole locations on the rail for mounting to wall studs (adjust for stud spacing other than 16 inches). With a ⅛-inch countersink bit, drill holes for #8 wood screws.

2 Position the support rail (C) between the two side supports (B) and check for a flush fit. Apply woodworkers glue to the ends of the support rail, position the side supports to the ends, and clamp in place. Set aside and let the assembly dry.

Hanging the shelf on your wall

1 Most wood-frame homes are built with wall studs spaced 16 inches on center. If you expect a shelf to support a load, you must mount it to the studs. Find studs with an electronic stud finder, then mark their location.

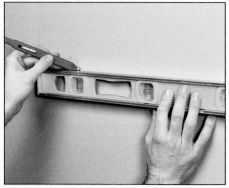

2 Use a long carpenter's level (or a smaller one on top of a straight 1×2) to draw a line on the wall between the marked studs. This will align with the bottom of the shelf's back support rail.

3 Have a helper assist you in lining up the shelf with the line, then insert a nail set through the screw holes and tap indentations into the wall. Remove the shelf and drill ⁵⁄₃₂-inch pilot holes into the studs.

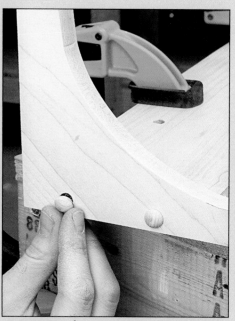

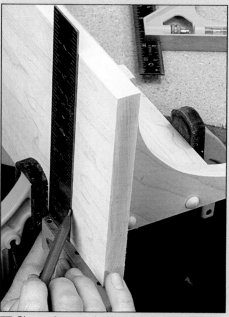

3 When the B/C assembly has dried, lay out and drill ⅜-inch-diameter holes ¼ inch deep from the outside of the side supports, shown on page 76. Center and drill ⁵⁄₃₂-inch pilot holes inside the ⅜-inch holes.

4 Drive #8×1½-inch flathead wood screws into screw holes in the side supports. Be sure the screws sink into the wood below the ⅜-inch holes. Then coat the holes with glue and press ⅜-inch maple mushroom screw hole plugs into place.

5 Clamp the top shelf and B/C assembly together; all back edges should be flush. Check the assembly and mark locations for #8×1½-inch screws to attach the top to the supports. Drill ⅜×¼-inch-deep screw holes with a centered ⁵⁄₃₂-inch pilot hole in each. Drive in the screws. <u>Cover with plugs.</u>

4 Reposition the shelf over the holes, then drive the #8×3-inch flathead wood screws into the shelf and wall. Complete the installation by pressing in (don't glue) finished mushroom-head screw hole plugs.

WHAT IF...
You want to hide the hangers?

The simple hangers shown above, which fit over nails or screws in the wall, are less visible. Use them only if you plan to display lightweight items on the shelf; they're not strong enough for heavy loads.

COVER WITH PLUGS
Sand the plugs smooth

Mushroom screw hole plugs make an attractive accent, but they're an obstruction on the top. Instead, glue in ⅜-inch-diameter wood plugs, then cut them off and sand them flush.

FLOATING SHELVES

With no visible means of support, these shelves appear to float on a wall. The secret is in their construction: They are built around a cleat that attaches them to the wall. The shelves' clean lines do nothing to distract from the objects placed on them. Their simple construction means you can easily make several to create an entire display wall for a collection.

Sizing for studs

The instructions here show how to build a 24-inch shelf that spans two wall studs spaced 16 inches apart on center, but you'll have no trouble increasing the length to 36 or even 48 inches. Basic construction remains the same.

Visible options

Visit a home center and survey the variety of preshaped moldings available for trim options, from contemporary to traditional. Almost any style will fit on the framework. Finish options are just as wide and varied, from natural to painted.

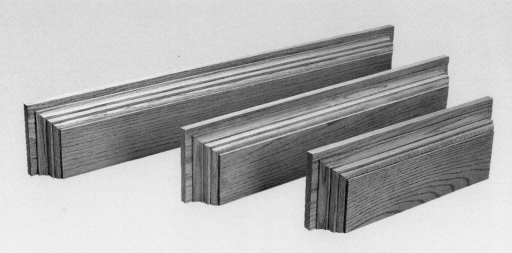

Built of red oak, these shelves employ a simple mounting cleat (D, below) to give the effect of having no support at all. The same construction applies to all sizes.

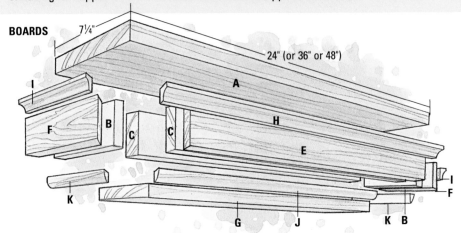

PRESTART CHECKLIST

☐ **TIME**
An afternoon or evening to construct, plus an hour or two for finishing

☐ **TOOLS**
Tape measure, try square, electric drill/driver, ⅛" drill bit, countersink bit, hammer, nail set, power mitersaw (or miter box and backsaw), clamps, level, stud finder, circular saw

☐ **SKILLS**
Sawing (making miter cuts), gluing, clamping

☐ **PREP**
Find studs at shelf location

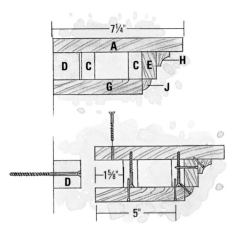

MATERIALS NEEDED

Part	Finished size			Mat.	Qty.
	T	W	L		
A top	¾"	7¼"	24"	RO	1
B end blocks	¾"	1½"	5"	P	2
C front & back rails	¾"	1½"	18"	P	2
D wall cleat	1½"	1½"	17½"	P	1
E front rail	¾"	1½"	21"	RO	1
F side rails	¾"	1½"	5¾"	RO	2
G bottom	¾"	5"	19½"	RO	1
H cove molding	¾"	¾"	22½"	RO	1
I cove molding	¾"	¾"	6½"	RO	2
J quarter round	½"	½"	20½"	RO	1
K quarter round	½"	½"	5½"	RO	2

Material key: RO–red oak, P–pine
Hardware: 4d, 6d finishing nails, #16×⅝" brads, #8×1¼", ×1½", ×2", ×4" FHWS
Supplies: Glue, wood putty, sandpaper, stain, clear finish

1 Crosscut the 7¼-inch-wide top (A) to 24 inches long with a mitersaw. Make sure that the ends are square before proceeding.

2 Cut end blocks (B) and rails (C) to length. Position as shown, glue, and clamp. Check for square by measuring diagonally (page 65); if misaligned, reposition.

3 When the glue has dried, drive 6d finishing nails through the end blocks and into the rails to strengthen the joints.

4 Clamp the assembly B/C to the underside of the top (A), the end blocks flush with the back edge of the top. Fasten with #8×1¼-inch flathead wood screws in countersunk holes.

ENDS ARE SQUARE
Cut once, check it twice

Clamp a layout square tightly against the board to guide a circular saw cut.

Don't assume that the ends of a board are square. Check each end with a try square. If you can see light between it and the board, it's not square.

COUNTERSUNK HOLES
Two-in-one bit

When you need to countersink screw heads and counterbore for plugs, do them both at once with a countersink bit of proper size.

5 Dry-fit the front rail (E), which has been miter-cut at each end, and mitered side rails (F) to the front and sides of the B/C assembly. Glue and clamp them in place.

6 Strengthen the attachment by driving 4d finishing nails through starter holes in the front (E) and side rails (F). Sink the nailheads below the surface with a nail set, then fill the holes with wood putty.

7 Turn over the shelf assembly and apply glue to the exposed edges of parts B and C, then position the bottom (G), and clamp. Secure the bottom with 4d finishing nails and set the heads. FIll the nail holes.

ON THE WALL
Clasping a cleat

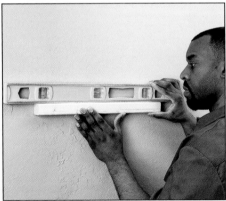

1 Use a stud sensor to locate the nearest wall studs. Position the cleat so it extends over them. Using a level, draw a pencil line on the wall at the top of the cleat. Fasten the cleat to the wall with two #8×4-inch flathead wood screws.

2 In order to attach the shelf to the wall cleat, you'll have to drill two countersunk screw holes in the top of the shelf for #8×1½-inch flathead wood screws.

3 Slide the shelf onto the wall cleat. Mark the screw hole locations on the cleat by inserting a finishing nail through the screw holes in the shelf and tapping lightly. Remove the shelf and drill pilot holes in the cleat.

8 From 2×2 material, cut a wall cleat (D) to length. Sand smooth all surfaces of the cleat, then insert it in the cavity at the back of the shelf to test for fit. There should be a ¼-inch gap at both ends.

9 Miter-cut cove molding (parts H and I) to size. Apply glue to the back of the cove molding pieces and clamp them in place against the bottom side of the top (A). Secure the cove molding with #16×⅝-inch brads. Set the heads and putty the holes.

10 Complete the shelf by miter-cutting the quarter-round molding (parts J and K) to size. Apply glue to the molding back and position at the bottom of the front rail (E) and side rails (F). Fasten with brads, set the heads, and putty the holes.

4 Reposition the shelf on the wall cleat and align it with the screw hole locations. Fasten it in place on the cleat with 1½-inch wood screws driven into countersunk holes flush with the top.

WHAT IF...
The walls are masonry?

Several types of fasteners can be used for mounting shelves to brick, concrete, or stone. Sleeve and wedge anchors expand in predrilled holes in the wall.

STANLEY PRO TIP

Drill starter holes with a nail

Driving finishing nails into hardwood moldings can be difficult. A simple, fast solution: Chuck a finishing nail of the size you're using into the drill, then use it to drill a starter hole.

MODULAR BOXES

These modular boxes, sometimes called shadow boxes, satisfy various needs, from a catch-all in a child's room to a striking showcase for collectibles. Because they stack, you can easily move or rearrange them. Best of all, you can build seven 12×12×12-inch boxes from a single 4×8-foot sheet of plywood.

Measure before cutting

You'd think that a sheet of plywood labeled ¾ inch thick would actually be ¾ inch thick. However, that's not always the case. Because much of the plywood sold is of Asian origin (even if it's made with North American wood), it may be slightly smaller than its stated thickness. That inconsistency will throw off your measurements for the sides of these boxes, which are sawed to 10½ inches wide to allow for joining to two thicknesses of ¾-inch plywood at top and bottom (see the exploded view drawing *below right*). So before cutting, measure the plywood's thickness, then deduct twice that from 12 inches for the width of the box sides.

Painting the birch plywood box and adding the distinctive ash veneer tape to the edges *(bottom left)* creates a distinctive look. For a bright design option, completely paint the box *(bottom right)*. Or you can accent the birch plywood with walnut plugs and veneer *(top)*.

PRESTART CHECKLIST

☐ **TIME**
About four hours to build seven boxes, plus finishing time

☐ **TOOLS**
Tape measure, clamps, electric drill/driver, 1½" spade bit, ¹⁄₁₆" drill bit, tablesaw or portable circular saw, 40- to 60-tooth blade, handsaw, try square, framing square, hammer, nail set

☐ **SKILLS**
Sawing, gluing, clamping

☐ **PREP**
Assemble materials; prepare work area

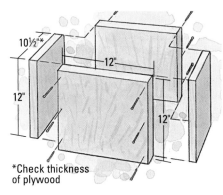

*Check thickness of plywood

MATERIALS NEEDED

Part	Finished size			Mat.	Qty.
	T	W	L		
PER BOX					
A sides	¾"	10½"	12"	BPW	2
B top/bottom	¾"	12"	12"	BPW	2

Material key: BPW–birch plywood
Hardware: 4d finishing nails
Supplies: Glue, wood putty or filler, ash veneer tape, primer, semigloss enamel

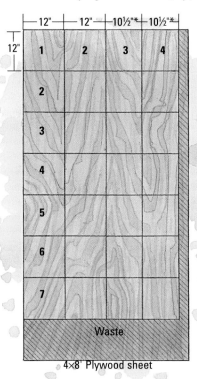

4×8' Plywood sheet

A. Cutting parts

1 To cut the tops and bottoms of the boxes, set the tablesaw fence to rip 12 inches wide (or use a portable circular saw and clamped straightedge for a guide).

2 Rip two 12-inch-wide lengths from the 4×8 plywood sheet. Then rip two pieces 10½ inches wide (or to your measurements) from the remaining stock.

3 To support plywood during crosscutting, attach an auxiliary fence of ¾-inch stock to the miter gauge with screws. Keep it about ⅛ inch from the fence to avoid binding.

4 Set the tablesaw blade and auxiliary fence to get a 12-inch-wide cut. Crosscut all the plywood lengths so you have 14 pieces 12×12 inches and 14 pieces 10½×12 inches.

SAFETY FIRST
Guard against kickback

When wood encounters a spinning saw blade, kickback can occur very suddenly. On a tablesaw, the wood can fly back at you. If you're using a portable circular saw, the saw jumps back at you.

Wood pinching the blade is the usual cause of kickback. Avoid pinching by using a splitter in the saw kerf (the gap left by the blade) behind the blade (page 50) and make sure that the material you're cutting is fully supported. Also, stay out of harm's way. At the tablesaw, don't stand directly in front of the blade. Don't overreach when using a portable circular saw.

AUXILIARY FENCE
Check to ensure straight cuts

Square setup: To make sure that all the box pieces are square (if they're not, they won't fit together properly), use a framing square to check the auxiliary fence before making a cut.

Test cut: Use some scrap plywood to make a test cut. With the framing square, check the test piece. Adjust the setup if necessary.

B. Assembling the parts

It's easy to go astray when assembling so many units, so build a clamping jig like the one shown in Steps 1–3 to help with assembly. Use it to hold the four sides square to each other while gluing and clamping. You can clamp the jig in just one corner, as shown in Step 3. If one corner is square, the opposite one is also square.

Sand with caution

When finishing these modular boxes, remember that hardwood plywood such as the birch plywood shown has a thin face veneer. If you sand too heavily in one area, it's possible to sand right through the veneer, an error that will show through the final finish. Always maintain a light hand with abrasives, even those with fine grit. Most plywood is fairly smooth to begin with, especially on the face side, so it doesn't take much sanding to prepare a surface for finishing.

1 To make a clamping jig, first clamp together (don't glue) a box top (B), bottom (B), and two sides (A). Be sure to assemble the pieces correctly. Measure the inside of the clamped box.

2 Cut scrap of ¾-inch plywood to the box's inside dimensions, minus about 1 inch on each side. Bore 1½-inch holes with a spade bit in a drill about 1 inch in from two adjacent edges. These holes will accommodate the clamp heads.

Apply the finishing touches

1 Fill all plywood edges, except those at the front of the box, with wood putty or filler.

2 Sand all filled edges smooth and lightly sand box surfaces. Remove sanding dust.

3 Apply a coat of primer to the box (except unfilled edges). Then sand lightly again.

3 Assemble the top, bottom, and two sides with glue, then clamp the box, using the clamping jig to check for square. Make any needed adjustments before the glue dries.

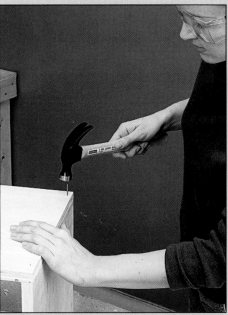

4 After the glue has dried, remove all the clamps and drive 4d finishing nails into the corners to reinforce the assembly. Be sure the nails enter the wood squarely. A finishing option: Use screws and plugs.

5 Drive the heads of all the finishing nails below the surface of the wood with a nail set. Fill the holes with wood putty or filler and later sand them flush.

4 Touch up any blemishes, then paint on one or two finish coats of semigloss enamel.

5 When the paint is dry, add ash veneer tape to the unfilled edges. Miter-cut the corners of the tape (page 44).

FINISHING OPTION
Use walnut plugs for accent

Join the pieces with screws in countersunk holes; plug the holes with walnut dowels for contrast. Then apply walnut instead of ash veneer tape and coat with a clear finish.

MISSION-STYLE UTILITY STAND

This Mission-style utility stand isn't just shelving; it's furniture. During the Arts and Crafts Movement of the late 19th and early 20th centuries, it could have served as a library table. Today it could be used as a home-office printer stand, with the lower shelves for paper and book storage.

Build it with an adjustable flat shelf, or modify it with the V-shape shelf. The drawings *below* show how to alter its height, width, or depth to fit your needs. All of these options follow the same step-by-step construction.

Material and finishing
The stand is made of oak, a popular wood for Mission-style furniture. After staining, it is coated with clear penetrating oil. If the stand will sustain heavy use, provide extra protection with a polyurethane finish.

This Mission-style stand in oak makes an efficient home-office addition, but it would fit into a living room, too, as a TV or stereo stand.

An optional V-shaped shelf replaces the adjustable flat shelf, to hold videos or CDs.

28"
Expand

28"

22"

Expand

You can change the dimensions of the piece to make it wider or deeper to, for example, hold a large-screen TV. Expand the appropriate dimension in both directions from the lines shown at right.

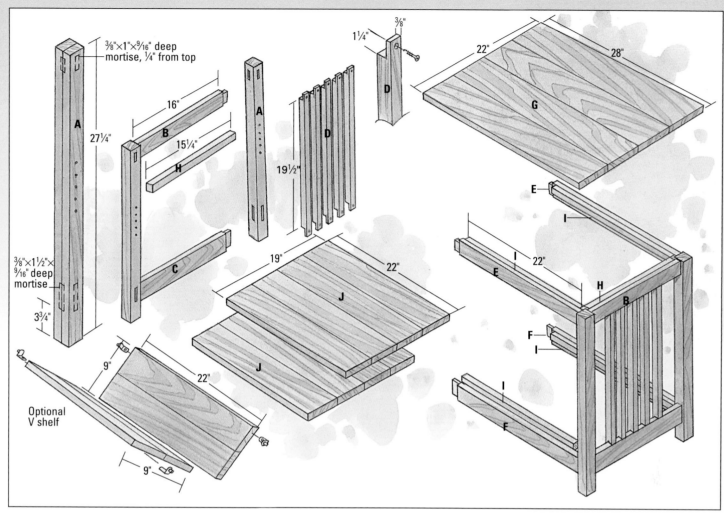

MATERIALS NEEDED

Part		Finished size			Mat.	Qty.
		T	W	L		
A	legs	1½"	1½"	27¼"	LRO	4
B	side top rail*	¾"	2"	17"	RO	2
C	side bottom rail*	¾"	2½"	17"	RO	2
D	spindle	¾"	1"	22"	RO	10
E	front top rail*	¾"	2"	23"	RO	2
F	front bottom rail*	¾"	2½"	23"	RO	2
G	top	¾"	22"	28"	ERO	1
H	cleats	¾"	¾"	15¼"	RO	2
I	cleats	¾"	¾"	22"	RO	4
J	bottom & shelf	¾"	19"	22"	ERO	2

Material key: LRO–laminated red oak, RO–red oak, ERO–edge-joined red oak
Hardware: #8×¾", ×1", ×1¼" FHWS, shelf pegs
Supplies: Glue, sandpaper, stain, clear oil finish
* Length includes tenons

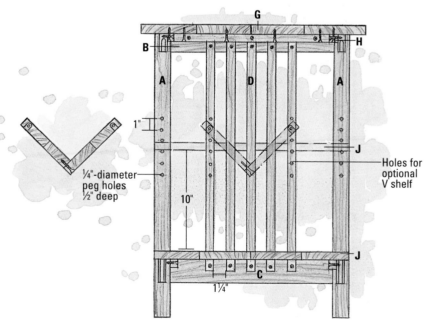

A. Make the legs

1 Make the four legs (A) by ripping ¾-inch-thick oak into eight 1½-inch pieces. Crosscut the pieces to 27¼ inches long.

2 Glue and clamp two pieces to form a 1½×1½-inch leg. (See the Pro Tip *below.)* Repeat for the three remaining legs.

3 Lay out and mark ⅜×1-inch mortises centered on the inside surfaces at the top of the legs, ¼ inch from the top (see exploded view, page 89). Lay out and mark the locations for ⅜×1½-inch bottom mortises, 3¾ inches from the bottom.

Get the grain right

When gluing two pieces of wood to form a single piece (laminating), first dry-fit the pieces. Arrange them so that the grain in each piece runs in opposite directions. When glued, the leg will be stronger and more resistant to any dimensional changes due to fluctuations in humidity that may actually split the wood.

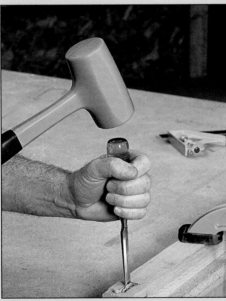

4 Chuck a 5/16-inch brad-point or Forstner bit in an electric drill and bore overlapping holes to 9/16-inch mortise depth within the layout lines.

5 Use a chisel to clean out and square the mortises. Drive the chisel with a dead-blow hammer; make sure the chisel is sharp.

B. Cut tenons in the rails

1 Rip and trim all rails (B, C, E, F) to length (finished size on page 89 includes the length of the tenon). Install a dado set in the tablesaw. Adjust the blades and spacers to cut ½-inch-long tenons to fit the mortise. (The length of the tenons is ¹⁄₁₆ inch shorter than the depth of the mortise.)

2 Use some scrap wood to test the cut of the dado set. Cut the tenon's outside shoulders (the wider ones) first. Check its fit in the mortise. Make any necessary adjustments to the dado blades and fence. When the saw settings are correct, cut the outside shoulders on all rails.

3 Check the setup for cutting the thin part of the tenons' shoulder with a test cut on the scrap wood used in Step 2. Cut one of the rails, then check the tenon's fit in one of the mortises. If it fits, complete the tenon cuts on the rest of the rails. Miter-cut the ends of the tenons.

What If...
You are cutting tenons with a handsaw?

1 To cut tenons with a backsaw, first mark the cuts on the end of the piece (remember the length is ⅛ inch shorter than the depth of the mortise). Clamp the part in a bench vise and saw two of the shoulders.

2 Turn the piece and reclamp it. Saw the remaining two shoulders of the tenon. Clean up the cuts with a sharp wood chisel.

B. Cut tenons in the rails
(continued)

4 Attach two legs to a side top rail (B) and side bottom rail (C) with glue and clamp. Check for square. Repeat assembly with two more legs and side rails. When glue dries, add the front top rails (E) and front bottom rails (F) to joined assemblies. Glue, clamp, check for square.

C. Add the spindles

1 Before you begin making the spindles (D), verify their length by measuring between rails B and C. Allow for a 1¼-inch-long notch ⅝ inch deep at either end to fit the rails.

2 Set up your tablesaw to rip 10 spindles 1×22 inches long (or to your measurement) from ¾-inch-thick oak stock. Use a push stick that's narrow enough to fit between the rip fence and the saw blade.

SAFETY FIRST
Close the gaps for thin rip cuts

1 When ripping thin pieces (less than 1 inch), make and install a zero-clearance insert to keep thin pieces from falling through the slot. Trace the shape of the original insert on material of the same thickness.

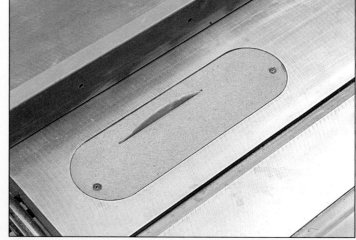

2 Cut out the new insert piece and install it in the arbor (with the blade all the way down). Start the blade and slowly raise it up through the piece, cutting a thin slot just big enough for the blade.

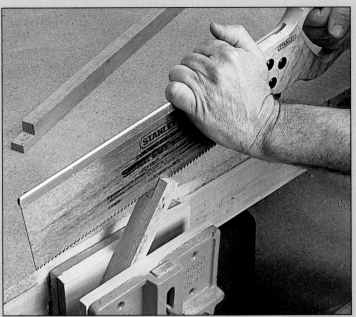

3 To cut the notches at the ends of each of the 10 spindles, refit your tablesaw with a dado set. Or use a backsaw to cut them, securing the wood in a bench vise and cleaning up each notch with a sharp chisel.

4 With an electric drill and counterbore bit, drill countersunk screw holes on the back (the side away from the notch) of each spindle end, shown in the drawing on page 89, then attach them to the side rails.

STANLEY PRO TIP

Oversize sanding block

A standard-size sanding block that holds one-quarter of an abrasive sheet tends to leave high and low spots when smoothing long, narrow pieces or panels more than a foot square. An oversize sanding block won't do that. Tape or glue one-half of a 9×11-inch abrasive sheet to a 3×11-inch block of wood. In much the same way as a long hand plane, it bridges the high and low spots across its length.

Do some finishing prep before assembly

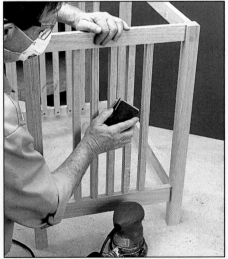

Clean off glue squeeze-out from the joints after joining all the subassemblies. It's easier to do a thorough job before final assembly.

Sand all the spindles while you can still easily get to them.

How to make up for width

Large, wide single pieces of wood will eventually crack and split because of changes in humidity. To avoid that problem, edge-join two or more narrow pieces to make up a wider piece. To make a 12-inch-wide top, for example, join three 4-inch-wide boards.

Make it a rule to never make up width using boards more than 6 inches wide. Narrower widths always work best.

As a further defense against warping, alternate the grain. Look at the arch formed by the growth rings on the end of each board, and place the boards so alternate arches face up.

The mating edges of the boards to be glued up must be true. That is, the sides have to make exact 90-degree angles with the tops and bottoms. Check this by butting all the boards together before gluing. Then, clamp them lightly and look for voids in the joints.

Be careful when clamping a wide piece from several narrower ones. Make sure the pieces remain absolutely flat as you apply and tighten the pipe or bar clamps. Don't overtighten.

D. Add the top and shelves

1 Rip and crosscut oak to get four 5½-inch-wide by 28-inch-long pieces to build the top (G). Arrange them for a pleasing grain effect, then edge-join them with glue and clamps.

2 Rip and trim cleats (H and I) to size from oak. Drill countersunk holes in the cleats for #8×1-inch flathead wood screws, as shown in the end view drawing (page 89). Attach the cleats (H, I) to the inside of the top and bottom rails with screws.

WHAT IF...
You'd like a V-shape shelf?

1 Rip and trim three ¾-inch-thick pieces to 4½ inches by 25 inches. Cut another of the same length to 5¼ inches wide. Edge-join two 4½-inch boards, then the remaining two.

2 When the glue is dry, remove any squeeze-out, sand the wood, and join the pieces together with glue and screws in countersunk holes as shown (see page 89).

3 Mark peg hole locations in the spindles as shown in the V-shelf end view drawing (see page 89). Drill holes using a brad-point bit fitted with a stop.

3 Drill countersunk screw holes in the undersides of cleats H and I. Position the top with an even overhang on all sides, then secure it with #8×1¼-inch flathead wood screws through the cleats.

4 Edge-join four 4¾-inch-wide by 25-inch-long pieces for the shelf (J). Repeat for the bottom. When the glue dries, check the shelf and bottom for fit in the stand. Trim with a tablesaw or circular saw to fit, then sand.

5 Refer to the drawing on page 89 for the shelf peg hole locations in the legs. Mark the holes and drill ¼-inch-diameter holes ⅜ inch deep in the legs. Use an electric drill fitted with a brad-point bit and a drill stop.

6 Insert pegs in the holes and test fit the shelf in the stand. Remove it for finishing. Test the fit of the bottom in the stand. Trim as needed, then attach to cleats with screws (or add it after finishing).

Color with stain and coat with oil

After a final sanding, use a pigmented oil- or water-base stain to give the oak a warm color. Apply at least two coats of a penetrating oil finish.

Remember—it's easier to stain and oil the shelf and the bottom before installing them in the stand.

UTILITY SHELVES

The basic design of this utility shelving unit is adaptable enough that it can be used in a garage, large storage closet, or basement. Add as many shelves as you want between the bottom and the top; just shorten the shelf supports for more shelves or lengthen them for taller spaces to store large items. You can easily change this unit's structural dimensions to make it deeper, longer, or taller.

Try functionally stylish

The unit uses softwood plywood and pine construction—materials readily available at home centers and lumberyards. Its only finish is a coat of marine spar varnish to make cleaning it easier. You could paint the piece in bright-colored enamel for use elsewhere in the house.

PRESTART CHECKLIST

☐ **TIME**
About four hours

☐ **TOOLS**
Tape measure, carpenter's square, power saw, electric drill/driver, countersink bit, drill bits, level, clamps, hammer, sander

☐ **SKILLS**
Sawing and measuring

☐ **PREP**
Organize tools and materials, prepare a work area

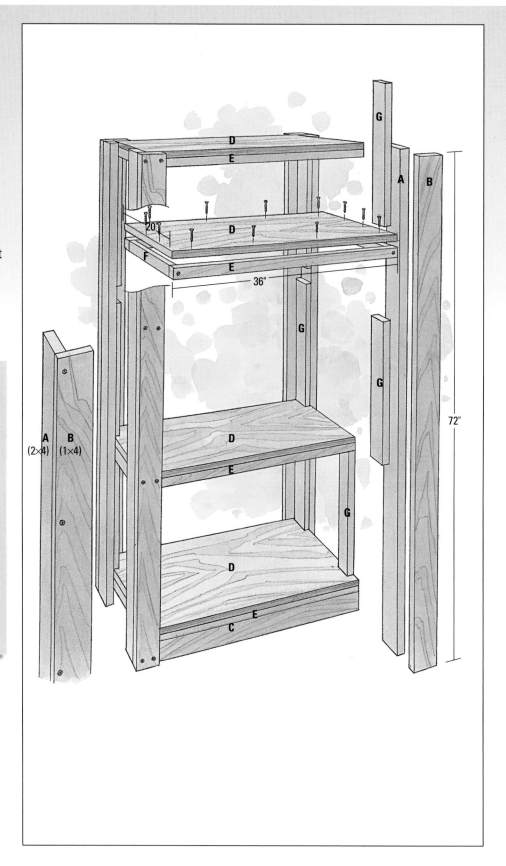

This utility shelf unit can be built quickly and easily with low-cost materials. Its size adapts easily to fit any situation.

MATERIALS NEEDED

Part	Finished size			Mat.	Qty.
	T	W	L		
A stiles	1½"	3½"	72"	NP	4
B stiles	¾"	3½"	72"	NP	4
C base rails	1½"	3½"	36"	NP	2
D decks	¾"	20"	36"	PW	4
E front/back rails	¾"	1½"	36"	NP	8
F side rails	¾"	1½"	18½"	NP	8
G supports	¾"	3½"	*	NP	12

*As needed, see instructions.
Material key: NP–nominal pine, PW–plywood
Hardware: #8×1½", ×1¼" FHWS
Supplies: Glue, shims, sandpaper, finish

A. Forming the stiles

1 Crosscut standard 2×4 material to 72 inches long to obtain the four stile parts (A) for the basic unit. Crosscut 1×4 material to 72 inches in length for the four stile parts (B).

2 Evenly apply glue to one edge of each 2×4 part A. Position one 1×4 part B on each part A with all ends and edges flush, then clamp and let glue dry. Clean off excess glue.

REFRESHER COURSE
Finish all sides

A finish's primary purpose is to protect the wood—from use and abuse, as well as dirt and moisture. Wood gets the most protection (especially from moisture) when all exposed sides are equally coated. With a wooden shelf, for instance, put as many coats on the bottom as you did on the top. That's especially important if the shelves will be in a harsh environment, such as a garage.

STANLEY PRO TIP

Stock off the shelf

Project plans normally include a bill of materials that lists the amount and sizes of all the wood parts needed. Think of this as the start of your shopping list. Rewrite it, listing the number of 1×4s, 2×4s, and other material you'll need before you go to the lumberyard or home center.

And when you get there, select the wood carefully. Set aside boards with obvious cosmetic defects and noticeable warp (page 34). Reject boards with even slight cupping or twisting. Check by placing boards on the floor to see if they lie flat. Bring a crayon to mark the ones you're keeping.

B. Building the framework

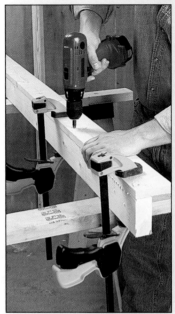   

1 Measure 2 inches in from each end of 1×4 (B) in stile assemblies. Drill five evenly spaced, countersunk holes for #8×1½-inch flathead wood screws. Drive the screws, then sand the edges.

2 Crosscut 2×4 material to 36 inches in length to make two base rails (C). Break the rail edges (page 77) with sandpaper.

3 Using a stop block to ensure identical length, crosscut 1×2 material to length for front and back rails (E). Repeat for eight side rails (F).

4 Clamp a straightedge as a guide and crosscut two 36-inch-long pieces of plywood 48 inches wide. Cut two pieces 20 inches wide from each to make the four 20×36-inch shelf decks (D).

Brush on glue

Use a small foam or stiff-bristle brush to spread glue on narrow surfaces, such as the edge of a 2×4. Either squeeze ribbons of glue directly from the bottle or dip the brush into a small container of glue.

USE A STOP BLOCK
Cutting a consistent length

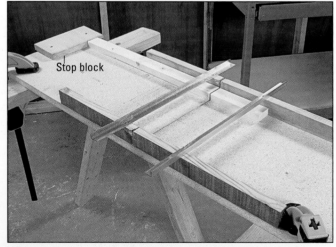

Stop block

When you have several parts to crosscut to the same length, clamp a stop block to your crosscutting jig or worktable at the desired length. Butt each board up to the stop block to make the cut.

C. Assemble shelves

1 Form a 20×36-inch base frame for each shelf by gluing and clamping two 1×2 front/back rails (E) to the ends of two 1×2 side rails (F).

2 Secure each shelf base-frame assembly by drilling holes in the front/back rails and driving #8×1½-inch flathead wood screws into each corner of the base frame.

3 Apply glue to the top of each shelf base frame (E/F). Position a 20×36-inch deck (D) on the top of the shelf base frame. Check for square. Realign as needed, then clamp.

4 Mark and drill evenly spaced countersunk holes for #8×1½-inch flathead wood screws through the deck top, into the base frame. Drive the screws to secure assemblies.

SAFETY FIRST
No chopping with a chop saw

Power mitersaws, often called chop saws in the building trade, are accurate tools that simplify crosscutting and cutting at angles. They cut quickly, but users sometimes try to rush the cut by forcing the blade into the wood, or chopping, which is dangerous.

Let the blade cut the wood at its own pace. Use one hand to pull on the saw with just enough force to lower it; keep the other hand away from the blade, firmly holding the board in place against the fence.

CHECK FOR SQUARE

To avoid the aggravation and wasted time of having to adjust work that's out of square, check for square every step of the way.

Use a carpenter's square to check the ends of boards for square before and after cutting. Use a try square to check the corners of a miter joint and the ends of smaller boards, as well as for squaring a tablesaw blade to the table or a portable circular saw blade to the saw plate.

Diagonal measuring is one way to check for square on a four-sided assembly, such as a face frame or bookcase carcase. Use a tape measure to find the length diagonally from one corner to another. Then measure diagonally between the other two corners. If both measurements are exactly the same, the assembly is square.

D. Assemble the framework

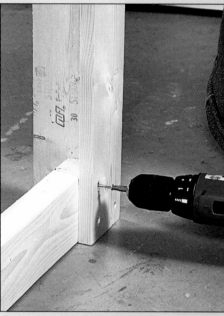

1 Join one end of a base rail (C) to one stile assembly (A/B) with a clamp. With a carpenter's framing square, check the assembly. Drill countersunk holes for two #8×1½-inch flathead wood screws in the face of the stile and fasten with screws.

2 Add a second stile to the base rail/stile assembly and repeat Step 1. Repeat the steps to attach the two remaining stiles and the remaining base rail. Be sure to check for square at each rail/stile joint with a carpenter's framing square.

3 Position the bottom shelf on one rail/stile assembly. Drill countersunk holes for #8×1½-inch flathead wood screws in the rail/stile through to the shelf. Then drive screws into the shelf and rail/stile assembly. Add the second rail/stile assembly and fasten to the shelf.

A finish to make it last

1 It may not be fine furniture, but you still want this shelving unit to feel smooth. Sand the surfaces with 120-grit abrasive, then follow with 180-grit. Soften all sharp edges too.

2 This storage unit may go into a garage or basement, often damp places. An exterior finish such as spar varnish will protect it from moisture as well as help you keep it clean. Finish all sides.

4 With the unit lying on the floor, position the top shelf in place between the stiles, as shown in the drawing on page 96. Drill countersunk holes in the stiles; fasten with #8×1½-inch flathead wood screws.

5 Cut 1×4 material for the 12 support spacers (G). To install a middle shelf, stand up the unit and clamp a support spacer to the inside of each stile. Fasten it with #8×1¼-inch flathead wood screws in counterbored holes.

6 Slide a shelf into place on top of the support spacers. Add other shelves by repeating Step 5. You can change the height of the middle shelves by shortening or lengthening the support spacers.

Leveling and installing the shelves

1 If the unit sits on an uneven floor, tap in shims under the stiles to level it. Check progress with a level.

2 Cut a spacer if there's a gap between the back of the top shelf and the wall. Screw through the shelf rail and the spacer, into the wall.

DESK HUTCH SHELVES

All your supplies will be within easy reach with this handy and handsome desk organizer. It provides 3 feet of various-sized cubbyholes to hold papers, envelopes, and other supplies. You can make yours longer or shorter to fit your desk. Eliminate the drawer, if you like, or make more drawers.

Material and finishing
The ¾-inch-thick parts of the organizer are made of preprimed, finger-jointed pine. This material is as easy to work with as solid pine, but it has less tendency to cup because it is made of multiple pieces that interrupt the grain pattern. There are no knots to bleed through the paint, and the preprimed surface allows you to paint without priming. For a different look, you can use knotty pine or hardwood, such as oak, with a clear finish.

PRESTART CHECKLIST

☐ **TIME**
About six hours for construction, plus finishing time

☐ **TOOLS**
Tape measure, framing square, combination square, hammer, nail set, four bar clamps, tablesaw or circular saw with rip guide and crosscutting jig, router with ⅜-inch piloted rabbeting bit, dado set for the tablesaw or ½-inch straight bit for the router, hand miter box or power mitersaw

☐ **SKILLS**
Measuring, sawing, routing

☐ **PREP**
Assemble tools and materials, prepare work area

MATERIALS NEEDED

Part		Finished size*			Mat.	Qty.
		T	W	L		
A	top and bottom	¾"	9"	34½"	PFJ	2
B	sides	¾"	9"	16½"	PFJ	2
C	long dividers	¾"	8¾"	16½"	PFJ	2
D	shelves	¾"	8¾"	11⅞"	PFJ	4
E	shelf	¾"	8 ¾"	7¾"	PFJ	1
F	short dividers	½"	5¼"	8¾"	pine	4
G	back	¼"	17¼"	33¾"	LP	1
H	top face trim	¾"	1"	36"	pine	1
I	top side trim	¾"	1"	9¾"	pine	2
J	bottom face trim	¾"	¾"	36"	QR	1
K	bottom side trim	¾"	¾"	9¾"	QR	2
L	drawer front	½"	6⅝"	7⅝"	pine	1
M	drawer sides	½"	6⅝"	8½"	pine	2
N	drawer back	½"	6⅛"	6⅝"	pine	1
O	drawer bottom	¼"	7 1/16"	8 7/16"	LP	1

Parts initially cut oversize, see instructions.

Material key: PFJ—preprimed finger-jointed pine, LP—lauan plywood, QR—quarter-round molding
Hardware: 4d finishing nails, 1-inch brads
Supplies: Glue, 80- and 150-grit sandpaper

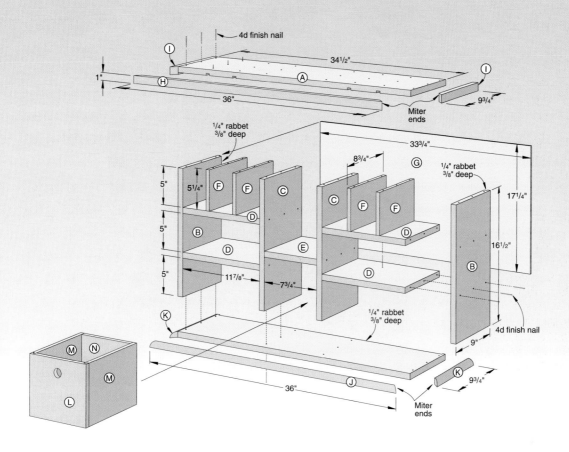

Finger-jointed stock

Painting pine is difficult because the knots are likely to bleed through paint and make a stain—sometimes even after a coat of shellac-based stain-stopping primer. Knot-free clear pine is becoming more expensive.

Finger-jointed pine stock—short clear sections of pine joined end-to-end with finger joints—provides a solution to this problem. Because the product is usually painted, it's usually sold preprimed.

WHAT IF...
You want oak?

Perhaps you want your organizer to match that nice oak desk. You can easily find ½-inch-thick and ¾-inch-thick oak boards as well as oak quarter-round at home centers and lumberyards. Construction is the same, but you'll need to predrill ⅛-inch holes so you don't bend the finishing nails when you drive them into the hard oak. Sand the whole project with 80-grit and then 150-grit sandpaper before applying a clear finish.

A. Cutting the parts

1 Use a tablesaw or a circular saw with a rip guide to rip a 10-foot 1×10 to 9 inches wide for the top and bottom (A) and the sides (B), an 8-foot 1×10 to 8¾ inches wide for the two long dividers (C) and the shelves (D and E). Rip ½×6-inch stock 3 feet long to 5¼ inches wide for the short dividers (F).

2 Use a crosscutting jig with a circular saw to cut the top and bottom pieces (A), the sides (B), the two long dividers (C), the shelves (D and E), and the short dividers to the lengths listed in the Materials Needed chart on page 102.

3 Use the tablesaw rip fence to cut a strip 17¼ inches wide from a sheet of ¼-inch lauan plywood. Have a helper support the long end of the plywood as you move it through the saw. If you don't have a tablesaw, make the cut with a circular saw and straightedge jig (page 50).

4 Cut a piece 33¾ inches long from the 17¼-inch-wide plywood to make the back (G). Make the cut with a circular saw guided by a straightedge jig.

5 As the drawing at the top of page 103 shows, the short dividers fit into two ½-inch-wide, ¼-inch-deep dadoes in the bottom of the top piece. Use a framing square to lay out these dadoes as shown above. Then place the top and bottom side by side, ends flush, and lay out positions of the long dividers (C).

B. Assembling the organizer

1 The four dadoes in the bottom of the top piece are ½ inch wide and ¼ inch deep. Cut them with a dado set on the tablesaw or with a router guided by a router straightedge guide.

2 Apply glue to the top edges of the sides. Place the top on the sides, and secure with 4d finishing nails. Do the same to attach the bottom to the sides. Use a framing square to make sure the box is square before the glue dries.

3 Set a ⅜-inch piloted rabbeting bit in the router to cut ¼ inch deep. Before rabbeting all four sides to receive the back, clamp a piece of 2×4 flush with the back to provide more support for the router base. Square the rabbet corners with a chisel.

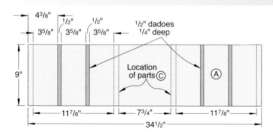

TOP SECTION VIEW

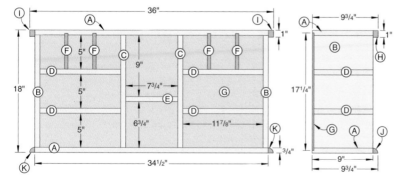

FRONT SECTION VIEW   **SIDE SECTION VIEW**

4 Put the long dividers side by side, with their ends flush. Use a framing square to lay out the position of the middle shelf (E). Flip the dividers over and lay out the positions of the side shelves (D). Then use the dividers to transfer the side shelf positions to the side pieces (B).

B. Assembling the organizer (continued)

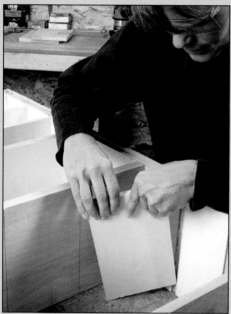

5 Apply glue on the ends of the long dividers, position them in the box flush with the front, and check for square before securing with 4d nails through the top and bottom. Glue and nail the short dividers into the dadoes, flush with the front.

6 Use glue and 4d nails to attach one of the shelves (D) to the short dividers. Use a combination square to hold the dividers square to the shelf while you nail. Then nail through the sides and long dividers into the end of the shelf. Install the opposite shelf the same way.

7 Glue and nail the middle shelf (E) in place between the long dividers. Then glue and nail the lower side shelves (D) between the sides and long dividers. The assembly template (right) will make it easier to align the lower side shelves.

8 Put the back in place with its good side temporarily facing out. Scribe the positions of the shelves and dividers on the inside. Remove the back and apply glue on the rabbets, shelves and dividers. Place the back in position with the lines showing the shelf locations up, and then secure it with 1-inch brads using the lines as a guide.

C. Adding the trim

1 Make stock for the top trim pieces (H and I) by ripping ¾-inch-thick solid pine to 1 inch wide. Cut one piece at least 36½ inches long with a 45-degree miter on one end and two pieces at least 10¼ inches long with a 45-degree miter on one end.

ASSEMBLY TEMPLATE
A spacer speeds the work

Because all the side shelves (D) are spaced 5 inches apart, you can assemble them more quickly and accurately by ripping a 9-inch-long piece of scrap to 5 inches wide. Put this assembly template against opposing walls, then put a shelf in place against the template.

2 Place the long piece of trim stock in place at the top of the organizer with the mitered end aligned with the corner. Mark the other end of the trim piece and use a square to extend the mark at 45 degrees over the top of the piece. Cut the miter.

3 Install the front trim piece with glue and 4d nails. Put the mitered end of one of the short pieces in place on one side and mark for a cut flush with the back. Do the same with the piece on the other side. Cut and install the pieces.

4 The bottom trim pieces (J and K) are made of ¾- by ¾-inch quarter-round molding. Mark, cut, and install it the same way as the top molding. Wipe off any glue squeeze-out with a sponge before it dries.

ROUTER STRAIGHTEDGE GUIDE
Use a simple jig for accurate ½-inch dadoes

You can make this jig in minutes to quickly and accurately align your router bit to the dado layout lines. Just screw a 12-inch-long piece of 1×2 at an accurate 90-degree angle to a 6-inch-wide piece of ¾-inch plywood that's about 3 inches longer than the workpiece width. Set the router bit to the depth you need and rout the dado in the crosspiece. Now you can align this dado to the layout line, clamp the jig in place, and rout the dado.

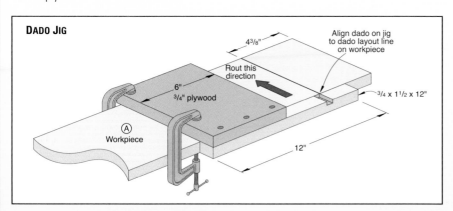

DADO JIG

4³⁄₈"

Align dado on jig to dado layout line on workpiece

Rout this direction

6"
¾" plywood

¾ x 1½ x 12"

Ⓐ Workpiece

12"

5 Set all the nails and fill the holes with wood putty. When the putty dries, use 80-grit sandpaper to smooth and slightly round all the edges. Prime the bare cut edges. Don't paint inside any spaces where you will add a drawer.

D. Building the drawer

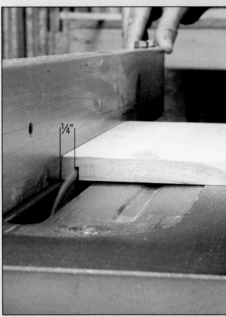

1 Rip 32 inches of ½-inch-thick pine to 6⅝ inches wide. Cut one piece to 7⅝ inches to make the drawer front (L), two pieces to 8½ inches for the sides (M), and one piece to 6⅝ inches for the back (N). Rip the back down to 6⅛ inches.

2 Set your tablesaw blade height to ¼ inch. Set the fence ¼ inch from the blade and cut a groove along the bottom inside edges of the front and sides. Run the ends of the drawer fronts against the fence to cut a dado from top to bottom.

3 Reset the fence so the outside of the blade is ½ inch from the fence. Run the pieces through again to widen the grooves and dadoes to ¼ inch.

Hutch Drawer

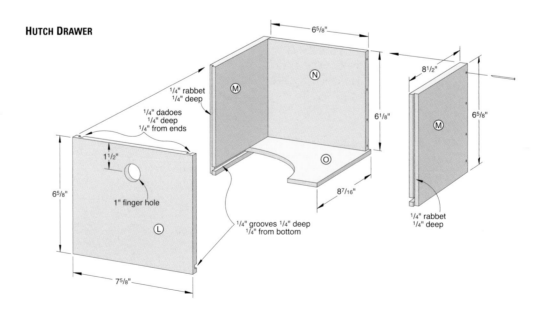

1½"

1" finger hole

6⅝"

7⅝"

¼" dadoes
¼" deep
¼" from ends

¼" rabbet
¼" deep

¼" grooves ¼" deep
¼" from bottom

6⅝"

6⅛"

8⁷⁄₁₆"

8½"

6⅝"

¼" rabbet
¼" deep

4 Lay out a line on the top edge of each sidepiece ¼ inch from the front end. Put a sidepiece against the miter gauge, align the blade to the line, and cut a groove. Move the piece and make another pass to remove the rest of the waste and create a ¼-inch rabbet ¼ inch deep.

5 Apply glue to the ends of the back and attach it between the sides with four 4d finishing nails into each side. Apply glue in the dadoes in the drawer-front ends and on the rabbets in the sides. Assemble these joints with clamps. Check for square.

6 Cut ¼-inch plywood to 7¹/₁₆ inches by 8⁷/₁₆ inches. Slide it into the grooves in the sides and front and nail it to the bottom with four 1-inch brads. It will be slightly loose to ease assembly and allow for wood movement. Don't use glue.

STANLEY PRO TIP

Set blade height with a combination square

To set the height of your tablesaw blade, first set your combination square to the height you need—in this case ¼ inch. Then crouch down so the saw table is at eye level and raise the blade until the topmost tooth touches the body of the square. Make a test cut and use the square to check the groove depth.

WHAT IF...
You want to hang the organizer

To save desk space, you can hang the organizer on the wall. Make three 1½-inch-wide hanging cleats from ¾-inch-thick pine. Cut the cleats to fit under the top between the sides and the first short divider on each side and between the long dividers. Glue and nail them in place. Hang the organizer with 2-inch drywall screws into studs or toggle bolts into hollow drywall.

7 Add a knob to the front or drill a 1-inch diameter finger hole as shown. Sand all the edges of the shelf and the finger hole.

ENTRY SHELF AND BENCH WITH SHELVES

Here's the perfect entryway combo—a bench to sit on while removing muddy sneakers or snow-covered boots, topped by shelves to stow hats and gloves with hooks for coats. The bench is open at the front to store sneakers or boots out of the way.

The bench and shelf combination shown here is 34 inches wide to fit the entryway they'll be in. You could easily make the units wider, perhaps adding another vertical divider to each. An upholsterer can make a 2-inch-thick foam cushion to fit the bench.

The exposed parts of the units shown here are made of birch plywood and poplar solid wood because both woods take paint well. You also can use oak plywood and solid oak with a clear finish. Or paint the birch plywood and make the seat border pieces of oak with a clear finish.

PRESTART CHECKLIST

☐ **TIME**
Eight hours to build the bench, four hours to build the shelves, plus finishing time

☐ **TOOLS**
Tablesaw or circular saw with straightedge jig, power mitersaw or miter box, router with ⅜-inch piloted rabbeting bit and ⅜-inch roundover bit, framing square, combination square, backsaw, bar clamps, chisel, mallet, hammer, nail set, tape measure, utility knife

☐ **SKILLS**
Sawing (making miter cuts), making dadoes and rabbets, gluing, clamping

☐ **PREP**
Organize tools and materials, prepare a work area

MATERIALS NEEDED

Part		Finished size*		Mat.	Qty.
	T	**W**	**L**		
BENCH					
A top	¾"	13"	34"	BP	1
B bottom	¾"	13"	33¼"	BP	1
C sides	¾"	13"	13¾"	BP	2
D divider	¾"	12¾"	13¾"	BP	1
E base supports	¾"	2"	9"	BP	2
F base support	¾"	2"	30"	BP	1
G base support	¾"	2"	28½"	BP	1
H seat border	¾"	3½"	35½"	PL	1
I seat border	¾"	3½"	14⅛"	PL	1
J back	¼"	13¾"	33¼"	LP	1
K blocks	¾"	2"	4"	BP	4
SHELF	(PAGE 118)				
L top face edging	¾"	1½"	35½"	PL	1
M top side edging	¾"	1½"	10¾"	PL	2
N top rail	¾"	1½"	32½"	PL	1
O top	¾"	10"	34"	BP	1
P bottom	¾"	8½"	32½"	BP	1
Q back	¾"	17¼"	32½"	BP	1
R divider	¾"	8½"	10"	BP	1
S sides	¾"	10"	17¼"	BP	2
T inside corners	¾"	¾"	10"	QR	2

Parts initially cut oversize, see instructions.

Material key: BP—birch plywood, PL—poplar, LP—lauan plywood, QR—Pine quarter-round molding
Hardware: 4d finishing nails, 1¼-inch coarse-thread drywall screws, 1-inch brads, three clothing hooks
Supplies: ¾-inch birch veneer edge tape, glue, 80- and 150-grit sandpaper, paint

BENCH OVERVIEW

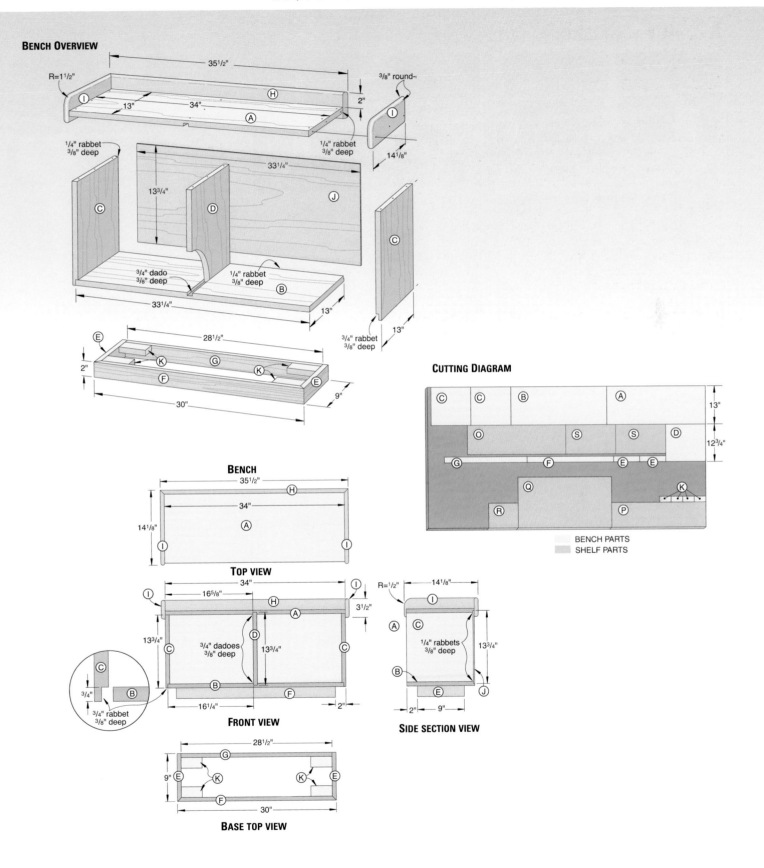

35½"

R=1½"

3/8" round

2"

1/4" rabbet
3/8" deep

13"

34"

H

I

A

I

14⅛"

1/4" rabbet
3/8" deep

33¼"

13¾"

C

D

J

C

3/4" dado
3/8" deep

1/4" rabbet
3/8" deep

B

33¼"

13"

13"

3/4" rabbet
3/8" deep

28½"

E

2"

K

G

K

F

E

30"

9"

CUTTING DIAGRAM

C   C   B   A   13"

O   S   S   D   12¾"

G   F   E   E

Q

K

R   P

BENCH PARTS
SHELF PARTS

BENCH

35½"

H

34"

A

14⅛"

I   I

TOP VIEW

34"

16⅝"   I

H

A

3½"

I

13¾"

C   3/4" dadoes
3/8" deep

D

13¾"

C

C   3/4"
B   3/4" rabbet
3/8" deep

B   F

16¼"   2"

FRONT VIEW

R=½"   14⅛"

I

A   C

1/4" rabbets
3/8" deep

13¾"

B

E   J

2"   9"

SIDE SECTION VIEW

28½"

G

9"   E   K   K   E

F

30"

BASE TOP VIEW

A. Cutting the bench parts

1 Set the tablesaw fence to 13 inches and rip-cut one piece from the sheet of ¾-inch birch plywood and one from the ¼-inch plywood. Then rip-cut 12¾ inches from the ¾-inch plywood. Or make the cuts with a circular saw and a straightedge jig (page 31).

2 After making preliminary cuts as described in the Safety First box *below*, use the miter gauge on your tablesaw to crosscut the top (A), bottom (B), sides (C), divider (D), and back (J). Or you can use a straightedge jig with a circular saw to make the cuts.

3 Use the tablesaw and a push stick to make the 2-inch rip-cut shown in the cutting diagram on page 111. Crosscut the pieces to length with a power mitersaw or hand miter box, making 45-degree miters on both ends of the two short pieces (E) and one of the long pieces (G).

SAFETY FIRST
Making preliminary cuts

If you have a small benchtop tablesaw, it can be awkward to rip-cut a full sheet of plywood. So make preliminary sizing cuts with your circular saw. To rip-cut the 13-inch and 12¾-inch pieces in Step 1 *above*, cut a piece 26½ inches wide from the full sheet using a circular saw and straightedge jig, then rip-cut the two pieces from it on the tablesaw.

It's dangerous to crosscut long pieces with the miter gauge on any size tablesaw. Instead, lay out lines and use your circular saw to cut the pieces slightly larger than you need before making final cuts on the tablesaw.

B. Making dadoes and rabbets

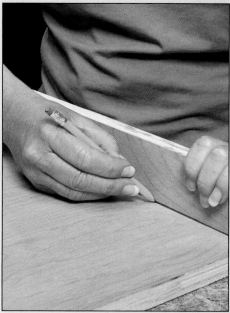

1 Mark one edge of the top (A) at 17 inches and one edge of the bottom (B) at 16⅝ inches. Lay the pieces together with these center marks aligned. Measure ⅜ inch to one side of the marks and strike a line. This is one side of the center dadoes.

2 Plywood is usually a little thinner than stated, so measuring may give you loose-fitting dadoes. Instead, align a scrap of the plywood to the first layout line and scribe the plywood's thickness across the top and bottom pieces. Scribe rabbets on the bottom of each side (C) by holding the scrap flush to the end.

3 Set your circular saw to cut ⅜ inch deeper than the base of your crosscut jig. Use the jig to cut both sides of the dadoes and the inside of the rabbets. Then make several passes across the joints to saw out most of the waste. Clean up with a chisel (page 55).

WHAT IF...
You cut dadoes with a router?

Because ¾-inch plywood is usually not quite ¾ inches thick, you can't use a ¾-inch-diameter bit to rout dadoes. Instead, use this simple jig to rout perfect dadoes with two passes of a ½-diameter bit set at ⅜ inch deep.

First, lay out the center of the dado on one side piece as shown at top right. Center the edge of a scrap piece of the plywood stock on the center line. Scribe both sides. Measure the diameter of your router base and divide by two to get the radius. Add ⅛ inch to the radius and strike a line this distance from each side of the dado. Use the lines to assemble the jig as shown at bottom right.

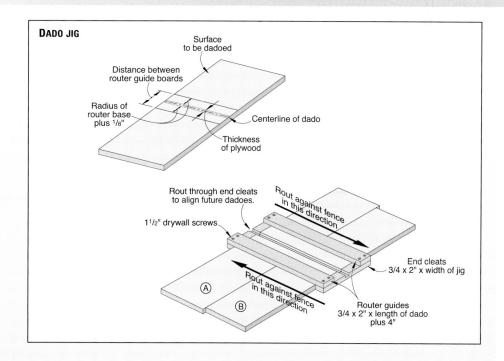

DADO JIG

Surface to be dadoed

Distance between router guide boards

Radius of router base plus ⅛"

Centerline of dado

Thickness of plywood

Rout through end cleats to align future dadoes.

Rout against fence in this direction

1½" drywall screws

End cleats 3/4 x 2" x width of jig

Ⓐ

Ⓑ

Rout against fence in this direction

Router guides 3/4 x 2" x length of dado plus 4"

C. Assembling the bench

1 Use glue and 4d finishing nails to assemble the center divider and then the sides to the bottom. Make sure the sides are flush at front and back. The center divider will be flush only with the front. It will be ¼ inch short at the back.

2 Apply glue to the top edges of the sides and center divider. Fit the dado in the top over the center divider and nail in place. Nail the top to the sides, making sure the ends of the top are flush to the front and the outside surface of the sides.

3 Put a ⅜-inch piloted rabbeting bit in your router and set the cutting depth to ¼ inch. Put the bench on its face. To give the router a wider surface to ride on, clamp a 2×4 flush with the top edge and then the bottom and each side before rabbeting the inside edges.

REFRESHER COURSE
Squaring the bench

Before the glue joints dry, and before you put the back in place, check that the bench is square. First check with a framing square. Then double-check: Measure diagonally between corners and then measure diagonally between the other corners. If the measurements are exactly the same, the bench is square.

Making the back rabbets on the tablesaw

You can use a tablesaw as described in "Rabbet joint" (page 61) to rabbet the back edges of the top, bottom, and sides before assembling the bench. However, because the rabbets will extend the full length of the pieces, there will be a small square hole at the bottom and top of each side. At the top, the seat borders will cover the hole. At the bottom, you can fill the holes with wood putty if you will be painting the bench.

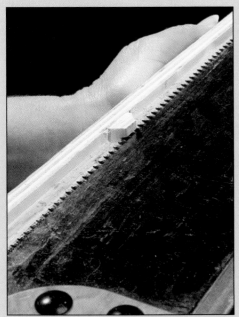

D. Attaching the base

4 Make a few strokes across with a backsaw and a quick slice with a chisel to complete the rabbets where the router bit's pilot bumped into the divider. Square the rabbet corners with the chisel.

5 Apply glue in the rabbets in the back of the bench and along the back of the center divider. Secure the back with 1-inch brads spaced about 4 inches apart. Be careful to nail straight down so the nails don't come through the sides.

1 Cut four 2-inch by 4-inch blocks of ¾-inch plywood (K). Using scraps to protect the outside surfaces, glue and clamp the long sides of the blocks to the long base support pieces (F and G). Make sure the ends of the blocks are flush to the inside ends and the top of the support.

SQUARE THE RABBET CORNERS WITH A CHISEL

1 Place the flat back of a chisel against the back of the rabbet. Hit the chisel with a mallet to chop straight down to the bottom of the rabbet.

2 Place the flat of the chisel against the bottom of the rabbet and slice back and forth to cut off the waste.

STANLEY PRO TIP

Pocket-holes for the blocks

If you have a pocket-hole jig (page 64), you can use it to attach the corner blocks, eliminating the need to clamp and wait for glue to dry. If you do use the jig, make the blocks from poplar instead of plywood. Use glue and four screws to attach each block to the base. Predrill the holes for screwing the poplar blocks to the bench.

D. Attaching the base (continued)

2 When the glue is dry, remove the clamps. Apply glue to the blocks and on the ends of the long base support pieces (F and G). Then clamp the short base support pieces (E) to the blocks, again using scrap to protect the outside surfaces. Make sure the base is square.

3 When the glue is dry, remove the clamps. Apply glue to the top surface of the blocks. Center the base on the bottom of the bench and attach the base to the bench with 1½-inch drywall screws—two screws into each block.

E. Adding the seat borders

1 Make all three seat border pieces (H and I) from a 6-foot length of poplar. Before cutting the stock, rout a ⅜-inch roundover on both sides of what will be the top edge of the border. Then make a ⅜-inch roundover on the bottom of the face that will be visible.

STANLEY PRO TIP: **Super-accurate scribing with your utility knife**

1 A sharp utility knife can be a more accurate scribing tool than a pencil. For example, use the knife to just nick the point where the seat border piece meets the back corner of the bench.

2 To lay out the miter, put your utility knife blade back in the nick it made. Slide your square up against the blade and scribe the exact position of the miter cut.

⅜-INCH ROUNDOVER
Setting your router for the perfect cut

You'll use a piloted ⅜-inch roundover bit to shape the edges of the seat border pieces. The key to a perfect roundover is getting the bit depth set correctly. You want just the round part of the bit wing to protrude from the router base—if any more protrudes, you'll have a roundover topped by a lip.

2 Use a mitersaw to cut a 45-degree miter on one end of the border stock. Cut the other end off square at about 36 inches. Have a helper align the miter with a back corner of the bench while you scribe the inside of the other miter on the other end.

3 Position the back border piece with 2 inches of its thickness protruding above the bench top, then secure it with glue and 4d finishing nails into predrilled holes. Cut the side border pieces 14⅛ inches long with a miter on one end and a square cut on the other.

4 Rout a ⅜-inch roundover on both edges of the end of each side border piece so that the fronts of the pieces will be fully rounded. Glue and nail the side pieces into place. Cover the front edges of the bench with edge banding (page 44) and sand all edges smooth.

OPTIONS TO CONSIDER
Skip the cushion

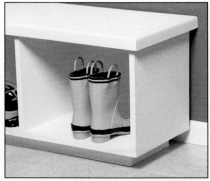

To make a bench with no cushion, make the border pieces only 1½ inches wide with a roundover on the outside edges only. Install them flush with the top of the bench. Add a fourth border piece to the front of the bench, then join it to the side pieces with miter joints.

POSITION THE BORDER PIECE
Lay out a line with your combination square

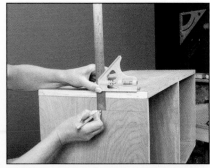

To help position the seat border pieces at the correct height above the bench, set your combination square to 2 inches and run it along the stock with a pencil against the blade to lay out a line. Keep the square set to 2 inches to quickly check the positions of the pieces as you nail them in place.

OPTIONS TO CONSIDER
Round slightly with sandpaper

Instead of completely rounding the edges of the seat border pieces with a router, you can gently round them with sandpaper after the pieces are installed. Use 80-grit sandpaper if you will paint the pieces, and follow up with 150-grit if you will use a clear finish.

F. Cutting the shelf parts

1 The cutting diagram (page 111) shows how the shelf parts are cut from the same plywood sheet as the bench parts. You'll have one piece about 10¾ inches wide. Rip this to 10 inches and crosscut it to make the sides (S) and top (O).

2 To make the back (Q), crosscut 32½ inches from the remaining piece of ¾-inch plywood and then rip that piece to 17¼ inches. Make an 8½-inch rip-cut, then crosscut as shown in the diagram to make the bottom shelf (P) and divider (R).

3 Lay out the cutouts at the bottom of the sides. Mark the layout on the outside faces, then score the lines with a sharp utility knife guided by a straightedge to prevent the veneer from chipping when you saw. Cut to the intersection of the lines with a circular saw.

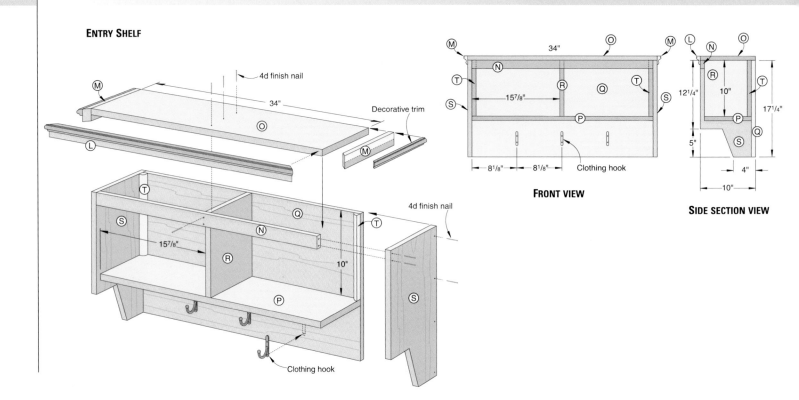

ENTRY SHELF

4d finish nail

34"

Decorative trim

4d finish nail

15⅞"

10"

Clothing hook

FRONT VIEW

34"

15⅞"

8⅛" — 8⅛"

Clothing hook

12¼" 10" 17¼"

5" 4"

10"

SIDE SECTION VIEW

G. Attach the top edging

4 You can't complete the cut with a circular saw without overcutting the intersection at the top. So turn the side pieces over and complete the cuts with a few strokes of a handsaw held vertically.

1 Put the top piece upside down on the bench. Square-cut one top side edging piece (M), put it in place against the top piece, and mark for a miter cut where it meets the top's front corner. Cut the miter with a hand miter box or power mitersaw.

2 Attach the first side piece with glue and 4d finishing nails in predrilled holes. Miter one end of the top face edging (L), mark the other miter in place, then cut and install. Miter one end of the other side piece, mark for the square cut at back, then cut and install.

OPTIONS TO CONSIDER
Alter edging for a custom look

Changing the top edging is a simple way to customize the look of your shelf. You can make it from a handsome hardwood such as oak, cherry, or walnut and give it a clear finish to contrast with the painted shelf. Or you can use a matching wood and finish for the seat borders on the bench.

Another way is to buy small pine molding, such as the base cap or panel molding shown at *right*. Glue and nail the molding onto the top edging and paint it with the rest of the shelf. A third way is to replace the poplar top edging with a 1½-inch-wide molding such as the shingle/panel molding shown at right.

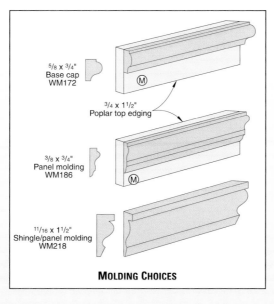

⅝ x ¾"
Base cap
WM172

¾ x 1½"
Poplar top edging

⅜ x ¾"
Panel molding
WM186

11/16 x 1½"
Shingle/panel molding
WM218

MOLDING CHOICES

REFRESHER COURSE
Predrilling nail holes

It's nearly impossible to drive nails through hardwood without bending them over. For this reason, you should always predrill in hardwood—use a 1/16-inch-diameter bit for 4d finishing nails.

It's also a good idea to predrill thin moldings to prevent splitting them, especially near the ends.

H. Assemble the shelves

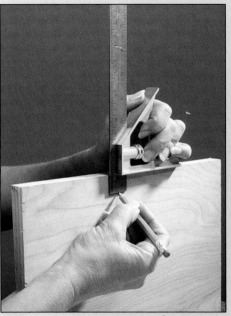

1 Attach the back between the sides with glue and 4d finishing nails, making sure all three pieces are flush at top. Cut quarter-round molding for the inside corners (T) to 10 inches and attach these pieces with glue and 1-inch brads.

2 Set a combination square to ¾-inch to lay out the position of the bottom (P) on the inside of the sides as shown. Apply glue to the ends of the bottom piece and align its bottom with the layout line. Check that the bottom is square to the back before securing with three 4d nails on each side.

3 Cut the top rail (N) to fit between the sides. Apply glue to the ends and position the rail flush with the top of the sides. Attach with two 4d finishing nails driven through predrilled holes in the sides.

Using dadoes and rabbets

Simple butt joints and glue are strong enough for a small shelf unit like this. But it will be easier to square up the project if you assemble it with dadoes and rabbets. If you rabbet the back into the sides, you don't need the quarter-round molding.

Making these joints will be easy if you already made the router jig (bottom, page 113) for the bench. Don't forget to add ¾ inch to the length of the bottom, divider, and back, as well as ¾ inch to the width of the back.

1 The bottom stops ¾ inch short of the front of the sides. In addition to laying out the bottom of the shelf dado on the sides, mark where the dadoes will stop.

2 Rout the stopped dado for the bottom on each side. Position the jig's end cleats to fit the side and rout a dado to the stop line on each side. Reposition the end cleats to fit across the top and bottom pieces together and rout the dadoes for the divider.

4 Apply glue to the bottom of the divider (R), center it across the bottom, and nail it in place. Center the divider across the top rail and secure with one nail.

5 Place the top upside down and apply glue to the inside of the poplar edging pieces. Apply glue along the top edges of the sides and top rail. Now lay the shelf unit on its back and attach the top with 4d finishing nails every 4 inches.

6 Cover all the exposed plywood edges with edge-banding veneer (page 44). Sand all the edges of the veneer flush with the shelves and sand the solid poplar edging flush with the top. Fill nail holes, paint, then screw three evenly spaced clothing hooks to the front face of the back.

3 The router cut will be rounded at the end of the stopped dadoes in the sidepieces. Square the dadoes with a chisel.

4 Make router guides long enough to fit the length of the top and bottom, then reattach the jig's end cleats. Position the jig along the back edge of the back so it will rout a ¾-inch-wide rabbet. After routing the top, rout the bottom and sides, resetting the cleats as necessary.

STANLEY PRO TIP

Attaching the shelf to the wall

Draw a level line on the wall for the top of the shelf. You'll need four points of solid attachment—just below the top and the bottom, a couple of inches from each side. If you are attaching the shelf to studs, use 2½-inch drywall screws. Use toggle bolts for hollow drywall or plaster, sleeve or wedge anchors for masonry walls.

BOOKCASES TO FIT YOUR HOME'S STYLE AND NEEDS

Building a bookcase is relatively simple, even for a novice woodworker. In its basic form, it has a framework called a carcase that includes the sides, a top, and a bottom, and a shelf or two inside. You'll learn to build that basic bookcase design, starting on page 124. You can make it with nominal-size, right-off-the-rack lumber.

If you're up to more of a challenge, you can add a back to the carcase and some adjustable shelves. That's the larger bookcase described on page 130. It features some distinctive trim options, too, that help set it apart from the ones at the local furniture store.

To really impress your friends with your woodworking skills, construct the built-in-look bookcase on page 138. Don't let its size or features scare you—it's a lot easier to build than it looks. And you can customize the unit to match any decorating style.

For a whimsical yet practical way to encourage children to learn to store their books, build the children's book rack featured on page 148. For yet another variation on a standard bookcase design, look at the ladder bookcase on page 154. It combines the storage of a traditional bookcase with the look of the ladders used in many high-ceilinged libraries.

Craft a step at a time

As with all projects featured in this book, you'll find step-by-step photos to follow, plus professional tips to help along the way. Study the exploded view and detail drawings that show how parts go together, as well as the materials lists, which provide dimensions for each part.

Wherever possible, the projects are broken down into subassemblies to help construction proceed smoothly so you can plan and divide your project into manageable time segments.

Practical parts

All five bookcases were designed with materials you'll easily find at home centers and lumberyards, including the specified moldings and hardware. Remember, however, that you can always substitute other materials. For instance, you might choose walnut for the painted birch plywood in the built-in-look unit. Remember that few retail suppliers carry a full line of moldings in other than the most commonly marketed woods. Check your local stores as you plan a project.

To get exactly the piece of furniture you want, build it yourself.

CHAPTER PREVIEW

Fixed-shelf bookcase
page 124

Adjustable-shelf bookcase
page 130

Built-in bookcase
page 138

An easy way to make adjustable bookcase shelves is to install shelf rails on the sides. For a cleanly finished look, rout grooves in the sides so the rails attach flush with the boards. (See "Groove Joint" on page 61 for information.)

Children's book rack
page 148

Ladder bookcase
page 154

FIXED-SHELF BOOKCASE

Sized to be built from nominal, finish-grade pine, this simple bookcase can play several roles in your home. Because it has no back and is finished on both sides, you can use it as a room divider. You can add ready-made molding to the shelf for a more traditional style.

To make it more portable, build it with cutout handholds on the sides. Add cutouts at the bottom to give it a lighter look.

Material enlightenment

Pine, although not as strong as a hardwood like oak, withstands plenty of use and abuse. To give this bookcase the warm color of aged pine, it was first coated with orange shellac, then covered with polyurethane varnish for protection. Or you could paint it.

Hardwood plywood works nicely to upgrade the look. And a less expensive but durable version could be built using medium-density fiberboard.

At 30¾ inches tall, this single, fixed-shelf bookcase, finished on both sides, serves as a room divider as well as an attractive and handy storage unit.

PRESTART CHECKLIST

☐ **TIME**
About four hours for construction, plus finishing time

☐ **TOOLS**
Tape measure, layout square, 1½-inch spade bit, bar and C-clamps, tablesaw or circular saw with a straightedge, electric drill/driver, bits, jigsaw (optional), router, utility knife, compass

☐ **SKILLS**
Measuring and sawing, clamping and gluing (routing optional)

☐ **PREP**
Assemble tools and materials, prepare work area

MATERIALS NEEDED

Part		Finished size*			Mat.	Qty.
		T	**W**	**L**		
A	top shelf	¾"	13¼"	32"	EJP	1
B	sides	¾"	11¼"	30"	P	2
C	bottom shelf	¾"	11¼"	28½"	P	1
D	middle shelf	¾"	11¼"	28½"	P	1
E	toe-kick rails	¾"	3½"	28½"	P	2
F	side rails	¾"	1½"	8¼"	P	2
G	apron rails	¾"	1½"	28½"	P	4
H	top cleats	¾"	1½"	9¾"	P	2

*Parts initially cut oversize, see instructions.
Material key: EJP—edge-joined pine, P—pine
Hardware: #8×1½", ×1¼" FHWS
Supplies: Glue, sandpaper, paint or clear finish

Simple design options on the sides give this case a different look and make it easily movable.

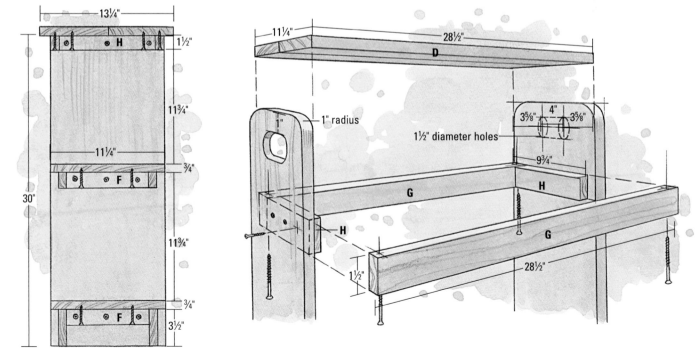

A. Cutting and preparing the parts

1 Glue and clamp two 1×8×32-inch clear pine boards to form the top shelf (A). Set aside to dry. Then remove the glue squeeze-out from the joint lines.

2 Measure and mark cut lines on 1×12 pine boards for sides (B) at 30 inches and for the bottom shelf (C) and middle shelf (D) at 28½ inches. Sand all sharp edges.

3 With a circular saw and a layout square as a guide, crosscut the sides, bottom, and shelf to the specified lengths.

STANLEY PRO TIP

Let wood move

Note that in this project no glue is used when fastening the framework for the top, middle, and bottom shelves. Only screws are used so the wood can move as the humidity changes. If the frames were glued, the wood might eventually split or crack.

OPTIONS TO CONSIDER
Add handles to the sides

Want a nifty portable unit? Build this bookcase as shown in the photo on the bottom of page 124 and you can easily move it anywhere. For this option, extend the sides to 34 inches tall and replace the top shelf (A) with another middle shelf (D).

The handhold cutouts are easy to create, as shown in the steps at right. To make the cutouts at the bottom of the sides, follow similar steps. Mark the cutouts along the bottom edge, 1½ inches in from the sides.

You can rout a slight roundover on the insides of all the cutouts, as shown in Step 4. Sand the roundovers if you don't have a router.

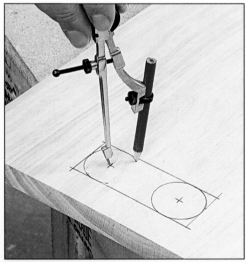

1 Draw two 1½-inch-diameter circles where shown on the optional handle drawing on page 125. Join them with straight lines to form an oval.

4 Using the setup in Step 3, mark and crosscut toe-kick rails (E) to length from 1×4 pine stock.

5 With a circular saw, crosscut the apron rails (G) and top mounting cleats (H) to length from 1×2 pine.

6 Use a tablesaw (or straightedge and a circular saw) to rip the top shelf (A) to 13¼ inches. Sand all edges.

2 Drill the holes with a 1½-inch spade bit. (When the bit's pilot point breaks through the back, flip the board and finish the hole.)

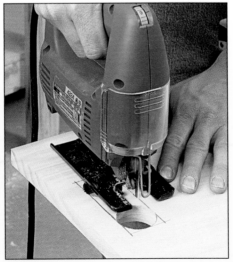

3 Complete the cutouts with a jigsaw.

4 Rout the inside of the cutout with a ⅛-inch roundover bit.

B. Assembling the pieces

1 Glue and clamp the toe-kick rails (E) to the side rails (F) to form the framework for the bottom shelf (C) as shown in the drawing (page 125). Follow the same steps to assemble the frame for the shelf (F, G).

2 Turn the bottom shelf (C) upside down on the bench and secure the framework assembly (E, F) to it with #8×1¼-inch flathead wood screws in countersunk holes. Repeat with the frame (F, G) and the middle shelf (D).

3 Place one side (B) on edge on the bench and position the bottom assembly on it. Clamp in place, with the toe-kick flush with the bottom of the side, and fasten with screws through the rails into the side. Repeat with the second side, supporting the first side with a piece of scrap lumber.

STANLEY PRO TIP

Use a sealer coat on pine

All pine tends to look blotchy when stained. That's why you should always give it a sealer coat of diluted shellac (50 percent denatured alcohol) or wood conditioner. The sealer keeps the stain from penetrating too deeply and unevenly. Unthinned orange shellac gives pine the pumpkin color of aged wood. Used by itself, however, it offers little protection from spills and wear.

FINISH THE BOOKCASE
Shellac warms up the wood tone

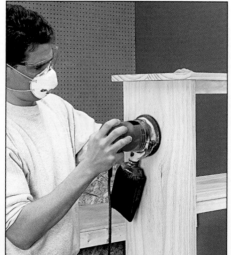

1 Sand the entire unit smooth, using progressively finer grits to 220-grit.

2 Remove sanding dust with a vacuum or tack rag, then seal with diluted orange shellac.

4 Glue and clamp the top cleats (H) to the apron rails (G). When the glue in the framework (G, H) dries, position and secure with screws to the bottom side of the top shelf (A).

5 Stand up the carcase and set the top assembly on it with the top cleats (H) fitted inside the sides, and clamp. Fasten the top with screws through the cleats into the sides. Be careful drilling, and be sure to use the proper-size screws so they won't come out the other side.

6 Measure between the bottom of the top frame and the top of the bottom shelf. Divide this distance by two to find the location for the middle shelf. Brace the shelf with 1×2s and fasten to the sides with screws. Again, be careful drilling and use the proper-size wood screws.

3 After the shellac thoroughly dries, sand the unit lightly with #0000 steel wool to smooth the seal coat.

4 Wipe off or vacuum all sanding dust and apply a finish coat or two of polyurethane varnish to all surfaces.

ADJUSTABLE-SHELF BOOKCASE

This bookcase has two adjustable shelves. Its double-wall construction adds strength to the unit while concealing the plywood edges and creates flush sides that allow you to slide books out without catching them on the face frame. You can easily make it taller, and its subassembly construction goes so quickly that you may want to build two of them at the same time to flank a window or fireplace.

Other materials
Red oak plywood is the material of choice here, but you can save money by using melamine-coated fiberboard and concealing the edges with veneer tape. Painted birch plywood is another practical option, and it's stronger than fiberboard. Built as shown, the bookcase makes an impressive addition to your home.

Three feet wide and 4 feet tall, this adjustable-shelf oak bookcase holds dozens of tomes, or displays your treasures.

To add more visual interest to the design, cut this shape into the front base. The cutout is made 5 inches from each end, ½ inch deep, with a ½-inch-radius corner.

PRESTART CHECKLIST

☐ **TIME**
About eight hours to build, plus finishing time

☐ **TOOLS**
Tape measure, try square, framing square, electric drill/driver, bits, countersink bit, tablesaw, circular saw, bar clamps, router, router bits, hammer, nail set, needle-nose pliers, sander

☐ **SKILLS**
Measuring, sawing

☐ **PREP**
Assemble materials and tools, prepare large work area

MATERIALS NEEDED

Part	Finished size			Mat.	Qty.	Part	Finished size			Mat.	Qty.
	T	W	L				T	W	L		
A sides	¾"	11"	42¼"	RPWD	2	I front base	¾"	3½"	36"	RO	1
B top/bottom	¾"	11"	33"	RPWD	2	J side base	¾"	3½"	12¾"	RO	2
C base rail	¾"	3½"	33"	Any	1	K top panel	¾"	12"	34½"	RPWD	1
D end rails	¾"	3½"	10½"	Any	2	L front edging	¾"	1½"	36"	RO	1
E side panels	¾"	11¼"	47¼"	RPWD	2	M side edges	¾"	1½"	12¾"	RO	2
F stiles	¾"	1½"	47¼"	RO	2	N back	¼"	33"	43¾"	RPWD	1
G top rail	¾"	1½"	31½"	RO	1	O shelves	¾"	11"	31½"	RPWD	2
H bottom rail	¾"	4½"	31½"	RO	1	P edging	¾"	1½"	31½"	RO	2

Material key: RO–red oak, RPWD–red oak plywood, Any–poplar, pine, etc.
Hardware: #8×1½", ×1¼" FHWS, #6×1" FHWS, 1" brads (optional)
Supplies: Wood putty, sandpaper, finish

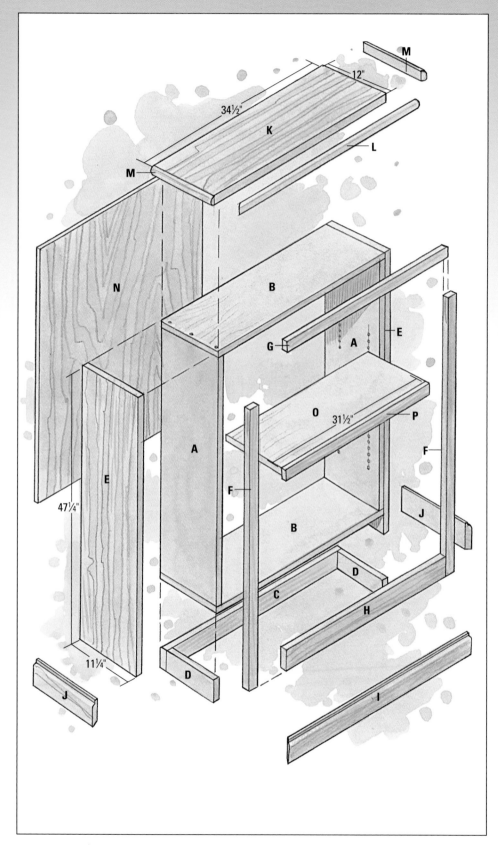

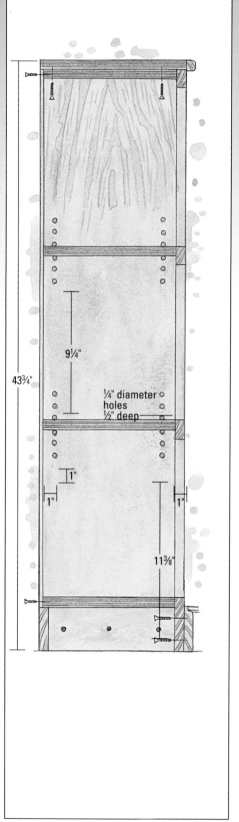

A. Drill shelf-pin holes

1 Cut and trim the sides (A) to size. Clamp a scrap of perforated hardboard (pegboard) to the sides as a template to lay out and mark locations for shelf-pin holes as shown in the exploded view drawing (page 131).

2 With sides on a bench, drill ¼-inch holes ⅜ inch deep at shelf-pin hole locations. Use an electric drill with a brad-point bit and a drill stop. Check the depth frequently; do not overdrill.

B. Join the inner carcase

1 Cut the top (B) to size. Join it to the end of one side (A) with glue and #8×1½-inch flathead wood screws in counterbored holes, with parts lying on the table as shown. Add the second side.

REFRESHER COURSE
Support plywood for ripping

To safely rip plywood with a portable circular saw, use 2×4 supports laying on sawhorses and a kerf splitter to prevent kickback.

STANLEY PRO TIP

No drill stop? Try tape.

You can control the depth of the holes you drill without a drill stop by wrapping tape around the bit as a visible guide to the proper depth.

2 Cut the bottom (B) to size. With the sides/top assembly in place, clamp and glue the bottom to the sides. Check for square by measuring diagonally. Fasten with #8×1½-inch flathead wood screws.

3 Rip and trim the base rail (C) and the end rails (D) to size. On a table, join the base rail to the end rails with glue. Secure with #8×1½-inch flathead wood screws in counterbored holes.

4 Trim the side panels (E) to size. Glue and clamp one panel to the side (A) of the carcase flush with the front edge. Glue and clamp the second side panel to the other side. Let the glue dry, then glue and clamp the base/end rails (C, D) in place.

OPTIONS TO CONSIDER
Make your own molding

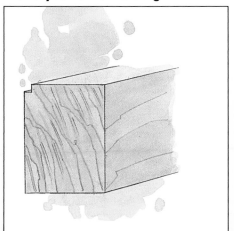

1 To profile the top molding, rip ¾-inch oak to 1 inch wide. Use a tablesaw or router to cut a ¹⁄₁₆×¹⁄₁₆-inch rabbet on one edge.

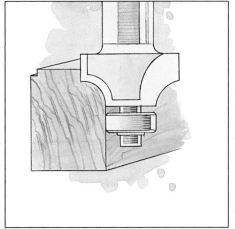

2 With a roundover bit in a router, shape a ¼-inch roundover ⅛ inch deep on the edge opposite the rabbet.

3 To complete the profile, chuck a ⅛-inch roundover bit into the router and shape a ⅛-inch roundover along the bottom edge.

C. Stick-build the face frame

1 Cut the stiles (F) and the top and bottom rails (G, H) of the face frame to size. Glue and clamp one stile to the face of the carcase, flush with the side. Dry-fit the other stile and the two rails to the clamped stile to check for fit. Trim as needed for a tight joint.

2 Glue and clamp the top and bottom rails to the carcase face flush with its sides and butted to the first stile. Dry-fit the second stile to check for fit. Trim as necessary, then glue and clamp in place to complete the face-frame assembly.

3 Rip and crosscut the front base (I) and the side bases (J) to size. Cut a rounded edge on the top edges using a ⅜-inch bit in a router. Measure and miter-cut both ends of the front base and one end of each side base. Glue and clamp in place on the carcase. Sand the subassembly.

REFRESHER COURSE
Dowel-jointed frame

Another way to build the face frame is to construct it as a separate assembly. Use dowel joints (page 59) to secure the stiles to the rails, then glue and clamp the frame to the carcase.

SAND THE SUBASSEMBLY
Make finishing easier

It may be difficult to finish-sand some parts of a project, such as the bookcase face frame, after assembly because you can't get into the corners and other tight places. Sanding a subassembly before adding it to the project ensures a thorough finish.

D. Make and install the top

1 Cut the plywood top (K) to size. Position it on the bookcase carcase, clamp, and fasten it in place with #8×1¼-inch flathead wood screws in counterbored holes from the inside. Drill carefully; don't go through the top and use screws the right length.

2 Rip and crosscut the top front edging (L) and the top side edges (M). Measure and miter-cut both ends of the front edging to length, then glue and clamp it to the front edge of the top.

3 With the front edging in place, double-check the mitered lengths for the side edges. Miter-cut one end of each and dry-fit to the top. Glue and clamp the side edges in place.

CONSIDER THE OPTIONS
Trim with cove molding

The design options for this bookcase include a top made of edge-joined solid oak. Round over top edges with a router and roundover bit, then add ¾-inch oak cove molding beneath it.

Top edge options

You can give the bookcase top a more finished look without adding edge molding. Rout its top and bottom with a ⅛-inch roundover bit *(top photo)*. Rout the piece on a router table before it's attached or by working with a hand-held router after it is attached to the case.

Another option is to add a profiled molding to the top edge. See the step-by-step instructions on page 133 to make your own.

E. Complete the basic assembly

1 Attaching the finish sides to the carcase created a rabbeted frame for the back. Measure inside that frame to get the final dimensions for the back (N).

2 Cut the back panel from ¼-inch-thick red oak plywood. Lay the bookcase face down on sawhorses and insert the back (N) to check its fit. Trim as necessary.

3 With the back in place, mark regularly spaced screw holes along its edges. Drill holes for short #6×1-inch flathead wood screws. Then remove the back for now.

REFRESHER COURSE
Cut the right side

All plywood has a good side and a not-so-good side. When working with expensive hardwood plywood, remember which is the best or face side because a saw blade leaves rough edges on the side where it exits the wood.

If you cut plywood with a portable circular saw, place the sheet with the good face down. The circular saw blade exits the wood on the side that's up. A tablesaw blade turns clockwise and exits the wood on the bottom, the side resting on the table, so you should saw with the best side of the plywood up (page 51).

REMOVE THE BACK
Finishing the back requires special attention

Finishing the back while it's attached to the bookcase will result in an uneven application, simply because it's hard to reach all of it. After fitting the back and drilling screw holes, remove it for sanding, staining, and finishing in a well-lit work area. When the back is dry, reinstall it in the bookcase and secure it with small wood screws. You may want to finish it on both sides for complete protection.

4 Cut the shelves' edging (P) to size from red oak and shape the edging as you want. Cut two shelves from plywood, then glue and clamp the edging to their fronts.

5 Install the shelf support pins in the drilled holes at the heights you want. Then temporarily install the shelves to check for fit. Trim the shelves as necessary, then sand.

6 Sand, stain, and apply a finish to the bookcase, shelves, and back. When the finish has cured, reinstall the back panel and secure it with screws.

SHAPE THE EDGING
Shelf edge options

Adding a solid wood edge to the red oak plywood shelves covers the unsightly plies and adds rigidity. A simple 1½-inch-wide strip ripped from ¾-inch-thick red oak will do *(top)*. Another attractive option is to rout ⅛-inch roundovers on the 1½-inch strip *(bottom)*. Cutting a ¹⁄₁₆×¹⁄₁₆-inch rabbet at the strip's back adds another detail.

SAND, STAIN, AND FINISH
Plywood requires a light touch

1 Modern hardwood plywood uses extremely thin face veneers. When sanding, make one pass with 180-grit sandpaper, a second with 220-grit. That's all you'll need before staining.

2 Apply stain and let it dry. We used a penetrating oil for a top coat, with two applications. Sand between coats with fine abrasive or #0000 steel wool for smoothness.

BUILT-IN BOOKCASE

Although the term *built-in* has an air of permanence about it, this bookcase doesn't require remodeling a wall to accommodate it. Creating a built-in look isn't complicated; the unit's construction follows the same approach used for previous projects: building subassemblies first, then joining them, as with the adjustable-shelf bookcase project on the preceding pages. You can trim this design with ready-made moldings selected to match your decorating scheme and furniture style.

Appearance options
To achieve a colonial look, the unit shown here was built of birch hardwood plywood because it accepts paint well. Paintable moldings are available in the same style. You could make the bookshelf of red oak or cherry plywood. Find out what materials are available locally and decide what best fits your budget and taste.

At more than 6 feet tall by 3 feet wide, this unit is an imposing piece that commands a wall and demands attention in a living room, dining room, or den.

PRESTART CHECKLIST

☐ **TIME**
About 16 hours to construct

☐ **TOOLS**
Tape measure, try square, carpenter's square, tablesaw, mitersaw or miter box and backsaw, coping saw, router, router bits, power drill/driver and bits, countersink bit, dowel pins, bar or pipe clamps, hammer, nail set, finish sander

☐ **SKILLS**
Measuring, sawing, drilling

☐ **PREP**
Assemble tools and materials; prepare a large work area

To conceal stored items, it's easy to add hinged doors to this bookcase unit when building it or even at a later date. The doors close against the lower shelf.

MATERIALS NEEDED

Part	Finished size			Mat.	Qty.
	T	W	L		
A stiles	¾"	1½"	76"	PL	2
B top rail	¾"	3"	36"	PL	1
C bottom rail	¾"	4¾"	36"	PL	1
D sides	¾"	11¼"	72"	BPW	2
E top/bottom	¾"	11¼"	36"	BPW	2
F finished sides	¾"	12"	76"	BPW	2
G top	¾"	13½"	40½"	BPW	1
H edging*	¾"	¾"	72"	PL	
I back	¼"	36"	72"	BPW	1
J shelves	¾"	10½"	36"	BPW	3
K shelf edging	¾"	1¼"	36"	PL	3
READY-MADE MOLDINGS:					
L colonial base	½"	4¼"	8'		
M quarter round	½"	¾"	8'		
N bed rail (or cove)	1⅛"	1½"	8'		

*Cut for three pieces, see instructions.

Material key: PL–poplar, BPW–birch plywood
Hardware: #8×1½", ×1¼" FHWS, #6×¾" FHWS, 4d and 6d finishing nails, shelf standards, shelf supports, wraparound hinges (optional), door pulls (optional), magnetic catch (optional)
Supplies: Glue, ⅜" dowel pins, putty or wood filler, sandpaper, primer, paint

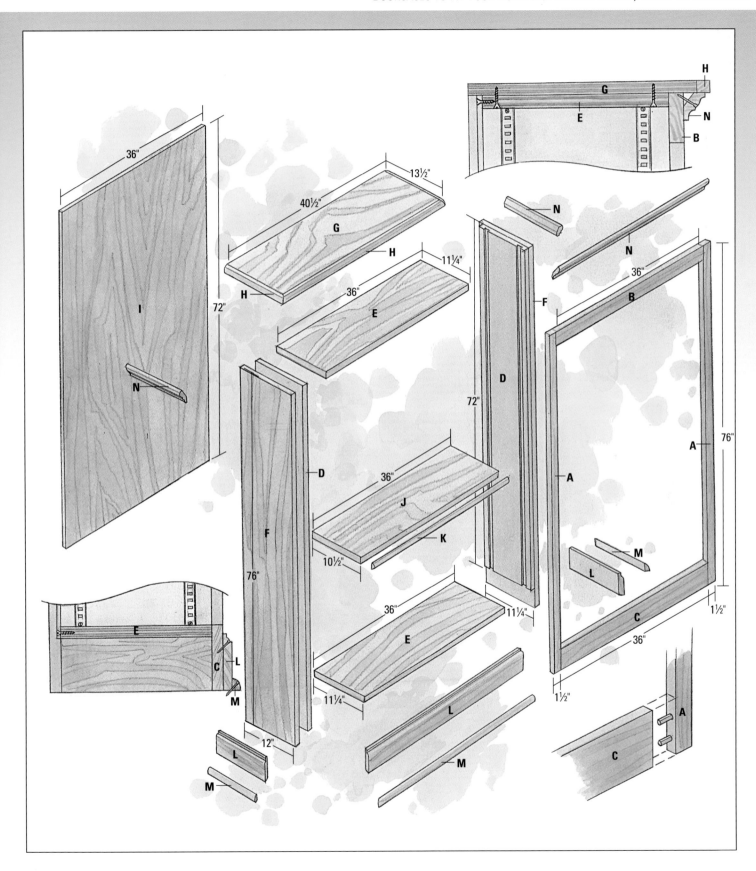

A. Building the face frame

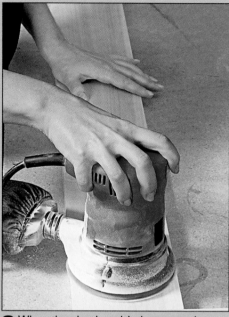

1 Rip and trim face frame stiles (A) and top and bottom rails (B, C) from solid stock. Refer to the exploded view and dowel joint detail drawings (page 139) to mark the dowel locations. Drill holes in parts A, B, and C where shown and insert the dowels.

2 Glue the dowel joints and assemble the face frame. Use bar clamps to hold the assembly. Before the glue dries, check the frame assembly for square by measuring diagonally. Loosen the clamps, adjust as necessary, then retighten clamps.

3 When the glue has dried, remove the clamps. Scrape off excess glue with a chisel or putty knife. Sand the face frame surfaces smooth with a finish sander or sandpaper and sanding block. Set the assembly aside.

CONSIDER THE OPTIONS
Add some doors

1 To make doors, rip and crosscut plywood to get two ¾×17¾×17¾-inch panels.

2 Add paintable veneer tape to their exposed edges (or fill and sand).

B. Building the carcase

1 From ¾-inch birch plywood, rip the two sides (D) and the top and bottom (E) to 11¼ inches wide. Then crosscut the sides, top, and bottom to the lengths specified in the Materials Needed box on page 138.

2 Measure the shelf standards you've chosen to get their exact width and thickness (they can vary by manufacturer). Later, you might have to trim them to exact length with a hacksaw.

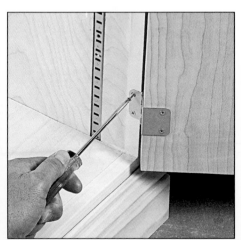

3 On the inside of the sides (D), lay out and mark locations for the shelf-standard grooves 1¼ inch from each edge and along the length of the sides (see the drawing on page 139). Double-check the locations.

3 Fasten a pair of wraparound hinges to each door. After finishing, mark the locations of pull knobs and latches, then drill the holes.

4 Install a shelf to the case. Dry-fit the doors in the opening to find and mark hinge screw hole locations on the face frame. Predrill the screw holes. Mark locations for latches.

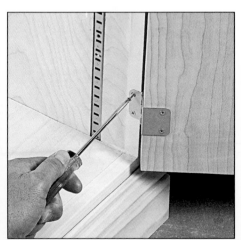

5 To hang the doors, support them with wood blocks and screw on the hinges. After fitting the hardware, remove it and the doors for finishing. Reassemble after finishing.

B. Building the carcase (continued)

4 Clamp a long straightedge to the sides (or use a router guide) to cut along the groove marks. Chuck a ⅝-inch (or your standard's width) straight cutting bit in a router and set its depth to the standard's thickness. Then rout the grooves.

5 Lay the sides, top, and bottom on the floor or workbench, apply glue to the ends of top and bottom (E), then glue and clamp to the insides of sides (D). Measure diagonally to check the assembly for square.

6 When the glue dries, remove clamps from the assembly and drill countersunk holes in the sides where they join with the top and bottom. Fasten the joints with #8×1½-inch flathead wood screws.

7 Rip and crosscut to specified size the finished ends (F), top (G), and shelves (J) from ¾-inch birch plywood. Then set the top and shelves aside until needed.

8 Apply glue to the inside of one finished end (F) and position it to a side (D). Fit the end of F flush with D at the front and top. Add the second finished end to the other side; glue, position, then clamp all in place.

9 Dry-fit the face frame to the front of the carcase with top and sides flush. Adjust as necessary; apply glue to carcase edges, then clamp face frame in place until the glue dries. Remove all glue squeeze-out.

10 Measure the area inside the rabbet formed at the back of the case. Cut the back panel (I) to those dimensions from ¼-inch-thick plywood and dry-fit in case.

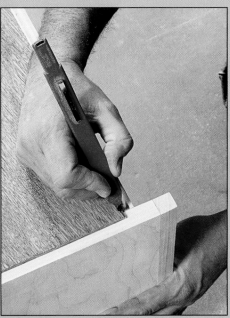

11 If the fit is too tight or slightly off, mark the areas that need trimming and plane or sand to remove excess.

12 Once you're satisfied with the fit, fasten the back in place by driving #6×¾-inch wood screws around the perimeter. If desired, you can later remove the back for finishing.

Add the base trim

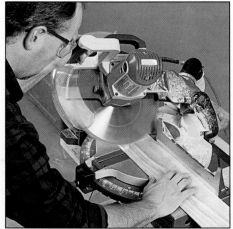

1 Buy an 8-foot length of colonial base molding 4¼ inches wide (or buy a molding style to match the existing molding on the wall). Measure for the front piece and miter-cut the ends.

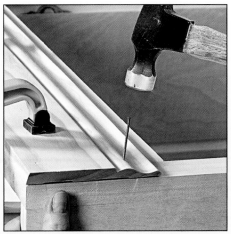

2 Glue and nail the front piece in place. Measure and cut the side moldings; miter one end of each. Leave the other ends square for a freestanding case. For a built-in look, see pages 146–147.

3 Dry-fit the side moldings and check the fit of the mitered joints. Attach the side moldings to the case with glue and 4d finishing nails. Sink the nailheads below the surface with a nail set.

C. Adding the top

1 From ¾-inch-thick stock, rip a 72-inch strip ¾ inch wide for the top edging (H). Crosscut the strip to obtain two 14¼-inch-long pieces and one 42 inches long. Miter-cut the ends of the long piece and one end of each side piece. Glue to the top (G).

2 When the glue has dried, clean off glue squeeze-out with a chisel or putty knife, then use a finish sander to sand the edging flush with the top. Sand the top and bottom edges of edging to obtain a rounded edge.

3 Position the top on the bookcase with an even overhang at the front and sides, then clamp in place. Drill evenly spaced countersunk screw holes for #8×1¼-inch flathead wood screws in the top of the case from inside. Screw the top to the carcase.

4 Miter-cut both ends of a piece of bed rail molding to fit under the front of the edged top (42 inches, but measure to be sure). Apply glue to the back edges of the molding, position it under the top, and secure it in place with 4d finishing nails. Sink the nailheads and fill them.

5 Measure the sides of the case from the back to the mitered front molding and cut two shorter pieces of bed rail molding to fit. Miter only one end of each piece to join with the front molding. Dry-fit to check its length, then glue and nail in place.

STANLEY PRO TIP

Avoid glue splotches

When edge-joining boards, you want to see glue squeeze-out so you know you've used enough to cover the joint. But if you get the glue on your hands, you can leave splotches that will mar your finish. Have both a damp and a dry cloth nearby as you work. Wipe your hands with the damp cloth, then dry them with the dry one so you won't dampen the wood. Pare off the squeeze-out with a chisel after the glue dries.

D. Building the shelves

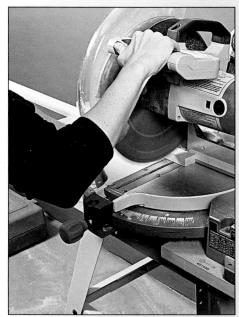

1 Rip and crosscut the shelves (J). Trim the shelf edging (K) to size. For shelf edge options, see pages 44-45, 133, and 137. For a more finished look, cut shelf-pin recesses in the bottom of the shelves.

2 Glue and clamp the shelf edging in place. Sand and paint.

3 Dry-fit and trim the shelf standards as needed. Rather than masking off the shelf standards, install them after you've finished the bookcase. Set them aside until the finishing is done.

SHELF-PIN RECESSES
Make a jig for the router

Measure and mark the shelf-pin recesses on the bottom of the shelves. With a straight-cutting bit in a handheld router, rout the recesses in the shelves. A jig made from scrap pieces limits router travel and simplifies repetitive cuts.

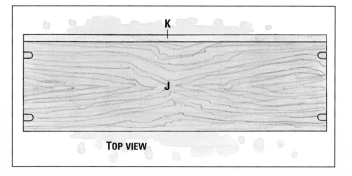

K

J

TOP VIEW

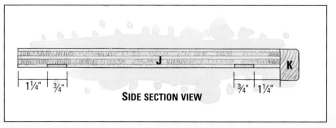

J

K

1¼" ¾"   ¾" 1¼"

SIDE SECTION VIEW

E. Finishing the pieces

1 When you're planning to paint, you don't need the extra-fine sanding grits used to sand wood for a clear finish. Sand first with 120-grit, then finish with 180-grit. Even if you use an electric sander, keep a sanding block on hand for corners and crevices.

2 The curves and troughs in moldings as well as other details are best sanded with fine mesh sanding pads that hug the contours. Be sure to vacuum or use a tack cloth to wipe off all sanding dust.

3 A coat of primer allows you to spot and correct any slight imperfections you may not have noticed when sanding. Primer also provides a good base for the finish coat.

STANLEY PRO TIP

Speed up the painting

A bookcase with several removable shelves usually requires twice the painting time as you wait for one freshly-finished side to dry before turning it over to coat the other side.

To speed things up and to avoid the need for touch-up painting, drive ¾-inch brads through some pieces of ½-inch-thick scrap wood. After you've coated one side of a shelf, pick it up by the ends and place it on the brad points of several of these homemade holders to keep the painted side off the work surface while you coat the other side. You'll never notice the tiny pin pricks left in the paint by the brads' sharp points. But if you do, you can quickly touch them up when the entire shelf is dry.

ACHIEVING A BUILT-IN LOOK
Cutting a profiled molding

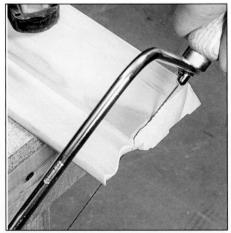

1 To make room for the bookcase, cut out and remove a section of the wall's base molding as wide as the bookcase.

2 Miter-cut the side base molding of the bookcase at the wall end. Pencil on the profile of the wall molding, then cut the molding to the profile with a coping saw.

F. Completing the assembly

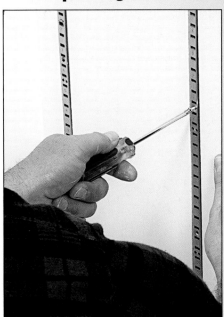

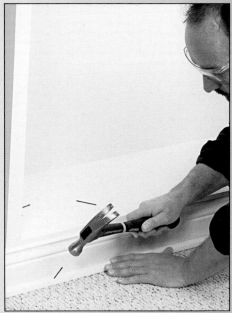

4 Brush on (or spray) semigloss enamel, carefully avoiding runs on vertical surfaces. This usually requires two coats for complete coverage and a smooth final finish.

Install the shelf standards. Unless you want to mask off the standards before painting, save time and labor by installing them after the unit has been finished.

Attach the shoe molding after the unit is in place against the wall. If there are any slight gaps between the bookcase and the floor, the molding will hide them.

3 Place the back of the bookcase against the wall. Fit the coped molding end against the wall molding; mark the length of the piece to join the front base molding. Miter-cut the side molding to fit.

SAFETY FIRST
Fasten the bookcase to the wall

1 You may want to secure this unit to the wall with #10×3-inch roundhead wood screws because of its height. Locate the studs in the wall behind the unit (one will do, two is better). Mark the screw locations on the upper back of the cabinet to match stud locations.

2 Drill holes in the back and in the wall for the screws. Position the cabinet against the wall and drive screws into the wall studs.

CHILDREN'S BOOK RACK

This bookcase is designed to let young children get to their favorite books easily. It's only 36 inches tall and attached to the wall just over the baseboard. The books are stored with their covers facing out, held in place by rows of dowels. Even children too young to read will recognize their favorite covers, encouraging them to select a book on their own. Maybe they'll put the book away on their own too.

Materials and finishing

The sides of this bookcase are made of poplar, a relatively inexpensive hardwood that's durable and has a tight grain that takes paint well. Semigloss or gloss enamel paint is a durable, easy-to-clean paint for a children's room. The back is beadboard—a ¼-inch-thick plywood paneling with a face veneer that looks like beaded boards. You can use ¼-inch lauan plywood if you don't like the beaded look.

PRESTART CHECKLIST

☐ **TIME**
An afternoon or an evening plus an hour or two for painting

☐ **TOOLS**
Tablesaw, circular saw with straightedge jig or mitersaw, jigsaw, palm sander or sanding block, router with ⅜-inch piloted rabbeting bit, drill with ⅛-inch bit, ½-inch spade bit and ¾-inch spade bit, tape measure, framing square, chisel, C-clamp, 4-foot level, angle square, needle-nose pliers

☐ **SKILLS**
Measuring, sawing, routing, drilling, gluing

☐ **PREP**
Prepare work area, gather materials, select location for bookcase

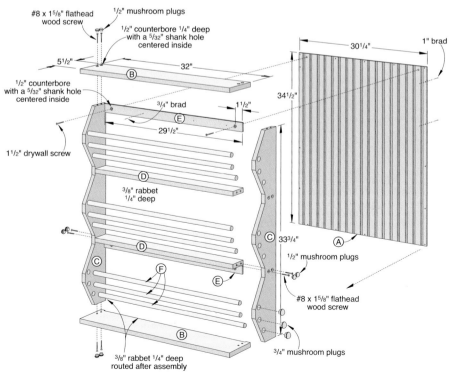

A. Cutting the parts

1 To make the back (A), use a circular saw with straightedge jig (page 31) to rip 30¼ inches from a 4×8 sheet of ¼-inch beaded board. Or use a tablesaw, with a helper to support the sheet. Use a circular saw and edge guide to crosscut the piece to 34½ inches.

2 Cut two pieces of 1×6 poplar to 32 inches long to make the top and bottom (B). Then crosscut two pieces of 1×6 poplar to 34½ inches for the sides (C). You can make these cuts with a power mitersaw or with a circular saw guided by a crosscutting jig (page 31) or guided by an angle square.

3 Use a tablesaw or a circular saw with ripping guide to rip one 6-foot length of 1×4 poplar to 2¾ inches wide and another 6-foot length into two 1½-inch-wide pieces. Cut the pieces to 29½ inches long, making the shelves (D) and cleats (E).

MATERIALS NEEDED

Part	Finished size			Mat.	Qty.
	T	W	L		
A back	¼"	30¼"	34½"	BB	1
B top and bottom	¾"	5½"	32"	PL	2
C sides*	¾"	5½"	33¾"	PL	2
D shelves	¾"	2¾"	29½"	PL	2
E cleats	¼"	1½"	29½"	PL	2
F dowels	¾" diameter		30¾"	Wood	9

Parts initially cut oversize, see instructions.

Material key: BB—beaded board, PL—poplar
Hardware: #8×1⅝" wood screws, 1" brads, ¾" brads, ½"-diameter screw-hole buttons, ¾"-diameter screw-hole buttons, molly bolts if hanging on hollow wall, 1½" drywall screws if attaching to studs
Supplies: Glue, finishing supplies

Make a push stick for narrow cuts

A push stick is a simple and essential piece of safety equipment for making narrow rip-cuts on the tablesaw. The one shown here is made from a scrap of poplar 1×6. Cut it out with a jigsaw and smooth the edges with sandpaper. The shape of the handle doesn't have to be exact; just shape it to fit comfortably in your hand.

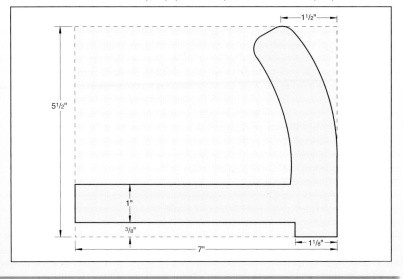

B. Cutting and drilling the sides

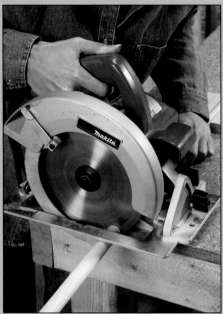

4 Cut nine pieces of dowel 30¾ inches long. These cuts don't need to be absolutely square; just make a mark on each one and cut through it with the circular saw. Be sure to grasp the dowel tightly so it doesn't turn during the cut.

1 The diagram *below left* shows how to lay out the sides, the positions of the shelves, and centers of the dowel holes. Lay out opposing shelf positions together with the sides laid back-to-back. Then lay out the shape on each side.

Scrap wood to prevent splintering on back

2 Lay out the center points for the dowel holes on one side. Clamp that side atop the other and drill through them together to make the ¾-inch-diameter dowel holes.

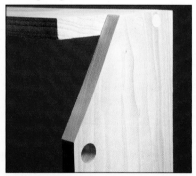

SIDE

5½"
3"
4¼"
10⅝"
©
33¾"
Location of part Ⓓ
13¾"
10⅝"
2"
2"
2"
¾"

4⅜"
1½"
4⅜"
1½"
4⅜"
1½"
4⅜"
1½"
4⅜"

¾"
¾" holes
¾" from front edge

OPTIONS TO CONSIDER
A slightly slicker bookcase

For a more streamlined look, eliminate the top and bottom overlaps. Instead make the top and bottom pieces the same length as the shelves, and make the sides 1½ inches longer. Install the top and bottom between the sides. You can also cover the screw and dowel holes with flush plugs instead of the button.

STANLEY PRO TIP

Prevent drill-bit blow-out

A drill bit, especially a large spade bit, can splinter the back surface of the wood as it exits the hole. If both sides of the hole will be visible in the finished project—such as the dowel holes in the bookcase—you can prevent this by clamping a block of wood under the workpiece when you drill.

C. Assembling the shelves

3 Use a saber saw to cut the shape on the front of each side piece. Don't try to cut them together—saber saw blades tend to wander when making thick cuts. Use a palm sander or sandpaper on a block to smooth the cuts and slightly round the front edges.

1 To locate where the top and bottom will overlap the sides, lay out lines ½ inch from each end of the top and bottom pieces. Mark the top and bottom pieces for two screws into each side. Locate the screw 1 inch and 2 inches from the back and ⅞ inch from the ends.

2 Position the top on the sides and predrill ⅛-inch pilot holes through the top into the sides where you marked for screws. Remove the top and use a ½-inch spade bit to counterbore to the depth required for the screw hole buttons. Repeat the process for the bottom-to-side connections.

OPTIONS TO CONSIDER
Round over the edges

1 Before assembly, consider routing a complete roundover on the front and side edges of the bookcase. To make it on ¾-inch-thick stock, put a ⅜-inch piloted roundover bit in your router and set the depth to ⅜ inch. Rout both sides of all front edges and the side edges of top and bottom pieces.

2 When routing the sides of the top and bottom pieces, you'll go across the grain, which may cause slight splintering at the front corner. So, rout the sides first; the splintered corner will be removed when you rout the front edge.

REFRESHER COURSE
Counterboring

Predrilling makes a hole for the screw's shank. Countersinking widens the top of the hole so the head can be driven flush. Counterboring makes that wider hole deeper to make room for filler or a plug. Spade bits are good for counterboring because they have a point you can stick into the predrilled hole. Use tape to mark the depth of the counterbore on the bit.

C. Assembling the shelves (continued)

3 Install the top and bottom with glue and 1⅝-inch-long #8 wood screws. Lay the bookcase front down. Set a ⅜-inch piloted rabbeting bit to ¼-inch deep and rout a rabbet clockwise around the inside perimeter. Clamp a straight 2×4 flush with the back of each side to support the router.

4 The routed rabbets will be rounded at the corners. To square them, place the flat back of a sharp chisel against the side of the rabbet and chop down to the bottom of the rabbet. Then hold the chisel horizontally and slice off the waste.

5 Put glue in the rabbets and insert the back with the beaded face down. Secure with 1-inch brads, being careful to nail straight down so the nails don't protrude through the sides. Turn the bookcase over. Wipe off excess glue inside the bookcase and check for square before the glue dries.

PRE-PAINT DOWELS
Make the job easier and neater

Painting the dowels after you install them would be difficult. Instead, make this dowel holder. In each of two pieces of 2×4, drill nine ¾-inch-diameter, ¼-inch-deep holes. Insert the dowels between the 2×4s and screw scrap pieces across both sides of the ends to keep the 2×4s in place. Now you can easily paint around the dowels.

NAIL STRAIGHT DOWN
Needle-nose pliers can help

To get a brad started straight without hitting your fingers with the hammer, hold the nail with needle-nose pliers while you start it.

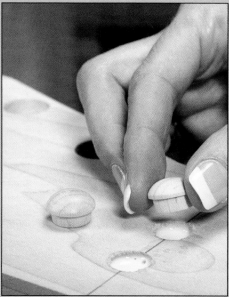

6 Position the shelves inside the bookcase. Predrill and counterbore screw holes as in Step 2. Drive in two screws per connection and center the holes 1 inch and 2 inches from the back. Screw the shelves into place.

7 Glue ½-inch screw-hole buttons into the screw holes at the top, bottom, and sides of the bookcase. Use a wet sponge to wipe off any excess glue before it dries.

8 Put glue on the back of each cleat and use ¾-inch brads to nail them to the front of the back piece, one butted under the top piece and one under the lower shelf.

D. Finishing and hanging the bookcase

1 If the dowels will be different colors from the bookcase, finish the bookcase before you install the dowels. Start by rounding the edges of the bookcase with 80-grit sandpaper using a sanding block or a palm sander. Prime and paint the bookcase.

2 Prepaint the dowels. Let the paint dry thoroughly, then insert the dowels into the holes in one side and through to the hole on the other side. Glue the ¾-inch-diameter buttons into the dowel holes. Paint the buttons and touch up any paint scuffs on the dowels.

3 Mark both sides of each cleat at 1½ inches from the sides. Place the bookcase on top of the room's baseboard and predrill a ⅛-inch hole through the cleat and back and into the wall. Counterbore the holes for ½-inch screw-hole buttons.

4 If you hit a stud, attach the bookcase with 1½-inch drywall screws. For hollow walls, put a toggle bolt through an enlarged hole in the cleat, thread on a toggle, and insert it into an enlarged hole in the wall. Plug the cleat holes and paint.

LADDER BOOKCASE

This handsome and unusual bookcase leans against a wall like a ladder. Each shelf is deeper than the one above, providing a place for books or display items of all sizes.

While the bookcase has a beautiful hand-crafted look, it is actually quite simple to construct. Consider building more than one bookcase; once you set up for each step, it takes very little time to repeat the step. And this bookcase makes a terrific gift.

Material and finish

This bookcase is crafted of oak, which is readily available at home centers. You can use any hardwood you like, such as cherry, walnut, or ash. If you want to stain the bookcase, maple or poplar are two woods that take stain evenly. The bookcase is finished with wipe-on polyurethane that's easy to apply and allows the beauty of the wood to shine through.

PRESTART CHECKLIST

☐ **TIME**
An afternoon or evening to build plus an hour to finish

☐ **TOOLS**
Hammer, nail set, bar clamps; tablesaw or circular saw with rip guide, power mitersaw or circular saw with crosscutting jig; electric drill/driver with stop, ⅛-inch bit and ½-inch spade bit; jigsaw, tape measure, compass, sander

☐ **SKILLS,**
Sawing, gluing, clamping

☐ **PREP**
Prepare a work area

MATERIALS NEEDED

Part		Finished size			Mat.	Qty.
		T	W	L		
A	rails	1½"	5½"	72"	Oak	2
B	bottom shelf*	¾"	10" *	22½"	Oak	2
C	lower shelf*	¾"	8" *	22½"	Oak	2
D	upper shelf*	¾"	7" *	22½"	Oak	2
E	top shelf*	¾"	5" *	22½"	Oak	2
F	shelf backs	¾"	3½"	22½"	Oak	4
BB	bottom shelf sides	¾"	3½"	20¾"	Oak	2
CC	shelf sides	¾"	3½"	16¾"	Oak	2
DD	shelf sides	¾"	3½"	14¾"	Oak	2
EE	top shelf sides	¾"	3½"	10¾"	Oak	2

Each pair of shelves will be glued into a finished size that is twice the width indicated.

Material key: #8×1⅝-inch wood screws, ½-inch-diameter screw-hole buttons, 4d finishing nails, wipe-on polyurethane wood finish
Supplies: Glue, sandpaper

SIDE VIEW

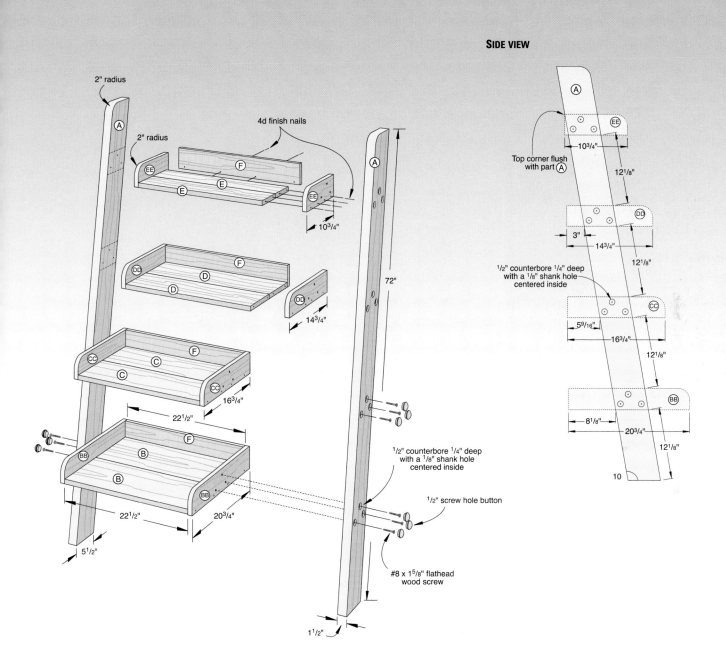

A. Cutting the parts

1 To make the rails (A), use a power mitersaw to cut two pieces of 2×6 oak to 72 inches long with a 10-degree angle on the ends. If you don't have a mitersaw, use a protractor to lay out the 10-degree angles and cut with a circular saw.

2 Cut a scrap piece of 1×6 to 12⅛ inches long with 10-degree angles at both ends. You'll use this assembly template later for positioning the shelves on the sides.

3 To make the stock for the shelf bottoms, rip-cut pairs of 4-foot lengths of oak 1×12 to10 inches (B), 1×10 to 8 inches (C), 1×8 to 7 inches (D), and 1×6 to 5 inches (E). Make the cuts on a tablesaw or use a circular saw with a rip guide.

USE A PROTRACTOR
Lay out 90 degrees first

It's difficult to start an angled circular-saw cut at the corner of a board. Instead draw a 90-degree layout line about ½ inch from the board's end. Align the protractor to this line when you are laying out the 10-degree cut on the ends of the rails.

SAFETY FIRST
Be sure to clamp for angled cuts

Starting an angled cut with a circular saw can be difficult because one side of the saw's guard contacts the wood first and the pressure pushes the saw to one side. To prevent this, lift the guard slightly as you start the cut. This makes cutting a two-handed operation, so be sure to clamp the workpiece firmly to the bench or sawhorse.

OPTIONS TO CONSIDER
Add an edge detail

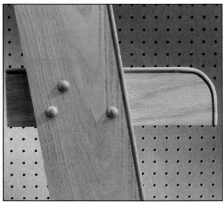

Add visual interest to your bookcase by routing a detail along the top and front edges of the shelf sides and rails. The detail can be an edge bead like the one shown here, a chamfer, a roundover, or anything else you like. Rout before you attach the shelves to the rails.

4 Crosscut the 4-foot pieces into 22½-inch-long pairs. Make the cuts with a stop block setup on your power mitersaw or crosscutting jig (page 31). Or you can set up a stop block on the tablesaw as shown below. Crosscut 1×4 oak to make the pairs of sides (BB, CC, DD, and EE).

5 Lay out the pivot point as shown in the drawing *below*. Use a compass to draw a 2-inch radius at the top front corner of the rails and each side piece. Cut the radii with a jigsaw.

STOP BLOCK ON THE TABLESAW
Make multiple cuts the safe way

The workpiece should never contact the rip fence when you make a crosscut—the piece can bind, causing dangerous kickback. However, there is a safe way to use the rip fence as a stop for several crosscuts of the same length.

First, clamp a block of wood to the fence and measure between the block and blade to set the fence for the length you need. Lock the fence, slide the block toward the in-feed side of the saw, and reclamp. Before turning on the saw, put a workpiece against the miter gauge, bump it against the block, then slide it forward. Make sure the piece will no longer contact the block when it reaches the blade.

DRAW A 2-INCH RADIUS
Use a compass for layout

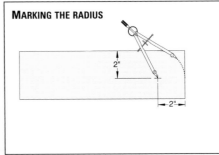

MARKING THE RADIUS

2"

2"

To lay out the 2-inch-radius cuts, measure 2 inches from both sides of the corner and mark where the measurements intersect. This is the pivot mark. Set a compass to 2 inches, set the point on the pivot mark, then draw the radius.

B. Assembling the parts

1 Edge-glue together the same-size pairs of stock (B, C, D, E) to make the shelves. Be sure the pieces are flush on the ends, then clamp them together with bar clamps. Let the glue squeeze-out dry, then pare it off with a sharp chisel.

2 When the glue is dry, remove the clamps. Sand the faces of all the parts. Attach the back to each shelf with glue and 4d finishing nails into predrilled holes. Then attach the sides the same way.

3 Sand the sides of all the project pieces and slightly round all the edges. Then, refer to the dimensions in the Side View drawing on page 155 and measure along the bottom of each shelf side from the back to mark where the bottom edges will meet the back of the rail.

STANLEY PRO TIP: **Alternate growth rings for gluing**

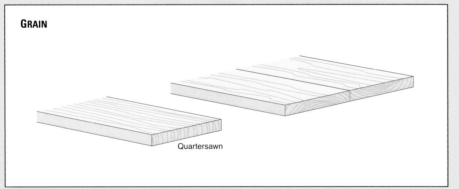

GRAIN

Quartersawn

Before you glue the pairs of pieces together to make the shelf bottoms, take a look at the growth rings at the end of the boards. You'll probably notice that the rings curve toward one face of the board. If so, glue up the boards with the rings facing up on one board and down on the other. This will resist any tendency for the boards to cup. If the growth rings go straight up and down you have a very stable quartersawn piece—just put the prettiest sides up.

SAND THE FACES
Remove the planer marks

It's important to thoroughly sand the board faces to remove the tiny ridges left by the lumber mill's planer. You might not even notice these ridges until finishing highlights them. Start sanding with 80-grit sandpaper on a sander or a sanding block, and then hit the surface again with 150-grit sandpaper.

Step head

4 Place the assembly template on the outside of a rail, flush with the bottom and sides. Scribe the top of the template. Put a scrap of 1×4 against the template and scribe that. Repeat until you have laid out where each shelf side will cross the rail.

5 Lay out the screw hole positions as shown *below left*. Clamp the assembly template to the inside of the rail, flush at top and bottom. Position the shelf against the template and align the mark on the bottom of the shelf to the back of the rail. Clamp the shelf to the rail.

6 Set a stop on the drill to 2 inches, and predrill ⅛-inch-diameter holes through the rail into the shelf side. Use a ½-inch spade bit to counterbore the holes for the screw-hole buttons. Attach the rail to the bottom shelf side with #8×1⅝-inch flathead wood screws.

HOLE LAYOUT

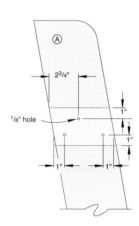

2¾"

⅛" hole

1"

1"

1"   1"

7 Clamp the pattern in the next position and repeat the process until you have attached the four shelves to one rail. Then, use the pattern to lay out screw holes on the other rail and then clamp it at each position to predrill, counterbore, and attach the rail. Use tape on the spade bit to mark how far to counterbore.

8 Sand off the layout lines on the outside of the rails. Put glue in each counterbore and insert a screw-hole button. Apply two or three coats of finish, and your bookshelf is ready for duty.

BUILT-IN STORAGE

Built-in bookcases, benches, and shelves add both style and storage space to your home. The nine projects in this chapter offer storage solutions ranging from utilitarian under-stair shelves to a beautiful floor-to-ceiling bookcase you can build next to a fireplace—or anywhere else you like.

The projects in this chapter lend themselves to custom touches so you can make them look like part of the home. The instructions show optional trim treatments and tell you how to make each project fit your space. Beyond that, you can build most of the projects so they can be painted to match or harmonize with your room or use wood that matches your existing woodwork.

Building custom built-ins is just as straightforward as the projects in other chapters. Most require skills only a few steps above basic woodworking. In all cases, careful measuring and attention to detail when joining pieces will ensure a pleasing final result.

You can combine projects to create the kind of built-ins you want. The built-in window seat on page 162, for instance, could be combined with the bookcases on page 180 to make a cozy retreat in a den or family room.

The recessed built-in shelves on page 176 are ideal for a den, living room, or dining room. But you also could build them into a hallway or stairway wall to create an attractive and unusual accent.

The closet organizer on page 212 is ideal for bedroom and dressing-room closets, but consider one also for the coat closet in your entryway. You could build the organizer from less-expensive wood for basement utility closets too.

You can alter and combine parts of projects too. To make a medicine cabinet or a laundry-room utility cabinet, you could build the recessed built-in shelves and add a door modeled after the ones for the cabinets on page 200 or the corner linen closet on page 228.

As you look through the chapter you'll see other projects you could adapt to particular needs in your home. And for every project, think of the plan as simply a starting point for your own custom design. Choose any wood and finish you like, alter the size to meet different needs, change the style of trim, add or remove shelves, and make any other changes.

Built-ins increase your storage space and enhance the looks of your home.

CHAPTER PREVIEW

Built-in window seat
page 162

Basement under-stair storage shelves
page 170

Recessed built-in shelves
page 176

Built-in fireside bookcase
page 180

Modular, contemporary built-ins
page 190

Cabinets with cushions or shelves
page 200

Closet organizer
page 212

Built-in kitchen bench
page 218

Corner linen cabinet
page 228

BUILT-IN WINDOW SEAT

This handsome storage bench is designed as a built-in window seat. It's a place to enjoy the sun or a great view. You can easily customize the seat to fit under any window just by adjusting the lengths of the top, side, front, and back pieces.

It's a built-in unit, so the chest doesn't need a bottom. You can add a bottom to make the bench a freestanding chest that's ideal as a blanket chest at the foot of a bed or even as a child's toy chest.

PRESTART CHECKLIST

☐ **TIME**
About four hours to build plus two hours to finish

☐ **TOOLS**
Tape measure, clamps, electric drill/driver, screwdriver, hammer, nail set, tablesaw or circular saw with straightedge jig, router with piloted ⅜-inch rabbeting bit

☐ **SKILLS**
Sawing, gluing, clamping, routing

☐ **PREP**
Prepare a work area

Customizing to fit your décor
The chest shown here is painted to match the room. The box itself is made of birch plywood that's painted the main wall color. The trim is made of ¼-inch pine that's painted to match the room trim. The chest would also look very elegant made of oak plywood and solid oak trim with a clear finish.

MATERIALS NEEDED

Part	Finished size			Mat.	Qty.	Part	Finished size			Mat.	Qty.
	T	W	L				T	W	L		
A lid	¾"	19⅜"	50"	BP	1	H cross support	1¼"	1½"	46½"	pine	1
B hinge rail	¾"	2"	50"	BP	1	I front horizontal trim	¼"	1½"	48½"	pine	2
C sides	¾"	16"	19"	BP	2	J side horizontal trim	¼"	1½"	19"	pine	2
D front	¾"	16"	48"	BP	1	K side horizontal trim	¼"	1½"	16¼"	pine	2
E back	¾"	16"	48"	BP	1	L vertical trim	¼"	1½"	13"	pine	9
F upper supports	¾"	3½"	19"	BP	3	M angled trim	¼"	1½"	13¾"	pine	2
G lower supports	¾"	3½"	16⅞"	BP	3	N bottom*	½"	17¾"	46½"	BP	1
						O bottom cleats*	¾"	3½"	23⅝"	BP	4

Material key: BP—birch plywood
Hardware: 48-inch piano hinge, lid support, 1¼-inch coarse-thread drywall screws, ¾-inch brads
Supplies: Glue, wood putty, 120-grit sandpaper
*optional

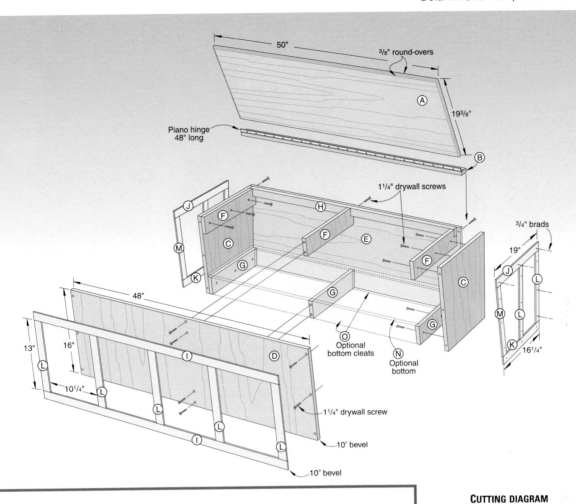

50"

³/₈" round-overs

A

19³/₈"

Piano hinge
48" long

B

J

F

H

1¹/₄" drywall screws

M

C

F

E

³/₄ brads

19"

K

G

F

J

L

C

G

M

L

48"

G

K

16¹/₄"

13"

16"

D

I

L

Optional
bottom cleats

O

N

Optional
bottom

L

10¹/₄"

L

L

1¹/₄" drywall screw

I

L

10° bevel

I

10° bevel

SAFETY FIRST
A top priority

Lid supports are spring-loaded mechanisms
that hold the lid open, then make it close
gently so it won't slam down on your head or
fingers. If children are around, it's important to
install a lid support on a low bench like this
one.

CUTTING DIAGRAM

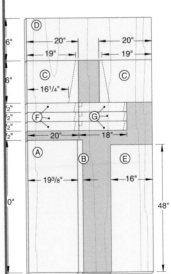

D

6"

20"   20"

19"   19"

C   C

6"

16¹/₄"

2"
2"
2"
2"

F   G

20"   18"

A   B   E

19³/₈"   16"

0"

48"

³/₄ x 48 x 96" birch plywood

A. Cutting the bench parts

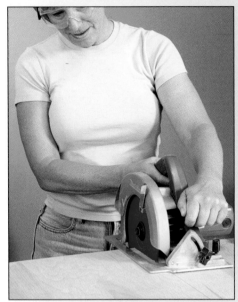

1 Guide a circular saw with a straightedge jig (page 31) to crosscut two 16-inch-wide pieces and one 50-inch-wide piece from a sheet of ¾-inch birch plywood as shown in the cutting diagram at the bottom of page 163. Use the circular saw alone to cut two 20-inch-long pieces (C) from one of the 16-inch-wide pieces.

2 On each side piece (C), mark one edge at 19 inches and the other at 16¼ inches as shown on the cutting diagram. Draw a line between these points. Starting at the 16¼-inch mark, cut to these lines with the circular saw guided by the straightedge jig.

3 To make the lid (A) and hinge rail (B), use a tablesaw or a circular saw with straightedge jig to rip a 21½-inch-wide piece from the 50-inch-long section of plywood. Working counterclockwise, rout a bullnose on one long side and both ends of this piece.

OPTIONS TO CONSIDER
Customize the lid edge

A bullnose is only one of many ways you can finish the edges of the lid and hinge rail. For a square painted edge, just coat the edge with wood filler and sand smooth. For a square edge with a clear finish, use edge-banding tape (page 44). Or pick a ¾-inch or slightly wider molding to glue and nail to the edges. Reduce the dimensions of the lid and hinge rail to fit the thickness of the molding.

ROUT A BULLNOSE
Use two passes to complete this roundover

When an edge is completely rounded over, it is called a bullnose. To make a bullnose on a ¾-inch-thick piece of stock, use a piloted ⅜-inch roundover bit. Rout around the top of the workpiece. Then turn the workpiece over and rout on the other side.

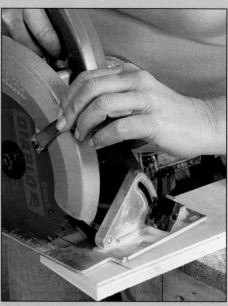

4 Set the tablesaw fence at 19⅜ inches. Rip the hinge rail from the lid by running the 21⅜-inch-wide piece through the saw with the long bullnose against the fence. Make sure the remaining piece is 2 inches wide for the hinge rail.

5 Rip 16 inches from the remaining 50-inch-long piece. Crosscut this piece to 48 inches to make the back (E). Rip-cut three 3½-inch-wide pieces from the remaining piece, then crosscut these into three 20-inch pieces and three 18-inch pieces for the supports (F and G).

6 Lay out the cuts for the upper and lower supports as shown in the diagram below. Clamp the stock down and make the angled cuts with a circular saw. Then cut the notches in the upper supports with a jigsaw or handsaw.

WHAT IF...
You want a clear finish?

Routing a bullnose on plywood works fine if you intend to paint the lid because you'll fill voids and hide the plywood layers with wood putty.

If you want to give your bench a clear finish, start out with a piece of plywood 20⅝×48½ inches for the lid and hinge rail. Glue and clamp a ¾×¾-inch hardwood edge to both ends and one long side of the piece, using miter joints at the front corners. You can use 4d finishing nails instead of clamps, but be sure to center them top to bottom and set them deeply. Rout the bullnose, then rip the hinge rail from the lid.

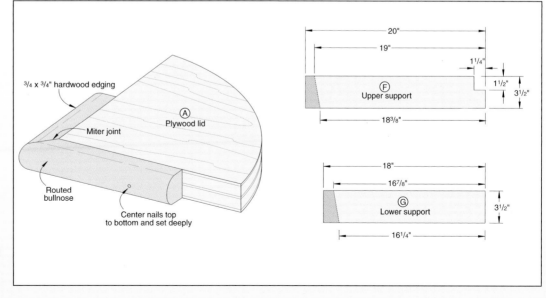

B. Assembling the bench

1 Attach a top support and lower support to the inside of each side with glue and 1¼-inch drywall screws. Make sure the upper supports are flush with the front and top of the sides. Make sure the lower support is flush with the front and bottom of the sides.

2 Apply glue on the back edges of the side pieces. Put the back in place, making its edges flush with the outside, top, and bottom of the sides, and then secure it with 1¼-inch drywall screws. Attach the front to the sides in the same way. Check for square.

3 Cut a piece of 2×2 or 2×4 to 46½ inches long and then rip it to 1¼ inches wide to make the cross support (H). Attach the cross support with glue and clamps into the upper support notches and with glue and screws through the back.

OPTIONS TO CONSIDER
Add a bottom for a freestanding chest

The optional bottom increases the versatility of the bench by turning it into a freestanding chest. The bottom rests atop the three lower supports (G) plus four cleats attached inside of the front and back. The bottom shown here is a single piece of ½-inch plywood. If you don't have a piece of plywood, don't buy a full sheet just for the bottom. Instead, use ½-inch- or ¾-inch-thick boards of any width you have, ripping one of the boards so the combined width spans from front to back.

1 To make the cleats (O), rip a 48-inch length of ¾-inch plywood to 3½ inches wide for the back cleats. Then tilt the saw blade 10 degrees and rip another 48-inch length for the front cleats. Crosscut the four 23⅝-inch pieces.

2 Attach the cleats to the front and back between the lower side supports and the center support using glue and 1¼-inch drywall screws. Install the two beveled cleats against the front with the beveled edge even with the tops of the support pieces.

C. Attaching the lid

1 Apply glue to the top of the cross support. Put the hinge rail in place and make sure it is flush with the front of the cross support and overhangs equally on both sides. Clamp the hinge rail to the cross support.

2 Put the lid in place making sure it is flush with both ends of the hinge rail. Use a quarter to gauge the space between the hinge rail and the lid, checking the space at the middle and both ends. Center the piano hinge over the space and predrill holes for the hinge screws.

4 Center the remaining top support and bottom support across the inside of the bench. Make sure they are square to the front and back and flush with the top. Then attach them with two 1¼-inch screws through the front and two through the back.

3 Cut the ½-inch-plywood bottom (N) to 17¾ by 46½ inches. Put glue on the tops of the cleats and lower supports. Install the bottom and secure it with a few 1¼-inch drywall screws.

STANLEY PRO TIP: **Use a simple stand as a third hand**

You might wish that you had a third hand to hold the sides of the window bench on edge while you screw them together. The job will be easier if you make a simple cabinet stand from ¾-inch plywood. Make a 6×12-inch base and two sides that are 4 inches tall by 12 inches long. Using two scraps of ¾-inch plywood as a 1½-inch spacer, screw through the bottom into the sides with six 1¼-inch drywall screws. Use the stand to hold up each side while you screw the back, and then the front, into the sides.

D. Trimming and painting

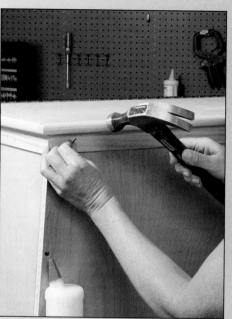

1 Cut two pieces of ¼-×1½-inch stock 20 inches long and two pieces 17 inches long for horizontal trim pieces (J, K). Put them in place at the top and bottom of the sides and scribe for the angled cut at the front of the chest. Make the cuts.

2 Attach the horizontal trim pieces (J, K) to the sides with glue and ¾-inch brads. Cut the front horizontal trim pieces (I) to fit overlapping the side horizontal trim, and then glue and nail them in place. Be sure the bottom trim piece is placed as shown in the drawing *below*.

3 Mark the 11 vertical trim pieces (L, M) for snug fit. Glue and nail them in place, spacing them as shown in the drawing *below left*. Note that on each side, both ends of trim piece M must be cut at 80 degrees to match the front angle.

LAYING OUT
VERTICAL TRIM PIECES

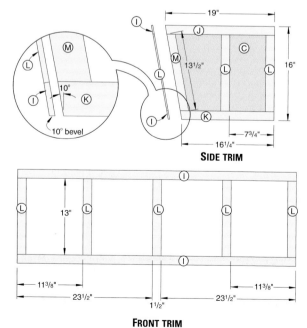

SIDE TRIM

FRONT TRIM

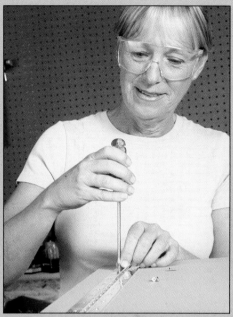

4 Coat the bullnosed edges of the lid and hinge rail with wood filler to fill voids and hide the plywood edges. Fill all nail holes. Slightly round all edges with 120-grit sandpaper. When the filler dries, sand the bullnoses smooth and the nail holes flush.

5 Prime and paint the bench inside and out. Prime and paint both sides of the lid. When the paint is dry, put the lid in place and screw the piano hinge to the lid and hinge rail. Use a screwdriver rather than an electric drill/driver to avoid stripping the small brass screws.

6 Install the lid support on either side of the upper support (F). Put the lid support in place on the upper support (F) and predrill holes for the screws. Attach the lid support, then predrill holes for the screws into the underside of the lid. Install the screws.

1 First prime the entire bench. Then put a first coat of paint on the trim. Let this coat overlap onto the plywood. Don't worry about painting a straight line—it's more important to work the paint into the joint between trim and plywood. When the trim dries, coat the plywood, letting the paint overlap the trim coat.

2 Put a second coat on the trim, this time working in long even strokes. Let the paint overlap just slightly onto the plywood.

3 Let the second trim coat dry. Dip about ½ inch of the brush into the paint. Paint down on the plywood about an inch away from the trim, then swoop the brush steadily toward the trim until the bristles just skim along the joint between plywood and trim.

BASEMENT UNDER-STAIR STORAGE SHELVES

Put that unused space under the basement stairs to work with these simple storage boxes. The design shown here gives you storage spaces of different sizes, including a tall narrow box for items such as brooms or skis. The boxes are so quick and easy to build that you'll have no trouble adapting them to your storage needs as well as to the size and pitch of the space under your stairs.

Materials and finishing
These boxes are built for utility, not beauty. They are made from inexpensive particleboard without finish, although you can paint them for a more attractive look. One word of caution: Don't build the boxes with particleboard if your basement is damp—particleboard readily absorbs moisture that makes it swell, and it will crumble if it gets wet. Use CDX plywood instead. This inexpensive grade of plywood, intended for exterior sheathing, is made with water-resistant glue.

PRESTART CHECKLIST

☐ **TIME**
About four hours

☐ **TOOLS**
Measuring tape, electric drill/driver, tablesaw or circular saw, framing square, chalk line, long clamps or bench vise

☐ **SKILLS**
Sawing, measuring, and gluing

☐ **PREP**
Measure the slope of stairs, assemble tools and materials, prepare a work area

MATERIALS NEEDED

Part	Finished size			Mat.	Qty.
	T	W	L		
LARGE BOXES					
A top and bottom	¾"	23⅞"	23⅞"	PB	6
B sides	¾"	22½"	23⅞"	PB	6
C backs	½"	23⅞"	24"	PB	3
SMALL BOXES					
D top and bottom	¾"	11⅞"	11⅞"	PB	6
E sides	¾"	10½"	11⅞"	PB	6
F backs	½"	11⅞"	12"	PB	3
TALL BOX					
G top and bottom	¾"	11⅞"	23⅞"	PB	2
H sides	¾"	23⅞"	70½"	PB	2
I back	½"	11⅞"	72"	PB	1

Material key: PB—particleboard
Hardware: #6 × 1½-inch particleboard screws
Supplies: Wood glue

Use particleboard screws

Like drywall screws, particleboard screws have a sharp point, an aggressive thread, and a bugle-shaped head. There's one important difference though: Particleboard screws have a self-tapping tip that pulls the screw into the particleboard without predrilling. If you can't find particleboard screws, use a ¹⁄₁₆-inch-diameter bit to predrill holes for drywall screws.

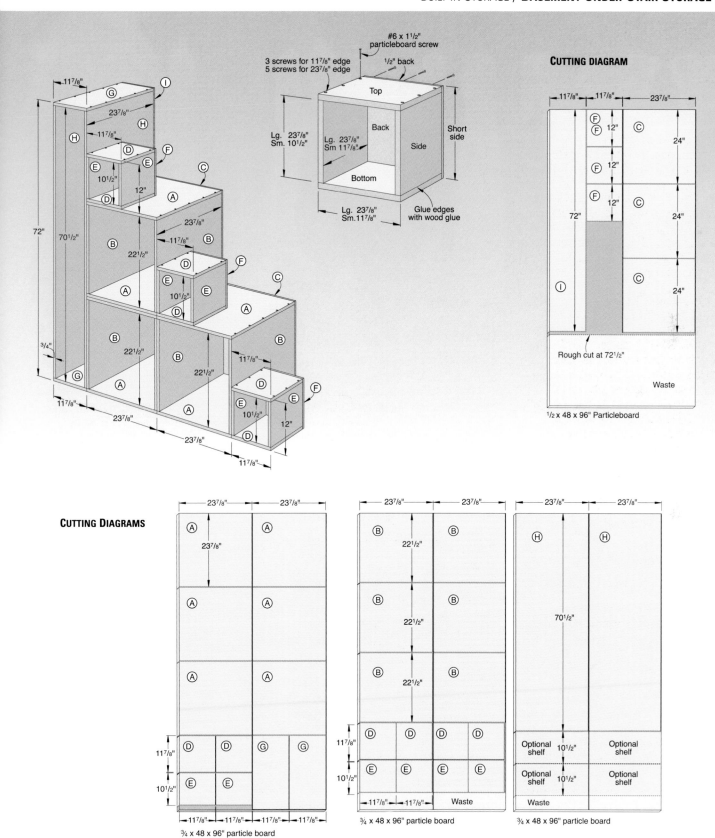

#6 x 1¹/₂"
particleboard screw

3 screws for 11⁷/₈" edge
5 screws for 23⁷/₈" edge

¹/₂" back

Top

Back

Lg. 23⁷/₈"
Sm. 10¹/₂"

Lg. 23⁷/₈"
Sm 11⁷/₈"

Side

Short
side

Bottom

Lg. 23⁷/₈"
Sm.11⁷/₈"

Glue edges
with wood glue

CUTTING DIAGRAM

12"

12"

12"

24"

24"

24"

72"

Rough cut at 72¹/₂"

Waste

¹/₂ x 48 x 96" Particleboard

11⁷/₈"

23⁷/₈"

70¹/₂"

72"

3/4"

22¹/₂"

22¹/₂"

22¹/₂"

10¹/₂"

12"

10¹/₂"

10¹/₂"

12"

11⁷/₈"

11⁷/₈"

CUTTING DIAGRAMS

23⁷/₈"

23⁷/₈"

23⁷/₈"

11⁷/₈"

10¹/₂"

11⁷/₈"

³/₄ x 48 x 96" particle board

23⁷/₈"

23⁷/₈"

22¹/₂"

22¹/₂"

22¹/₂"

11⁷/₈"

10¹/₂"

11⁷/₈"

Waste

³/₄ x 48 x 96" particle board

23⁷/₈"

23⁷/₈"

70¹/₂"

10¹/₂"

10¹/₂"

Optional
shelf

Optional
shelf

Optional
shelf

Optional
shelf

Waste

³/₄ x 48 x 96" particle board

A. Cutting the parts

1 Use a circular saw and straightedge jig (page 31) to crosscut one ¾-inch-thick particleboard sheet to 70½ inches long—the length of the tall box sides (H).

2 Although the lengths of the three backs (C) add up to 72 inches, you need a little more length to allow for the kerfs—the ⅛ inch of material that the saw blade turns into dust with each cut. Snap a line at 72½ inches across the ½-inch-thick particleboard sheet. Make a freehand cut with a circular saw.

3 Rip all four particleboard sheets to make eight pieces 23⅞ inches long. Rip-cut the particleboard on the tablesaw, and have someone support the sheet at the back of the saw table. Or use a circular saw and an 8-foot-long straightedge jig.

Have panels precut

Many lumberyards and home centers have a panel saw—the best tool for cutting sheet goods to size. A panel saw has a rack that holds the panel upright and a circular saw that runs on tracks to easily make accurate rip-cuts and crosscuts anywhere on the panel.

Ask your dealer to make the crosscuts described in Steps 1 and 2 and the rip-cuts described in Step 3. This will speed your work when you get home, and the smaller pieces will be easier to transport.

STANLEY PRO TIP

Save your setups

As you follow the steps on this page, you'll notice that all rip-cuts of a particular width are made at the same time. Remember this technique when you plan all your woodworking projects.

Whenever you set up a machine for any purpose, try to do all the operations calling for that setup at the same time so you don't have to repeat the setup later. This saves time, but more importantly, it ensures all like pieces will be exactly the same and your projects will fit together with ease. You can leave the setup in place until you need the machine again—just in case you have to remake a piece.

4 Use a circular saw with a straightedge jig to make all the cuts that go completely across the ripped pieces (see the cutting diagrams, page 171). These are parts A, B, and C, and the cuts that will separate parts D from parts E. Label all parts as you cut them.

5 If you have a tablesaw, set the rip fence to 11⅛ inches. Cut the remaining ¾-inch-thick pieces (D, E, and G). Leave the fence setting at 11⅛ inches. If you don't have a tablesaw, make these cuts with your circular saw and straightedge jig.

6 Rip-cut one long piece of ½-inch particleboard into two 11⅛-inch-wide pieces. With your circular saw and straightedge jig, crosscut one of these pieces to 72 inches to make the back (I) of the tall box. Cut three 12-inch backs (F) for the small shelves from the other 11⅛-inch piece.

CONSIDER THE OPTIONS

If you don't need tall storage, consider adding shelves to the tall box. Just rip the whole panel used to make the sides (H) into two 23⅞-inch pieces. Cut the sides to length, then use the offcuts to make up to four shelves.

1 Lay the tall box sides (H) next to each other, with edges flush. Draw lines across both pieces with a framing square to show where to locate the bottom of the shelves. Extend these lines across the outsides of the panels so you will see where to drive screws.

2 Attach the shelves before you attach the top and bottom pieces. Have someone help hold each shelf along the layout line as you glue and screw the shelf to one side. Then glue and screw the other side in place.

B. Assembling the boxes

1 Assembly is the same for large and small boxes. Apply glue to the top edge of one box side (B or E). Use a bench vise or clamps to hold the piece, glued edge up. Screw the top (A or D) to the side, using three screws for small boxes and five screws for large boxes.

2 Apply glue to the top edge of the other box side. Put the top in place, make sure the edges are flush, then screw it in place, again with three screws for small boxes, five screws for large boxes.

3 Turn the box over and apply glue to the bottom edges of both sides. Put the bottom (A or D) in place, check that the edges are flush, and secure with three or five screws into each side.

WHAT IF...
Your stairs have a different pitch?

The boxes shown fit under a staircase with a 45-degree pitch: For every 12 inches the stairs rise, they run (travel horizontally) 12 inches. The boxes step up and over in 12-inch increments.

If your stair slope is more gradual, your boxes will need to be wider to fit; more steep and the boxes will be narrower. To find out, hold a tape measure vertically with the hook on the floor. Move the tape along the bottom of the stair until the distance to the floor is 36 inches. Use a 4-foot level to make sure the tape is plumb, then mark the point on the floor. Measure from the floor mark to the point where the bottom of the stair meets the floor. Let's say the distance is 46 inches. Divide 46 by 3 to get 15⅝ inches. Now you know your small boxes and tall box need to be 15⅝ inches wide while your large boxes should be 30⅝ inches wide.

4 The back piece helps make the whole box square, so be sure to put backs on before glue sets. Lay the box on its face and screw the back in place—five screws per edge for large boxes, three screws per edge for small boxes.

5 Apply glue to the top edge of a long side (H), and place the piece flat on a workbench. Put the top (G) in place and make sure it is flush to the front and back of the side. Attach with five screws. Do the same for the bottom (G).

6 Turn over the long box assembly, apply glue to the top and bottom edges of the second side, and screw it into place between the top and bottom. Finally, screw the back in place using 12 screws along each side, five screws across the top and five screws across the bottom.

Be prepared for squeeze-out

Always have a small bucket of water, a sponge, and a towel handy when working with wood glue. You can wipe away glue that squeezes out of joints with a damp sponge and dry your hands with the towel.

STANLEY PRO TIP

Wax paper protects your bench

When joining the top and bottom of the long box to the sides, put wax paper under the joint to keep glue squeeze-out off your bench. The wax paper will easily pull away without getting stuck to your project the way newspaper will.

OPTIONS TO CONSIDER

If your stairs are accessible from both sides, consider making two sets of boxes to place back to back. Since the stairs are unlikely to be 4 feet wide, you'll probably need to reduce their depth to fit.

RECESSED BUILT-IN SHELVES

This handsome shelf unit is designed to be recessed into the wall between two studs. It works great as display shelves in the living room or dining room or as handy extra shelving in a bathroom.

Materials and finishing

It's easy to adapt this versatile design to fit your space and home style. This unit is made of clear-finished solid oak with a lauan plywood back. The peaked top rail has a triangular cutout flanked by small diamond cutouts. You might instead want to match the window and door trim in the room—casing the unit just as you would a window. You can make the unit from any hardwood you like, or use pine with a painted or clear finish.

PRESTART CHECKLIST

☐ **TIME**
About four hours

☐ **TOOLS**
Tape measure, combination square, hammer, nail set, drywall saw, 4-foot level, pocket-hole jig or biscuit joiner, tablesaw or circular saw with straightedge guide, drill/driver with #6 counterbore bit and 1⁄16-inch-diameter bit, jigsaw, drywall saw

☐ **SKILLS**
Accurate measuring, sawing, joining

☐ **PREP**
Locate and prepare opening in wall

MATERIALS NEEDED

Part		Finished size T	W	L	Mat.	Qty.
A	sides	¾"	3"	32"	Oak	2
B	supports	¾"	3"	14½"	Oak	2
C	back	¼"	14½"	33½"	LP	1
D	shelves	¾"	3"	13"	Oak	3
E	side trim	¾"	3½"	32¼"	Oak	2
F	top trim	¾"	5½"	20¼"	Oak	1
G	bottom trim	¾"	3½"	20¼"	Oak	1

Material key: LP—lauan plywood
Hardware: 1½-inch coarse-thread drywall screws, 4d finishing nails, 1-inch brads, pocket-hole screws or #20 joinery biscuits
Supplies: Glue; 80-, 150- and 220-grit sandpaper; wood filler, polyurethane clear finish

Choosing a location

Install the shelves only on an interior wall so you don't have to remove insulation from an exterior wall.

Once you've chosen the wall and located the stud bay you want, make sure there are no plumbing pipes in the bay. Plumbing runs mostly vertically, so check in the basement to see if any pipes enter the wall directly below the bay. Also check for sinks, bathtub faucets, and showers directly above the bay.

Electrical wiring is more difficult to find. If there is no electrical switch directly to either side of the bay, there's probably no wiring. If you open the bay and find wires running up one of the studs, make the cabinet ½ inch narrower and be careful when you screw the cabinet to the stud.

A. Opening the wall

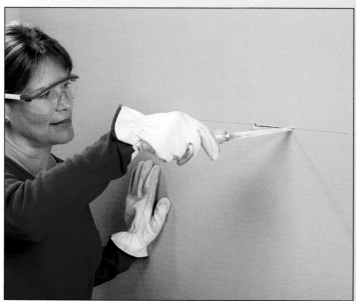

1 Stud spacing isn't always exact, so open the wall before you build the shelf unit in case you need to adjust the cabinet width. Use a 4-foot level to draw a line for the top of the cabinet. Then cut the line with a drywall saw until you run into a stud at both ends.

2 Measure down 32½ inches from both ends of each line and use the level to mark a plumb line along both studs. Then mark a level line across the bottom of the vertical lines. Cut along these lines with the drywall saw, and remove the cutout.

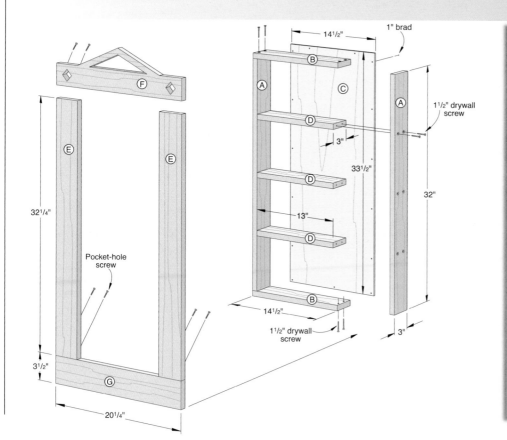

OPTIONS TO CONSIDER
Trim the shelves with casing

Here the shelving unit is trimmed with a colonial-style casing that has been painted to match the room's window and door casings. Just miter the casing and nail it to the shelf-unit sides and the wall studs—neither biscuits nor pocket-hole screws are necessary.

B. Making the shelves

1 Rip and crosscut the sides (A), top and bottom (B), back (C), and shelves (D). Sand the inside faces of the hardwood parts with 80-, 150-, and 220-grit sandpaper. Put the sides next to each other with the inside faces up and edges flush. Lay out the positions of the shelves as shown below.

2 Position the top on the sides and, if the sides are hardwood, predrill countersunk holes for two 1½-inch drywall screws. Then apply glue to the ends of the sides and drive in the screws. Attach the bottom to the sides the same way.

3 Attach the back with 1-inch brads and glue, making sure it is flush to all edges. Predrill with a ¹⁄₁₆-inch bit if you have trouble driving the brads.

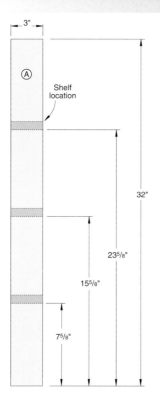

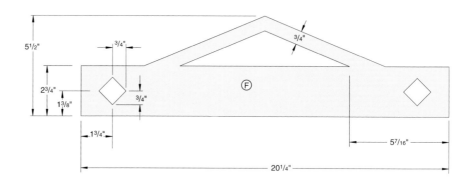

C. Making the trim

1 Transfer the shelf layout lines around to the outside and back of the unit. Put the shelf in place and predrill two countersunk holes into each side. Apply glue to the back and ends of a shelf. Secure the shelf with 1½-inch drywall screws and three brads through the back. Install the other shelves.

2 Rip (if necessary) and crosscut the trim pieces (E, F, and G) to size. Lay out the triangular and diamond-shaped cutouts on the top trim (F) as shown in the drawing, opposite page. Drill ¼-inch-diameter starter holes and make the cutouts with a jigsaw.

3 Join the top and bottom trim pieces to the side trim pieces with glue and one #20 biscuit or two pocket-hole screws (page 64) per joint. Set a combination square to ⅛-inch and use it to guide a pencil as you lay out a reveal around the unit's perimeter.

Caulk fills back gaps

Drywall is rarely as flat as it looks, so you may discover small gaps where the face trim meets the wall. If so, fill the gaps with painter's latex caulk. Smooth the caulk with a wet finger and let it dry. Then paint the caulk the same color as the wall.

D. Installing the shelves and trim

1 Sand the trim faces and slightly round all edges. Apply finish. Predrill the sides for 4d finishing nails, position the shelf unit in the wall, then drive and set the nails. Align the trim frame and secure it with 4d nails in predrilled holes into the studs and front edges of the unit.

2 Fill all nail holes with matching wood filler. When the filler dries, sand the filler flush and lightly sand the face frame with 220-grit. Wipe away sanding dust with a damp cloth. Add one more coat of finish to the face frame.

BUILT-IN FIRESIDE BOOKCASE

Add to the value and elegance of your home with this built-in bookcase next to the fireplace. A pair of doors at the bottom provides out-of-view storage, and a cut-out arch in the top rail adds visual interest. Yet there's no fancy joinery here, so this bookcase is the perfect beginner's project. If you have room, you'll want to build a bookcase for each side of the fireplace. The bookcase is 95½ inches tall to fit in a room with an 8-foot ceiling. You may need to adapt the height for the room.

Before you assemble the case (Step 4, page 184), make sure you will be able to move the case into its location and stand it up. If stairs, doors, or ceiling height will make it difficult to put the assembled case into position, assemble the case with the sides standing in place. Attach the top (B) with pocket-hole screws or cleats if you cannot drive screws in from the top.

Materials and finishing
This bookcase is made of oak, which is readily available at home centers. You can use any other hardwood you like, such as cherry, walnut, or ash. If you want to stain the bookcase, maple or poplar are two choices that take stain evenly. The bookcase is finished with wipe-on polyurethane that's easy to apply and allows the beauty of the wood to show.

PRESTART CHECKLIST

☐ **TIME**
About 16 hours to construct, plus several hours to finish

☐ **TOOLS**
Tape measure, hammer, nail set, combination square, framing square, bar clamps, power drill with ¹⁄₁₆-inch and ⅛-inch bits, tablesaw or circular saw with a straightedge guide, power mitersaw or hand miter box, pocket hole jig (optional), jigsaw finish sander

☐ **SKILLS**
Measuring, sawing, drilling

☐ **PREP**
Assemble tools and materials, prepare a large work area, prepare installation area

MATERIALS NEEDED

Part	Finished size T	W	L	Mat.	Qty.	Part	Finished size T	W	L	Mat.	Qty.
A sides	¾"	11⅞"	94¾"	RPWD	2	I bottom rail	¾"	2¼"	24"	RO	1
B top	¾"	11⅞"	30"	RPWD	1	J shelf rail	¾"	1½"	24"	RO	1
C shelves	¾"	11⅞"	28½"	RPWD	5	K center stile	¾"	1½"	25¼"	RO	1
D back	¼"	30"	95½"	RPWD	1	L top molding*	cove molding		33"	OC	1
E doors	¾"	11"	25¼"	RPWD	2	M top molding*	cove molding		15"	OC	2
F shelf cleats	¾"	¾"	11⅞"	Pine	10	N bottom molding*	base shoe		33"	OB	1
G top rail	¾"	5½"	30"	RO	1	O bottom molding*	base shoe		15"	OB	2
H side stiles	¾"	3"	90"	RO	2	P side molding*	¼"	1½"	95½"	RO	2

*Select moldings to match room and cut to fit. Initial size shown for moldings; see instructions.
Material key: RPWD—red oak plywood, RO—red oak, OC—oak cove molding, OB—oak base shoe
Hardware: 4d finishing nails, 1¼-inch brads, 1¼-inch drywall screws, pocket-hole screws (optional), #8×1¼" screws, four wraparound hinges, two magnetic catches, two door knobs or door pulls, drywall screws if attaching to studs
Supplies: Carpenter's glue, construction adhesive; 120-, 180-, and 220-grit sandpaper; stain; clear finish

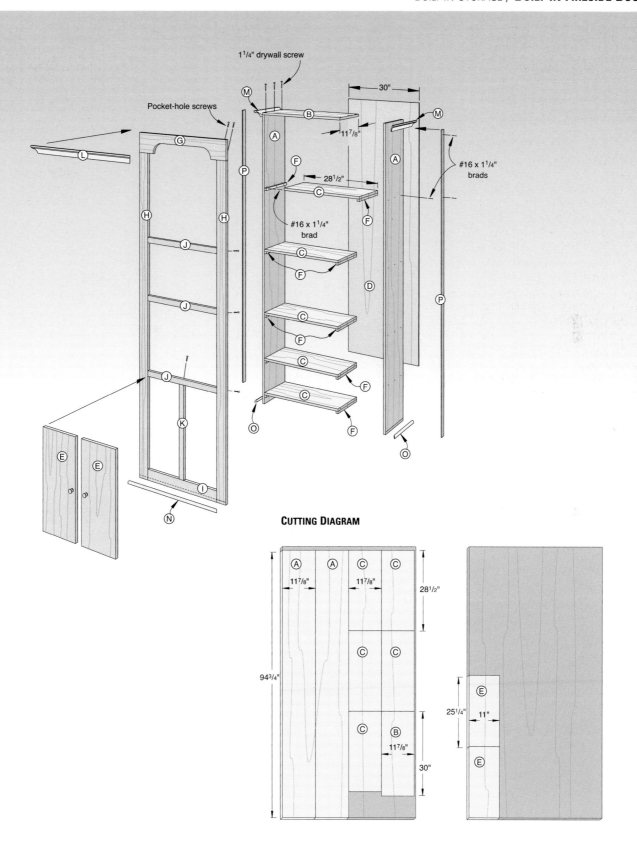

1¼" drywall screw

Pocket-hole screws

30"

11⁷⁄₈"

#16 x 1¼" brads

28½"

#16 x 1¼" brad

CUTTING DIAGRAM

94³⁄₄"

11⁷⁄₈"

11⁷⁄₈"

28½"

11⁷⁄₈"

30"

25¼"

11"

A. Cutting the case parts

1 On the tablesaw, rip a sheet of plywood into four 11⅞-inch-wide pieces as shown in the diagram on page 181. Rip 11 inches from another ¾-inch sheet and 30 inches from a ¼-inch-thick sheet. Or make the cuts with a circular saw and straightedge guide as described on page 31.

2 Use a straightedge guide with a circular saw to crosscut the sides (A), top (B), shelves (C), and doors (E) to the lengths listed in Materials Needed. Use the straightedge guide to crosscut the ¼-inch plywood to 95½ inches for the back (D).

3 Rip ¾-inch-thick pine to ¾ inch wide to make shelf cleats. Crosscut 10 pieces to 11⅞ inches long using a stop block with a mitersaw or tablesaw (see "Make multiple cuts the safe way," page 157). Or use a stop block on a circular-saw crosscutting jig, as shown *above*.

SAFETY FIRST
Have a helper for full-sheet cuts

Always have an assistant when you cut full sheets of plywood on the tablesaw. The assistant can move around the saw to support the sheet as you push the sheet through the blade. Make sure your assistant just holds the sheet level and doesn't pull on the sheet or lift it.

OPTIONS TO CONSIDER
Make the shelves adjustable

You can easily make the top two shelves adjustable by adding recessed standards as shown in the "Built-in Bookcase" project beginning on page 138. When you rout the grooves for the standards, stop just past the top of the shelf above the doors.

Eliminate the face frame and cleats from the top two shelves and cover their front edges with veneer tape, as you will do for the shelf concealed behind the doors.

STANLEY PRO TIP
Move the glue

When gluing the cleats to the sides, move the cleat slightly back and forth a few times along the layout line. This ensures even distribution of the glue and helps the glue grip—you can even feel the glue grabbing as you do this.

B. Assembling the case

1 Place the sides next to each other with their inside faces up and ends flush. Lay out the positions for the top of each shelf cleat (F) as shown in the drawing below. Mark the cleat positions with an X so you'll attach the cleats on the correct side of the lines.

2 Apply glue to each of the shelf cleats and secure them to the inside of the sides with 1¼-inch brads. Square each cleat to the front and back of the sides.

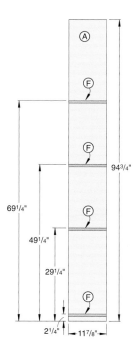

STANLEY PRO TIP: **Lay out nailing guidelines**

When nailing through the sides and back into the shelves, it's easy to misjudge a nail's position, causing it to poke through the inside of the bookcase. To prevent this, before assembly, extend the cleat layout lines lightly in pencil around the outside of the sides. Then, when you put the back in place, extend the lines onto the back. Nail about ⅜ inch above the lines. A little sanding will remove the lines from the sides.

B. Assembling the case *(continued)*

3 The second shelf from the bottom will be hidden behind the doors, not covered by the face frame. Cover the front edge of this shelf with oak veneer edge banding (page 44). Lightly sand with 120-grit sandpaper to round the front edge.

4 Apply glue on the top edges of the sides and install the top piece (B) with 1¼-inch drywall screws. Put glue on the bottom cleats and on the edges of one shelf (C). Hold the shelf firmly on the cleats while you drive 4d finishing nails through the sides into the shelves. Install the remaining shelves the same way.

C. Cutting the face frame

1 Crosscut an oak 1×6 to make the top rail (G) and an oak 1×2 to make the center stile. Then rip two 8-foot oak 1×4s to 3 inches wide and crosscut them to 90 inches to make the side stiles (H).

REFRESHER COURSE
Pre-finish the back

It's much easier to apply finish to the back before you install it, and you will get a much better result because you can apply the finish with long even strokes.

OPTIONS TO CONSIDER
Skip the doors

The bookcase is very easy to adapt if you want to eliminate the doors: Don't put veneer tape on the second shelf from the bottom. Instead, eliminate the center stile and add another rail to the face frame to cover the shelf that would have been hidden behind the doors.

STANLEY PRO TIP

Crosscutting with a circular saw

You can do an excellent job cutting the relatively narrow face-frame pieces simply by guiding a circular saw with an angle square. The secret to a clean cut is to put a 40-tooth finish blade on the saw. Don't force the cut—finer blades take longer to cut the wood.

2 Rip a piece of 1×4 oak to 2¼ inches wide for the bottom rail (I). Set up a stop at 24 inches on your mitersaw, tablesaw, or crosscutting jig. Use it to crosscut the bottom rail and then use it to cut three shelf rails (J) from oak 1×2s.

3 To lay out the arched cutout in the top rail (G), start by drawing a line along its length 2½ inches from the bottom as shown in the drawing below. Set a compass to a 2½-inch radius, set it on the pivot points shown, and draw the arcs.

4 Clamp the top rail to a bench or saw horses and use a jigsaw to cut out the arch in the top rail. Before cutting the curve, cut straight in from the edge to the curve layout at two or three points. These relief cuts allow waste to fall away and prevent the blade from bending too much as you cut the curve.

TOP RAIL

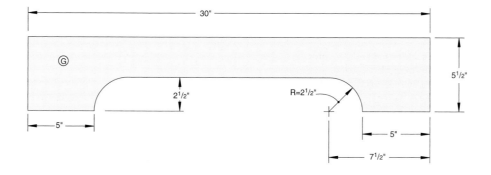

OPTIONS TO CONSIDER
Choosing knobs or pulls

The hardest part of installing knobs on your doors is deciding which ones to use. In fact, maybe you want to use pulls instead of knobs. To help you choose, take a look around the room where you'll install the bookcase. Are there knobs or pulls in the room you would like to match? What's the style of the room's trim and furniture? You'll find knobs and pulls designed to complement Mission, Shaker, Colonial, and other styles.

D. Assembling the face frame

1 Pocket-hole joinery is used to assemble the face-frame parts. To mark where the shelf rails (J) meet the side stiles (H), put the side stiles in place on the bookcase. Also mark where the center stile will meet the bottom rail and shelf rail.

2 Drill pocket holes in the backs of the parts—two holes into the top of the side stiles, two into the ends of the bottom rail, and one hole into each end of each shelf rail and the center stile.

3 After drilling all the holes, apply glue to mating pieces, butt them together, and drive screws into pocket holes. Wipe off the glue squeeze-out before it dries.

WHAT IF...
You don't have a pocket-hole jig?

Pocket-hole joinery is handy because you don't need clamps, but there are other ways to attach the face frame. The easiest is to attach all the pieces directly to the bookcase with glue and 4d nails. This method is particularly effective if you will paint because when filled, nail holes will disappear. Even with a clear finish, filled nail holes don't look bad if you use matching filler.

If you don't want to see nail holes, you can glue and clamp the face frame to the bookcase. If your clamp supply is limited, glue and clamp one piece at a time, giving the glue 30 minutes to set.

If you have a biscuit joiner or doweling jig, you can assemble the face frame as a unit and then glue and nail or clamp it in place.

Plugging pocket holes

The pocket holes in the bottom of the shelves will be mostly hidden by the face frame, but if you really want to make them undetectable, buy oak plugs designed to fill the pocket holes. Just glue them in place and sand flush.

4 Apply glue to the front edges of the bookcase and put the face frame in place. Drill three pocket holes in the bottom of each shelf, and drill the bottom of the top piece into the face frame. Drive one screw in the middle and one near each end. Screw the face frame in place.

E. Installing the doors and back

1 Cover the edges of both doors with wood veneer edge banding (page 44). Iron the edge banding in place, trim it flush at the corners with a sharp utility knife, then slightly round the edges with sandpaper. Position two wraparound hinges on each door, locating them 2 inches from the top and bottom. Predrill holes and screw the hinges into place.

2 The doors are sized to fit in their openings flush to the face frame with a ⅛-inch gap at all edges. Put each door in its opening with the hinges against the face frame. Shim to create an equal opening at top and bottom. Mark the side stiles for the exact location of the hinges.

OPTIONS TO CONSIDER
Enhance the doors with molding

A few pieces of molding can make the plywood doors look like traditional raised-panel doors. A 1¹⁄₁₆-inch-thick by 1⅛-inch-wide base cap molding normally used to top baseboard is shown. Use any narrow tapered moldings you like. Tapered moldings have one edge that is thinner than the other. Experiment with the molding you use to see whether it looks most realistic with the thin edge in or out.

1 Set your combination square to 2 inches and run it along the edges of the doors to mark layout lines with a pencil. You'll use these lines to locate the outside edges of the molding.

2 Miter-cut eight pieces of molding to fit the layout lines. Attach the moldings with glue and 1-inch brads.

E. Installing the doors and back *(continued)*

3 Use a square to extend your marks across the inside edge of the side stiles. Remove the hinges from the doors and align them to the layout lines, then mark the screw-hole locations. Predrill the holes.

4 Apply glue on the back of the sides and the backs of the shelves. Put the back in place and secure it with 1¼-inch brads. Nail the corners first, checking for square as you go. Make sure edges are flush as you complete the nailing.

F. Finishing and installing

1 Sand all edges of the bookcase to break (slightly round) the edges. Apply stain and clear finish or paint to the doors and bookcase separately. Also, pre-finish moldings (L, M, N, O, P) without cutting to length. When the finish is dry, put the bookcase in place and install the doors.

REFRESHER COURSE
Sand between coats for a smooth finish

1 Hardwood plywood has very thin face veneers that need no sanding for a paint finish. For a clear finish, sand lightly with 180-grit, then 220-grit sandpaper. If you sand too much or use a coarser sandpaper, you could actually sand through the thin veneer.

2 After applying stain and letting it dry, you can apply a clear finish. Apply two or three coats, lightly sanding by hand with 220-grit between coats. Sanding between coats smoothes out irregularities.

WHAT IF...
You need to fit the bookcase around baseboard?

If baseboard is installed behind the bookcase, just use a jigsaw or handsaw to cut a notch in the side of the bookcase.

2 The cove molding (L and M) will be attached to the ceiling and the top rail like a crown molding. Put a 33-inch length of molding upside down in the mitersaw—as if the saw base were the ceiling—and make a miter cut on one end.

3 Put the piece of cove against the front of the bookcase with the bottom of the miter aligned to one corner. Mark the bottom of the other corner for the opposing miter and then make the cut. Square-cut one end of the side cove pieces (M). Mark their miters in place, then make the cuts.

4 Install top molding on one side, then the front, and finally the other side. For each piece, squirt small dabs of construction adhesive on the surface that will contact the ceiling. Press the molding against the ceiling. Predrill $\frac{1}{16}$-inch holes and attach the molding to the cabinet front with 1-inch brads.

5 Shoe molding is used where the bookcase meets the floor. Fit the pieces (N and O) in place as you did for the cove and install with 4d finishing nails. Predrill and drive the nails at a slight downward angle so the molding is pressed against the floor but the nails go into the bookcase's bottom rail.

6 The side molding (P) covers the edge of the plywood back and any gap that might result if the wall is not perfectly plumb. Cut the pieces to fit between the top and bottom moldings. Press them against the wall and attach them to the bookcase sides with $1\frac{1}{4}$-inch brads.

7 Drill holes in the doors for the knobs $1\frac{1}{2}$ inches from the edge and centered top-to-bottom. Install the knobs. Attach magnetic catches to the bottom of the inside shelf and mating metal strikes to each door. Fill nail holes and touch up the finish.

MODULAR, CONTEMPORARY BUILT-INS

Modular construction makes it easy and efficient to customize your built-in cabinets and shelves. You just build a simple standard box, shelf, and door. There's a simple base made of 2×4s below, and plywood countertops above.

Once you set up to build any of these components, the main variable is the time it'll take to build however many you want. The completed project shown here has 10 boxes, four open shelves, and four doors. Mix these components in whatever way suits your needs and your space. The Materials Needed chart lists what you need to build one cabinet with a door and a shelf. The instructions explain how to adapt the base and countertops to your needs.

PRESTART CHECKLIST

☐ **TIME**
About four hours for the first cabinet, door, and shelf. Add about one hour for each additional cabinet or door and 30 minutes for each additional shelf. Allow additional time for finishing.

☐ **TOOLS**
Tape measure, hammer, nail set, combination square, 4-foot level, tablesaw or circular saw with straightedge guide, electric drill with stop, ¼-inch bit, ⅜-inch bit, 1⅜-inch Forstner bit, #6 counterbore bit, drill press jigsaw, straightedge or chalk line

☐ **SKILLS**
Measuring, sawing, gluing

☐ **PREP**
Measure installation space, configure built-ins, prepare workspace

MATERIALS NEEDED

Part	Finished size			Mat.	Qty.	Part	Finished size			Mat.	Qty.
	T	W	L				T	W	L		
A top and bottom	¾"	15¾"	23½"	BP	2	G base rails	1½"	3½"	to fit*	CL	**
B sides	¾"	15¾"	28½"	BP	2	H base crosspieces	1½"	3½"	10"	CL	**
C back	¼"	23½"	30"	BP	1	I countertops	¾"	17½"	to fit*	BP	**
D door	¾"	23¼"	29¾"	BP	1	J toe-kick covers	¼"	3½"	to fit*	BP	**
E shelf	¾"	15⅝"	21⅞"	BP	1	K filler panels	¾"	to fit*	to fit*	BP	**
F back supports	¾"	3½"	23½"	pine	3						

*See instructions.
** as needed
Material key: BP—birch plywood, CL— construction lumber (Douglas fir or spruce)
Hardware: 1¼-inch, 1½-inch, 2½-inch, and 3½-inch drywall screws—all coarse thread, 1-inch brads, European-style self-closing concealed hinges, door knobs or pulls
Supplies: Birch edge-banding veneer, glue, construction adhesive, 120-grit sandpaper, clear finish

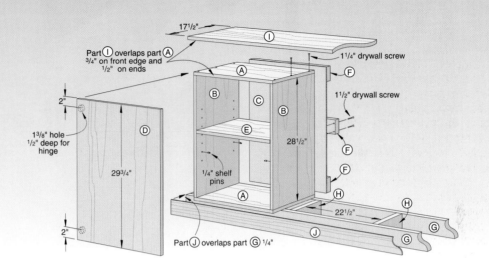

Materials and finishing

The units shown here are built with birch plywood, edged with veneer banding tape and given a clear finish. Birch plywood also takes paint very well. You might also check the price of medium density overlay (MDO) plywood that has face veneers that are designed to be painted. Oak or cherry plywood with a clear finish is another option.

CONFIGURING YOUR BUILT-INS
Size up the location first

The cabinets shown here are built between two walls. Of course, your cabinets can be flanked by one wall or by none. In any case, the length of the bottom run of cabinets will have to be divisible by 23½ inches—the width of each cabinet. With walls on both sides, you'll center the bottom run and install filler panels on each side. With one flanking wall, you might be able to butt the cabinets against the wall and install a piece of molding where the cabinet meets the wall. But if the wall is much out of plumb, you'll need a 2-inch-wide, custom-tapered filler panel.

The cabinets sit on a base made of 2×4s. For built-ins flanked by two walls, measure between the walls at the floor. Make the base to fit minus about ½ inch on each end. Make the toe-kick cover to fit exactly.

Each level of your built-in will have a countertop. Cut the countertops to length after you install the cabinets, adding an overhang of ½ inch on any side that doesn't abut a wall.

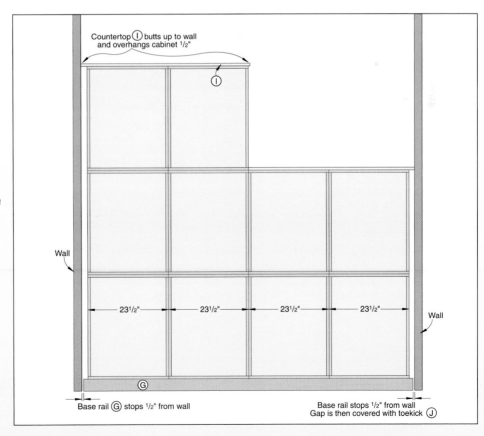

A. Cutting the cabinet parts

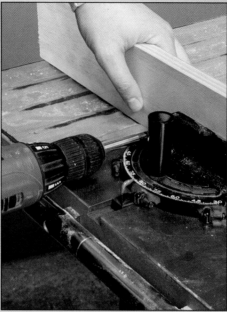

1 To rip stock for the top and bottom (A) and the sides (B) of the cabinet, set the tablesaw's fence to rip 15¾ inches wide. Have a helper hold up the unsupported end of the plywood while you rip 15 ¾ inches from a full sheet. Or use a circular saw with a straightedge guide (page 31).

2 To support plywood while crosscutting, use screws to attach an auxiliary fence (page 85) to the miter gauge. Make the fence of ¾-inch stock that's at least 3 inches wide and about 30 inches long. Or make the cuts with a circular saw and straightedge.

3 Crosscut the 15¾-inch-wide piece into two pieces for the top and bottom (A) and two sides (B). If you will make a number of cabinets, you'll save time if you set up a stop block on the tablesaw (page 157).

STANLEY PRO TIP

Pay attention to grain direction

When planning how you will cut parts from a sheet of plywood, consider how the wood grain will be oriented in the finished piece. Generally, the grain should run in the same direction as solid boards—vertically for sides, backs, and doors; and from side to side on top and bottom pieces and shelves. This is especially important for the doors and the cabinet sides with visible outside surfaces. It won't be as noticeable if horizontal grain is inside the cabinets.

OPTIONS TO CONSIDER
Add a dramatic hardwood edge

If you'd like to add a strong horizontal visual element to your built-ins, consider covering the exposed countertop edges with ¾-inch-by-¾-inch edging made from a contrasting wood instead of matching veneer tape. The rich dark brown of walnut or the deep red of cherry would both have a dramatic look. (Remember that cherry gets darker with age.) Attach the wood with glue and clamps or glue and 4d nails in predrilled holes. Make miter joints at the corners.

B. Drill shelf-pin holes

4 Rip and crosscut ¾-inch plywood to make the door (D). Then rip and crosscut ¼-inch plywood to make the back. Crosscut 1×4 stock to make three back supports (F). You can crosscut to a layout line with a circular saw or tablesaw or use a stop block on the tablesaw.

1 Make the shelf-pin drilling template shown below from a piece of ¼-inch plywood. To lay out the template holes, set a combination square to 2 inches and draw a line parallel to one side. Mark the centers of the holes along the line.

2 Set a stop on a ¼-inch drill bit to ⅞ inch so you'll drill ⅝-inch-deep holes. Put the template atop a side piece, flush with the front, and drill the holes. Then turn the template over, put it flush with the back of the side piece, and drill again.

Guaranteed alignment

Mark one end of your drilling template and one end of each shelf as "TOP." Match up the top designations when drilling and assembling. You'll have to turn the template over when drilling the second set of holes in a side. This way, all four holes for any shelf position will align perfectly, even if the template holes aren't perfectly spaced.

SHELF-PIN DRILLING TEMPLATE

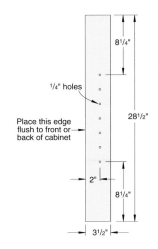

¼" holes

8¼"

28½"

Place this edge flush to front or back of cabinet

2"

8¼"

3½"

REFRESHER COURSE
Perforated hardboard makes a handy template

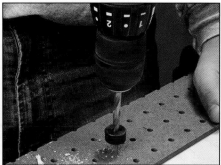

Perforated hardboard has ¼-inch-diameter holes centered 1 inch apart so drilling every other hole will give you the spacing you need for the shelf-pin holes. Make a template of the size shown at *left,* making sure one hole is located 8¼ inches from the top and 2 inches from one side.

C. Assembling the cabinets

1 Apply glue to the top edges of the side pieces. Put the top piece in place, make sure it is flush with the sides, then attach with 1¼-inch drywall screws. Attach the bottom piece the same way. Check the cabinet for square before the glue dries.

2 Apply glue to the back edges of the cabinet, then put the back in place. Check that the back is flush with the outside of the cabinet all around. Secure the back with 1-inch brads.

3 Attach the back support pieces (F) with glue and 1½-inch screws into the back edges of the sides. Center one crosspiece and attach the others flush with the top and bottom. If there is baseboard on the wall, raise the bottom crosspiece to clear it.

STANLEY PRO TIP

Speed the work with a power nailer

If you have a lot of cabinets to assemble, consider buying or renting a power finish nailer. These tools quickly drive and set finish nails, leaving a smaller hole than a hand-driven finish nail. There are air-driven models that require a compressor as well as battery-operated models. Use 1½-inch nails to assemble ¾-inch plywood cabinets.

WHAT IF…
You don't have a drill press ?

Hinge cup holes must be drilled to exact depth and be square to the surface. You can do this with a template and guide set designed specifically for locating and drilling hinge cup holes *(below right)*. A general-purpose drill guide *(right)* will help you drill cup holes and will be useful for other drilling tasks.

D. Installing hardware and finishing

4 Use edge-banding veneer (page 44) to cover the front edges of the cabinets and shelves. Cover all edges of the doors. Slightly round veneered edges with 120-grit sandpaper.

1 The doors are attached with European-style, self-closing, concealed hinges. Use a drill press with a 1⅜-inch-diameter Forstner bit to bore holes 2 inches from the top and bottom of the door. Typically the holes should be ½ inch deep and ³⁄₃₂ inch from the door edge, but check the hinge manufacturer's instruction sheet.

2 Place each hinge in its hole. Check that the hinge arms are 90 degrees to the door edge. The manufacturer's instructions will tell you the drill bit size (usually ³⁄₃₂-inch) you need to drill holes to fasten the hinge. The instructions will also tell you where to locate screws to fasten the hinge to the inside of the cabinet.

EUROPEAN-STYLE HINGES:
Make sure you get what you need

The streamlined look of doors that fully overlap the face of a cabinet built without face frames first became popular in Europe. European-style hinges were designed for this type of cabinet.

All European-style hinges close into a cup fitted into a hole on the inside of the door, so they are completely hidden when the door is closed. Usually, the hole is 1⅜ inches in diameter; European-made versions usually state this size as 35 millimeters. They are self-closing, so there's no need for a latch. They are all adjustable up and down and side to side after installation. More expensive ones can also be adjusted in and out.

Some European-style hinges have a separate piece that mounts inside the cabinet; others are one piece. Check the hinges before you buy them; some hinges sold as European style are designed to fit on the front or side of a face frame and won't work on frameless cabinets.

FORSTNER BIT
A special bit for
flat-bottomed holes

Forstner bits are specially designed to drill larger holes with a very cleanly cut circumference and a flat bottom—just what you need to drill cup holes for European-style hinges. The bits have a short pointed spur in the center to allow you to exactly locate the center of the hole and to keep the bit on track as it starts cutting.

E. Installing the cabinet

3 Drill holes in the doors for door pulls or knob screws. (See Pro Tip *below.*) Remove the hinges. Apply finish to the inside and fronts of the cabinets. Also finish the outside of any sides that will be exposed and both sides of the walls.

1 Cut 2×4s for the base rails (G) to length. (See "Configuring Your Built-Ins" on page 191.) Cut enough base crosspieces (H) to place them 24 inches on center. Lay out the crosspiece spacing on the rails and assemble the base with 2½-inch drywall screws or 10d nails.

2 Rip ¼-inch plywood to 3½ inches wide and cut it to the lengths you need to cover the front of the base and fit exactly between the walls. Attach these toe-kick covers (J) with 1-inch brads.

(See "Configuring Your Built-Ins" on page 191.)

STANLEY PRO TIP

Place handles at convenient heights

You'll probably want to place your handles or knobs about 2 inches from the door edge. For convenience and good looks in a three-tier configuration, place the handle or knob about 3 inches from the top of the door for the lowest tier, center it for the middle tier and place it about 3 inches from the bottom of the top-tier doors.

PREDRILL COUNTERSINKS
Countersink for neat holes

Most of the screws driven inside the cabinet will be out of direct view, especially if you are using doors. But you should still predrill a clean countersink—just deep enough for the screw head to sit flush to the surface. If you think the screw heads will mar the appearance of open cabinets, counterbore the holes about ¼ inch using a ⅜-inch bit. Fill the holes with matching ⅜-inch tapered face-grain plugs.

3 Put the base in position and use a 4-foot level to check front to back and side to side. Shim if necessary. Put the lowest row of cabinets in place, predrill countersinks, then attach the cabinets to each other with two 1¼-inch drywall screws. Attach each cabinet to the base with two screws.

4 Find the studs behind the first row by poking the wall with a finish nail or by using a stud finder above the cabinets. Drive 3½-inch drywall screws through the back of the cabinets into each stud. Drive the screws just under the cabinet tops where they will be inconspicuous.

5 Install the remaining cabinets. To determine the length of each 17½-inch-wide countertop (I), measure from the wall it will meet to the outside of the last cabinet it will cover. Add ½ inch for an overhang. Rip and crosscut the countertops.

WHAT IF...
You had to shim the base?

If you had to shim the base, the toe-kick cover will need to be wider than 3½ inches at one end. Measure the base height under the shim and rip the toe-kick ½ inch wider. Put the toe-kick against the base and scribe a cut line along the top. Cut the taper with a jigsaw.

6 Use veneer tape (page 44) to cover countertop edges that will be exposed. Slightly round the edges with sandpaper. Install the countertops with 1¼-inch drywall screws driven up through the cabinet tops. Use two screws per cabinet, one near the front and one near the back.

F. Installing filler panels and doors

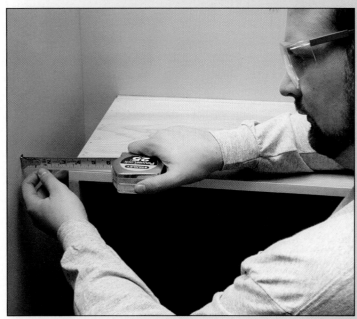

1 The walls on either side of the cabinets may not be perfectly plumb, so the filler panels (K) may need to be tapered to fit. To find out, measure the distance from the top of the cabinet to the wall and from the bottom of the cabinet to the wall.

2 To make the filler panels, cut plywood to the height of the cabinet minus the base. If the walls are plumb, rip the strips to the width you need. Otherwise, rip the strip to ½ inch wider than you need. Mark the top measurement on one end and the bottom measurement on the other end.

STANLEY PRO TIP: **Molding covers gaps**

Besides often being out of plumb, walls often aren't flat—they can bow in or out slightly anywhere along their height. The solution is to use 1-inch brads to install quarter-round molding where filler panels or countertops meet walls. The molding is flexible enough to follow a wavy contour and cover any gaps.

OPTIONS TO CONSIDER
Make a modular room divider

With only minor modifications, these versatile modular cabinets can make an effective room divider—perhaps between a living area and dining area in an open-plan home. Build one or two tiers of cabinets depending on how much privacy you want to create. Cover the backs of the cabinets with a run of wood paneling or beaded tongue-and-groove boards. Or make two rows of back-to-back cabinets.

3 Draw a line between the points you marked on the ends of the filler panel. You can use a straightedge for shorter panels or a chalk line for longer panels. Cut along the line with a circular saw.

4 Make filler panel cleats from any ¾-inch-thick scrap. Cut the cleats to fit, and attach them to the bottom of the countertops, the sides of the cabinets, and the walls. Set the cleats back ¾ inch from the cabinet face. Attach them to wood with glue and 1¼-inch drywall screws, to the wall with construction adhesive.

5 Check that your filler panels fit their spaces, then finish them. Put a bead of construction adhesive on the faces of the panels and press them onto the cleats. Reinstall the hinges and adjust them according to the manufacturer's instructions. Insert four shelf pins per shelf and install the shelves.

WHAT IF...
The walls have baseboards?

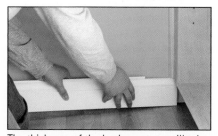

The thickness of the back supports will take care of the space created if you install the cabinets against baseboards. If your baseboard is less than 3½ inches tall, you can cut the kick plate cover to fit around it. Otherwise, the best solution is to carefully pry the molding off the wall. After installing the cabinets, measure and cut the molding to butt into the cabinet base, and reinstall. If the molding is taller than the base, you can notch it to fit around the end panels.

OPTIONS TO CONSIDER
Water-base finish gives a lighter look

If you finish birch plywood with an oil-base polyurethane or other oil-base finish, the wood will take on a mellow orange tinge *(right)* that many people find attractive. The cabinets shown in these instructions are coated with water-base polyurethane finish *(left)* to match factory-finished birch furniture.

CABINETS WITH CUSHIONS OR SHELVES

You can build this versatile wall-to-wall design as a built-in cushioned bench with storage cabinets underneath. Or, instead of the cushion, you can build open shelves above the cabinets.

If you are new to woodworking, don't worry. The cabinets are simple to build and the doors don't require complicated joinery. You can build as many cabinets as you want and you can easily adapt their sizes, along with the shelf lengths, to fit.

If you choose to make this into a bench, you can have an upholstery shop make the cushion to fit. Just pick a fabric, specify 2-inch-thick foam, and give the shop the cushion dimensions.

Materials and finishing
Birch plywood and solid poplar are used on the exposed parts of this project because both woods take paint well. Hidden parts are made of inexpensive particleboard.

PRESTART CHECKLIST

☐ **TIME**
About eight hours to construct the cabinets and four hours to make the shelves, plus finishing time

☐ **TOOLS**
Tape measure, combination square, framing square, angle square, tablesaw or circular saw with ripping guide, router with ½-inch piloted rabbeting bit, pocket-screw jig and bit, hammer, nail set, hand plane, flat-bladed screwdriver or putty knife, ½-inch chisel, spring clamps or C-clamps, 4-foot level

☐ **SKILLS**
Accurate measuring, sawing, routing

☐ **PREP**
Assemble tools and materials, prepare work area and installation area

MATERIALS NEEDED

Part	Finished size			Mat.	Qty.	Part	Finished size			Mat.	Qty.
	T	W	L				T	W	L		
FOUR CABINETS						L bench edge facing	¾"	¾"	12'	PL	1
A tops and bottoms	¾"	14¼"	35½"	PB	8	M door rails	¾"	1½"	15½"	PL	16
B sides	¾"	14¼"	15"	PB	8	N door stiles	¾"	1½"	15½"	PL	16
C backs	½"	16½"	35½"	PB	4	**SHELVES**					
D bench top	¾"	15½"	72"	BP	2	O bottom shelf	¾"	11⅞"	96"	BP	1
E base pieces	1½"	2¾"	35½"	CL*	8	OO bottom shelf	¾"	11⅞"	47⅞"	BP	1
F door panels	¼"	13½"	13½"	BP	8	P middle shelf	¾"	11⅞"	95⅝"	BP	1
G filler pieces	½"	1½"	19¼"	PL	2	PP middle shelf	¾"	11⅞"	47⅞"	BP	1
H top rails	¾"	1½"	35½"	PL	4	Q vertical dividers	¾"	11⅞"	13¾"	BP	6
I bottom rails	¾"	3½"	35½"	PL	4	R end panel	¾"	11⅞"	27½"	BP	1
J stiles	¾"	1½"	14¼"	PL	8	S top shelf	¾"	11⅞"	94"	BP	1
K middle dividers	¾"	3"	14¼"	PL	4	T shoe molding	½"	¾"	12'	Pine	

Material key: PB—particleboard, BP—birch plywood, CL—construction lumber (these pieces are ripped from spruce or Douglas fir 2×4s), PL—poplar
Hardware: Eight semi-concealed door hinges
Supplies: #6 × 1½-inch particleboard screws, 2½-inch single-lead drywall screws, pocket screws, glue, 4d finishing nails, glazer's points, 150-grit sandpaper

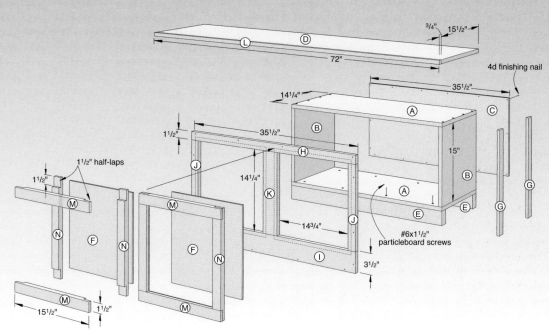

A. Cutting carcase parts

1 Set your tablesaw rip fence to 14¼ inches. Have someone hold the unsupported end of the sheets; rip five pieces from two sheets of ¾-inch particleboard. If you don't have a tablesaw or helper, use a circular saw with an 8-foot straightedge jig (page 31).

2 Crosscut the 14½-inch-wide pieces into the lengths shown in the cutting diagram *(below)* to make parts A and B. When cutting across full-length rips, it's easiest and safest to use a circular saw with straightedge jig. You can crosscut shorter rips with the miter gauge on the tablesaw. Label all parts.

3 With the tablesaw or straightedge jig, rip the sheet of ½-inch particleboard to 35½ inches as shown in the cutting diagram. Now use a shorter straightedge jig to crosscut four backs (C) to 16½ inches wide. Label the parts.

CUTTING DIAGRAM

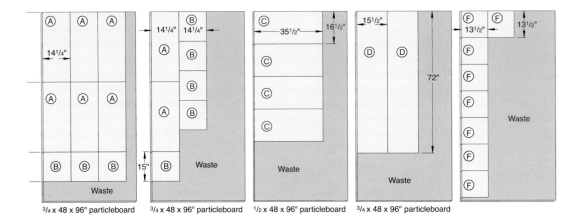

¾ x 48 x 96" particleboard   ¾ x 48 x 96" particleboard   ½ x 48 x 96" particleboard   ¾ x 48 x 96" particleboard

B. Assembling the cabinets

4 Rip-cut two 15½-inch pieces from ¾-inch particleboard to make the two bench tops (D). Crosscut the tops to 72 inches. To make the eight door panels (F), rip-cut two 13½-inch pieces from the sheet of ¼-inch plywood. Crosscut the pieces to 13½ inches.

1 Make the base pieces (E) by cutting 2×4s into six 35½-inch-long pieces with a mitersaw or circular saw. Then, rip each piece to 2¾ inches wide with a tablesaw or a circular saw and rip guide.

2 Apply glue on the top edge of two side pieces (B). Attach a top (A) to the side pieces with four #6×1½-inch particleboard screws into each side. Attach a bottom (A) the same way.

CROSSCUT
Make your straightedge into a custom crosscut jig

Need to crosscut several pieces from boards of the same width? For example, the tops, bottoms, and sides in this project all come out of 14¼-inch pieces. Here's an easy way to modify your straightedge jig to speed the work.

Put your straightedge jig across the first piece to be cut. Make sure it is square to the edges of the workpiece and clamp it in place as you normally would.

Now turn over the workpiece with the jig. Cut two 24-inch-long 1×2s, sandwich the workpiece between them and screw both to the bottom of the jig. Now you can just pop the jig onto the workpiece to make each cut without squaring and clamping the jig.

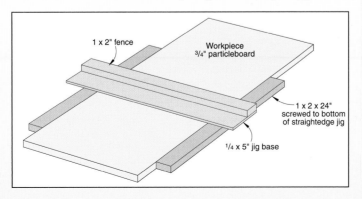

1 x 2" fence

Workpiece ³⁄₄" particleboard

1 x 2 x 24" screwed to bottom of straightedge jig

¹⁄₄ x 5" jig base

RIP GUIDE

A circular saw rip guide simplifies rip-cutting up to about 5 inches from the edge of the stock. The guides are available at home centers and hardware stores; be sure to buy one that fits your saw. Just mark the desired width on the end of the stock, align the saw blade with the mark, and set the guide against the stock edge.

B. Assembling the cabinets *(continued)*

3 Apply glue to the top edges of the base pieces and position them flush with the front and back of the carcase. Attach the pieces with 1½-inch particleboard screws driven down through the carcase. Use four screws for each piece.

4 Put the carcase face down on the bench and apply glue to all the back edges. Attach the back (C) with 4d finishing nails making sure the back is flush with the outside of the box all around. Repeat Steps 2 and 3 for other cabinets.

C. Making the face frames

1 Crosscut the top rails (H), bottom rails (I), stiles (J), and middle dividers (K) to length from poplar. (See Materials Needed, page 200.) The top rails and stiles are cut from 1×2s, and the middle dividers and bottom rails are cut from 1×4s. Rip middle dividers to 3 inches wide.

Cut panels on the floor

When ripping with a circular saw near the middle of a 4-foot-wide panel, it can be difficult to reach over sawhorses to guide the saw. Instead, lay the panel on the floor, good side facing down, atop two 8-foot 2×4s positioned to support the part of the panel you will use. Crawl along that part of the panel to make the cut.

OPTIONS TO CONSIDER
Different woods for different looks

Poplar is ideal for the face frame and door frames because it is a relatively inexpensive, widely available hardwood. It has tight grain that takes stain evenly and is an excellent surface for paint. If you plan to paint, you could use preprimed finger-jointed pine instead. Although not quite as strong as poplar, it needs no predrilling. It doesn't have pine knots that bleed through the paint, and saves work because you only have to prime surfaces you've cut.

If you like the look of wood, consider building the face frames and doors of solid oak and oak plywood. For a bit more money you can use cherry plywood and solid wood. If you make the shelving unit, use matching plywood and wood edge tape.

2 On the faces that won't show, mark both ends of each middle divider and the midpoint of its width. Make a mark halfway along the length of the top rail. Lay a bottom rail next to it, ends flush, and use a square to draw the centerline across both pieces. Do this for all rail pairs.

3 You can use dowels (page 59) or biscuits (page 64) to join the face frame parts, but pocket-hole joinery (page 64) is the easiest because you don't need clamps. Align the center marks on the middle dividers with the marks on the rails and join the parts with two screws.

4 Make sure the frames are flush with the top and sides of the carcase. Use glue and 4d nails to attach the face frames to the carcases. Predrill the nail holes with a 1/16-inch-diameter bit so you won't bend the nails when you drive them in.

Use a stop block for accuracy and speed

When you have several pieces to cut to the same length, such as for the face frames and doors in this project, using a stop block is not only faster than measuring, it is a more accurate way to make sure like pieces are the same length. If you are using a crosscutting jig with your circular saw, screw the block right to the base, as shown in Step 1 *above left.* Or you can clamp a stop block to a miter gauge extension on your tablesaw as shown to the *right.*

1 Screw a 3-by 24-inch extension of 3/4-inch plywood onto the miter gauge. Measure and cut the first (master) piece to length. Look closely at the teeth on the saw blade—one juts slightly left, the next slightly right. Put the master piece against the miter gauge, one end against a tooth that juts to the miter gauge side.

2 Put a stop block against the opposite end of the master piece and secure it in place with a spring clamp. Now you are ready to cut all the like pieces to length by butting them against the stop block.

D. Building the doors

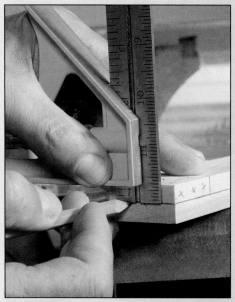

1 Cut 16 rails (M) and 16 stiles (N) to the lengths listed in Materials Needed. Make these cuts using a stop block screwed to the bottom of a circular saw crosscutting jig, a stop block on a power mitersaw, or the miter gauge extension with stop block described on the bottom of page 205.

2 Lap joints connect rails and stiles. Cut these with a backsaw like the half-lap joint on page 58 with one exception: In these full-lap joints both pieces will be cut. So, instead of Step 1 on page 58, set your combination square to ⅜ inch—half the thickness of the rails and stiles—to scribe the lap depth on each piece.

3 Apply glue to the lap joints and clamp the joints together to form each door frame. Use spring clamps in pairs at each joint or a single C-clamp at each joint. Use a framing square to make sure the door frames are perfectly square before the glue dries.

LAP JOINTS
Making this joint with a circular saw

1 Set your circular saw blade to cut ⅜ inch deep. Make a test cut in scrap to make sure the depth is exactly right. Draw a cut line at 1½ inches from the ends of the stiles and rails. Cut along the line, guiding the saw with an angle square.

2 Starting at the outside edge, make repeated passes over the waste area of the joint until all the material is removed. You don't need to mark or guide these cuts. Clean up the bottom of the joint with a sharp chisel.

C-CLAMPS

If you use C-clamps to glue up the face-frame lap joints, use pads of ¼-inch plywood or other scrap between the clamps and both surfaces of the wood. This will prevent damage to the workpieces and also helps to spread the clamping pressure.

4 When the glue has dried, unclamp the frames. Put a ½-inch piloted rabbeting bit in your router and set the depth to ⁵⁄₁₆ inch. To make the rabbets for the door panels, rout clockwise around the inside edge of the backside of each door frame.

5 The router will leave rounded corners. Square these up with a sharp chisel. Chop down at each side of the corner with the flat side of the chisel against the side of the rabbet. Put the flat of the chisel in the bottom of the rabbet to slice off the waste.

6 Put glue in the bottom of a door rabbet and set a door panel in place. Use a flat-bladed screwdriver or a small putty knife to push glazer's points into the side of the rabbets. Do this for all the door panels.

E. Installing the doors

1 The doors completely overlap the stiles and are attached with semi-concealed hinges (page 43). Attach two hinges to the back of each door 1½ inches from the top and bottom. Predrill holes for the screws.

2 To find where the top edges of the doors will meet the door frame, set your combination square to ⅝ inch and scribe a line ⅝ inch from the inside edge of each face frame top rail.

3 Have someone hold the top of each door along the layout line on the face frame top rail. With a stop on your drill bit set to ⅜ inch, predrill through the hinge holes. Screw the doors in place.

F. Installing the cabinets

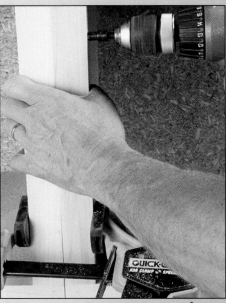

1 Center the cabinets between the walls, leaving equal gaps of about 1½ inches on both sides. Make sure the faces are all plumb and flush and the cabinets are level. Shim if necessary.

2 Clamp cabinets together and drill ³⁄₁₆-inch counterbored (page 54) pilot holes through the cabinet stiles and about ¼ inch into the adjoining stile. Screw the cabinets together with two or three 2½-inch screws through each pair of stiles.

3 Because walls are rarely plumb, filler pieces (G) are used between the outside cabinets and the walls. Cut the strips to 19¼ inches. On both sides, measure the gap at the top and at the bottom.

SCARF JOINTS
Overlapping joint looks neater

Where the ends of two pieces meet, a scarf joint looks neater than a butt joint. To make a scarf, cut the mating ends at opposing 45-degree angles so that one end overlaps the other. If your bench top (D) will remain exposed, join the two top pieces with a scarf. If you do, allow for the overlap when you measure the pieces. If the bench face edging or the shoe molding requires more than one piece, use a scarf.

OPTIONS TO CONSIDER
Add an edge lip

If you want a cushion on the bench, make the bench face edging 1½ inches wide instead of ¾ inch and allow the extra width to form a lip above the bench top. This will prevent the cushion from sliding off the bench. Use sandpaper to round over the top edges of the edge facing

4 If the top and bottom measurements are different, transfer the smaller measurement to one end of the filler piece and draw a cutting line between the mark and the other end of the filler piece. Clamp the piece in a bench vise and hand-plane to the line.

5 Secure the two bench top pieces with 4d finishing nails spaced about 12 inches apart around the edges. Rip the ¾-inch-square bench edge facing (L), then crosscut it to fit the length of the cabinets—you'll probably need two pieces. Glue it to the front edge of the tops and drive 4d nails in predrilled holes.

6 The shoe molding (T) covers any gaps between the bottom of the cabinets and the floor and eliminates a corner that's hard to sweep or vacuum. Cut it to fit and attach it to the cabinets, not the floor, with 4d nails.

G. Making the shelves

1 Rip-cut six 11⅞-inch-wide pieces from two sheets of ¾-inch birch plywood. Then crosscut as shown in the cutting diagram at *right* to make all the parts. Label the parts as you cut them.

CUTTING DIAGRAM

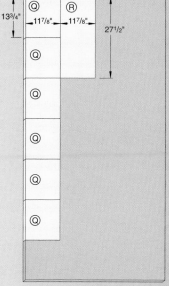

13¾" Q R 27½"
11⅞" 11⅞"
Q
Q
Q
Q
Q

¾ x 48 x 96" birch plywood

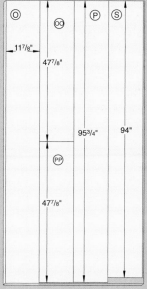

O O P S
11⅞"
47⅞"
95¾" 94"
PP
47⅞"

¾ x 48 x 96" birch plywood

G. Making the shelves *(continued)*

2 As the drawing *below right* shows, the vertical dividers (R) fit into ¾-inch-wide dadoes. Shelf sections P and PP (and O and OO) meet with ⅜-inch rabbets that form a dado. Use a framing square to lay out opposing dadoes and rabbets together as shown in the drawing on the *opposite page.*

3 Place one of the vertical dividers (Q) atop the side piece (R). Make sure the pieces are flush at the bottom and both ends. Then scribe a line along the other end of the vertical divider to lay out one side of the dado in the side piece. Use a scrap of ¾-inch plywood to lay out the other side.

4 Set your circular saw cutting depth to ⅜ inch to make the dado cuts with multiple passes as described on page 60. Make the rabbet cuts the same way, except you only need one guided edge cut. Clean out the joints with a sharp chisel.

DADOES AND RABBETS
Lay them out with a scrap template

Plywood sold as ¾-inch thick is usually slightly thinner than that. So, laying out dado widths by measurement may result in a loose fit. Instead, lay out one side of each dado. Then use a scrap piece of the project plywood to lay out the other side.

CABINET SHELVES

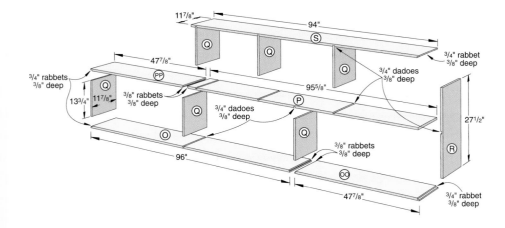

11⅞" 94" S ¾" rabbet ⅜" deep
47⅞" PP Q Q Q ¾" dadoes ⅜" deep
¾" rabbets ⅜" deep 95⅝"
13¾" 11⅞" ⅜" rabbets ⅜" deep Q P ¾" dadoes ⅜" deep 27½"
O Q R
96" ⅜" rabbets ⅜" deep
47⅞" OO ¾" rabbet ⅜" deep

H. Assembling the shelves

1 Apply glue in the dadoes that will join parts Q, S, and P. Assemble the parts to three vertical dividers with three 4d finishing nails into each joint. Then glue and nail the other shelves and dividers, and finally the side piece. Make sure the entire assembly is square before the glue dries.

2 Apply edge banding to all front edges (page 44), covering the horizontal shelf edges first so they run full length. Slightly round all the edges with 150-grit sandpaper. Now you're ready to paint or finish your project.

FRONT VIEW

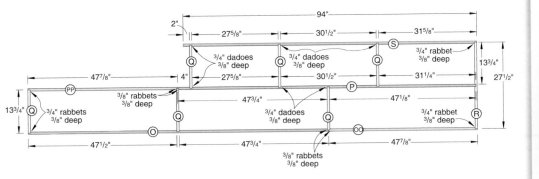

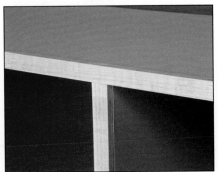

OPTIONS TO CONSIDER
Accent the shelves with solid hardwood edging

Consider painting the cabinet and shelves to match the wall and using solid hardwood such as oak or cherry as an accent. To do this, skip the edge tape and glue. Instead, nail ½×¾-inch strips of prefinished wood to the front edges. Use matching wood for the cabinet top edge facing (L).

CLOSET ORGANIZER

After assembling this organizer you'll think you've doubled the size of your closet. The key is efficient, accessible use of space. Instead of the usual single closet pole with a difficult-to-reach shelf, you'll have three poles at appropriate heights for shirts, pants, and coats. Instead of a jumble of shoes in the dark recesses of the floor, your footwear will be neatly stored in an easily accessible rack. At the center of the organizer is a stack of narrow shelves that's perfect for storing sweaters. There also are divided accessory shelves to the left of the sweater shelves and another shelf over the shirt pole. The organizer shown fits a closet that's 7 feet wide and 8 feet tall. If your closet is a different size, see the bottom of page 215.

Materials and finishing
This organizer is made of birch plywood and has a clear satin polyurethane finish. Of course, you can stain the plywood first or use oak plywood for a different look. Birch plywood also looks great with a painted surface. A semigloss paint will be more durable than flat paint.

PRESTART CHECKLIST

☐ **TIME**
About eight hours to construct, plus finishing time

☐ **TOOLS**
Tape measure, angle square, framing square, chalk line, tablesaw or circular saw, electric drill/driver, hammer, nail set, long bar clamps, utility knife, metal straightedge, stud finder

☐ **SKILLS**
Accurate measuring, sawing, gluing, clamping

☐ **PREP**
Clean closet, assemble tools and materials

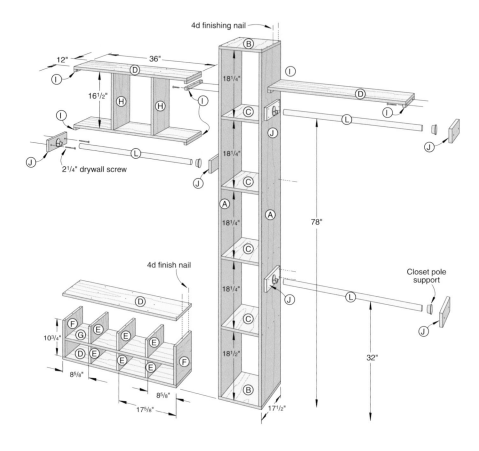

CUTTING DIAGRAM

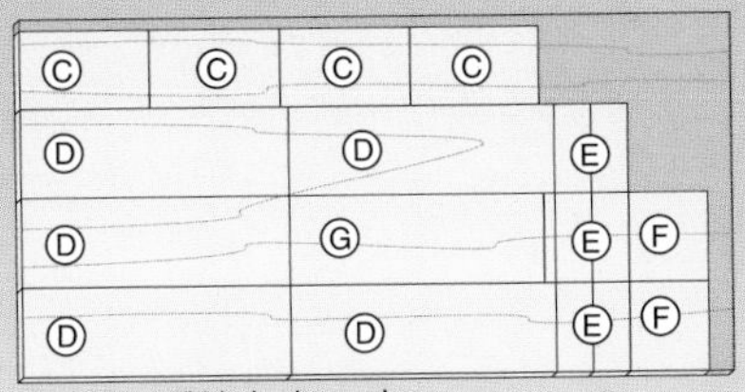

3/4 x 48 x 96" birch plywood

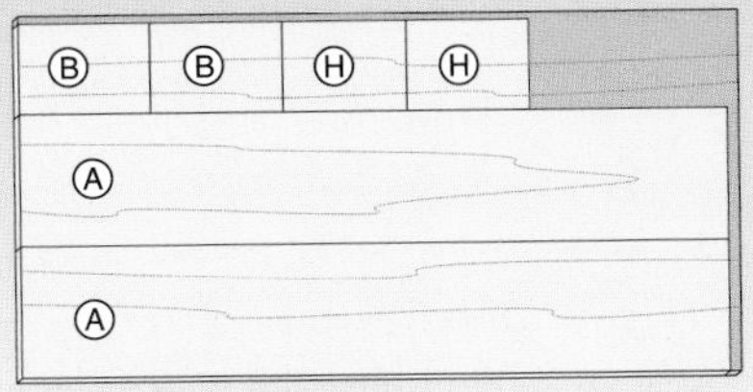

3/4 x 48 x 96" birch plywood

A. Cutting parts

1 This project uses two sheets of plywood with little waste. Use a tablesaw with a helper or a circular saw with a straightedge guide (pages 30-31) to rip the plywood into four 12-inch-wide pieces, two 17½-inch-wide pieces, and one 10½-inch piece as shown in the diagrams *above left*.

2 Crosscut all plywood parts to the lengths shown in the cutting diagrams. Attach a 2-foot length of ¾-inch stock to the miter gauge to better support the plywood. Alternately, use a circular saw with crosscutting jig (page 31). Use masking tape to label each part as you cut it.

MATERIALS NEEDED

Part	T	W	L	Mat.	Qty.
Finished size					
A sweater divider sides	¾"	17½"	94½"	BPW	2
B sweater divider top & bottom	¾"	12"	17½"	BPW	2
C sweater divider shelves	¾"	10½"	17½"	BPW	4
D shelves and shoe rack top & bottom	¾"	12"	36"	BPW	5
E shoe rack vertical dividers	¾"	5"	12"	BPW	6
F shoe rack sides	¾"	10¾"	12"	BPW	2
G shoe rack horizontal shelf	¾"	12"	34½"	BPW	1
H accessory shelf dividers	¾"	12"	16½"	BPW	2
I shelf cleats	¾"	1½"	*as needed	Pine	6
J pole cleats	¾"	3½"	*as needed	Pine	6

Material key: BPW—birch plywood
Hardware: 4d finishing nails, 2¼-inch single-lead drywall screws, three pairs standard closet pole hangers
Supplies: Glue, wood putty, sandpaper, stain (optional), clear finish, shelf edging, birch or oak edge tape, one 10-foot standard closet pole

WHAT IF...
You don't have a helper?

To cut a full sheet of plywood accurately and safely on a tablesaw, you must have a helper or support tables or rollers on three sides of the saw. Even with a helper and extra support, a lightweight benchtop saw could shift around dangerously during the cut.

The solution is to snap a chalk line on the sheet for a rip-cut that's about ¼ inch wider than the final width you need. Cut along this line with a circular saw—you don't need a guide because this cut doesn't have to be perfectly straight. Then set the tablesaw for the final width and rip off the extra ¼ inch.

B. Assembling the sweater divider

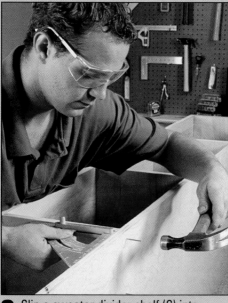

1 Place the sweater divider sides (A) next to each other with their inside faces up and tops and bottoms perfectly flush. Use a framing square to lay out lines for the bottom of the four divider shelves (C), as shown in the drawing on page 212.

2 Apply glue to the top edges of the divider sides (A). Attach the sweater divider top (B) with 4d finishing nails. Glue and nail the sweater divider bottom (B) in the same way. Use a framing square to check that the box is square before the glue dries.

3 Slip a sweater divider shelf (C) into place, carefully aligning its bottom to the layout lines. Attach it with 4d nails driven partway into the sides. Check for square and complete the nailing. Repeat for all the shelves.

OPTIONS TO CONSIDER

Birch plywood has a tight grain that takes paint well. However, if you will paint your closet organizer, you can build the organizer with less-expensive medium-density overlay (MDO) plywood, available at your lumberyard or home center. This plywood has top veneers that take paint evenly.

STANLEY PRO TIP: **Know the score**

When cutting hardwood plywood on a tablesaw, make sure the good side (the side that will show in the project) is facing up. When cutting with a circular saw, the good side should be down so any tear-out that occurs as the sawteeth exit the plywood will be hidden in the project.

You might want both sides of the cut to look good (the shoe rack sides, for example). Or it just might not be practical to cut from the correct side. If so, place a metal straightedge along your cut line and use a sharp utility knife to score the cut line. Make two or three passes with the knife, until you cut completely through the plywood's thin top veneer.

C. Assembling the shoe rack and accessory shelf

1 As you did for the sweater divider, lay the shoe rack top and bottom (D) and horizontal shelf (G) side by side to lay out the positions of the vertical dividers (E). Center the horizontal shelf so its ends are ¾ inch from the ends of the top and bottom.

2 Glue and clamp a vertical divider to the bottom. Make sure the divider is aligned to the layout, then secure with 4d finishing nails. Repeat for the other dividers. Attach the sides (F) the same way, making sure the ends of the bottom are flush with the sides.

3 Apply glue on the ends of the shoe rack horizontal shelf (G), then glue and clamp the shelf to the three vertical dividers (E). Check for square and nail in place. Nail the sides into the ends of the vertical shelf.

WHAT IF...
Your closet is a different size?

The wall organizer shown here is designed to fit in a closet with a back wall 7 feet wide and 8 feet tall. But your closet dimensions may be different.

If the height is different, all you need to do is adjust the height of the center sweater divider. If the closet is narrower, you just need to shorten the right shelf or the accessory shelf or both.

If your closet is wider than 7 feet, start by reviewing "Sagless Spans" on page 39. Although bookshelves made of ¾-inch plywood shouldn't span more than 36 inches, you probably won't store anything as heavy as books in the closet, so you can safely expand the right shelf to about 42 inches. The left accessory shelf can be as long as 48 inches if you add another vertical divider.

Another option for wide closets is to make the sweater divider wider or even make two or three side-by-side sweater dividers. Of course, the shoe rack can be widened or narrowed to any width you want.

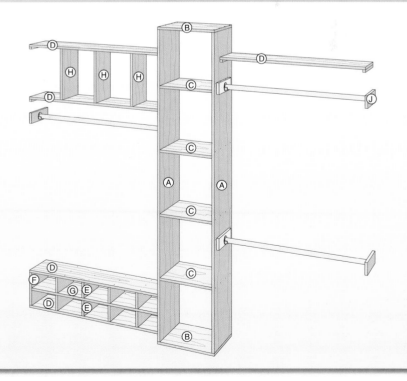

C. Assembling the shoe rack and accessory shelf (continued)

4 Glue and clamp one of the three remaining vertical dividers (E) to the top. Align it, then secure it with 4d finishing nails. Repeat for the remaining dividers.

5 Apply glue to the top edges of the sides and the bottoms of the dividers you attached to the top. Nail the top to the sides. Make sure the assembly is square, then secure each top divider into the horizontal shelf by toe-nailing at front and back.

6 Lay the top and bottom (D) of the accessory shelf side by side to mark the positions of the two vertical dividers (H). Glue and clamp the dividers in place and secure with 4d finishing nails. Cover all the front edges with edge banding as described on page 44.

STANLEY PRO TIP

Make carrying plywood easier

Full sheets of plywood are awkward to carry because of their 4-foot width. A panel carrier hooks under the sheets and extends your reach to give you better control and help prevent back strain. You can buy one at a home center or hardware store.

OPTIONS TO CONSIDER
Screen molding edge

Screen molding covers seams where screening is attached to a frame, but it's also ideal for covering exposed plywood edges. The molding is ¾ inches wide to match the plywood, and you can choose from several profiles, including flat molding with rounded edges or beaded.

Attach the molding with glue and 4d finishing nails. You can paint or apply a clear finish to match the project. Or, make a decorative contrast by prepainting the molding to apply to plywood with a clear finish, or prefinishing to apply to painted plywood.

D. Finishing and installing the organizer

1 Apply finish. Center the sweater divider in the closet and install the shoe rack. Lay out shelf-cleat heights on the divider and closet sides with a 2-foot level. Locate studs in both sides of the closet wall with a stud finder.

2 From 1×2s, cut six shelf cleats (I) long enough to extend 1 inch past the first stud from the closet's back corners or at least 10½ inches long. Attach the cleats with 2¼-inch drywall screws into the closet corner framing and first stud. Attach cleats to center divider with glue and 4d nails.

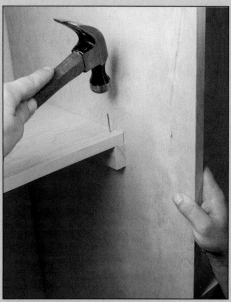

3 Install the right shelf and the left accessory shelf unit with two 4d nails driven down into each cleat. Fit cleats under the top of the accessory shelf assembly and install as you did the other cleats.

Choosing pole heights

When you build your own closet organizer, you are free to customize it to your needs, and even to your height. For example, the shirt pole is set 46 inches above the pants pole—enough room to hang long skirts from the pole. But for most shirts, you only need about 36 inches. So, if a short person will use the closet, you could set the shirt pole only 36 inches above the pants pole—at 68 inches instead of 78 inches. In that case, you could add a second shelf for items that are used infrequently.

4 Cut six closet pole cleats (J) to the same length as the shelf cleats. Lay out heights for the cleats as shown on page 212 and described *at left.* Attach with pairs of 2¼-inch screws into the wall studs and with glue and pairs of 4d nails into the divider.

5 Fill the screw and nail holes in the cleats. Paint or finish the cleats to match the closet and divider. Install pole hangers with their center screws located 8¾ inches from the back of the closet and 1½ inches from the cleat bottoms. Cut closet poles to length and install.

BUILT-IN KITCHEN BENCH

Do you have a nook in your kitchen that's just the place for a cozy bench? Maybe you already have a table and chairs there, but the space is tight, and getting in and out of the chairs is awkward. A bench solves this problem because you don't push it back as you slide in and out.

This bench offers more than sitting space; it offers storage space as well. Open the seat lid, and you'll find a handy place to store tablecloths or infrequently used dishes. There's even a box built into the side for storing cookbooks.

Materials and finishing

The bench shown here is built of oak plywood with solid oak edging to match oak kitchen cabinets. You might choose cherry or birch plywood to match your kitchen. Birch plywood also looks great when painted. Consider painting the base and back to match the walls and using a clear finish on the seat and trim.

PRESTART CHECKLIST

☐ **TIME**
About 16 hours to construct, plus finishing time

☐ **TOOLS**
Tape measure, hammer, nail set, utility knife, metal straightedge, sliding bevel gauge, protractor, utility knife, tablesaw, circular saw with rip guide, C-clamps, electric drill driver with ³⁄₆₄-inch bit for predrilling, handsaw or jigsaw, sanding block or random-orbit sander

☐ **SKILLS**
Accurate measuring, sawing, routing, drilling

☐ **PREP**
Assemble tools and materials, prepare a large work area, prepare installation site

MATERIALS NEEDED

Part	Finished size			Mat.	Qty.	Part	Finished size			Mat.	Qty.
	T	W	L				T	W	L		
A back	¾"	38"	45"	OP	1	L seat support	1½"	3½"	33¾"	CL	1
B sides	¾"	23⅛"	38"	OP	2	M bottom supports	1½"	2"	45"	CL	3
C seat back	¾"	21⅛"	46½"	OP	1	N box back	¾"	13"	17"	OP	1
D front	¾"	17¼"	46½"	OP	1	O seat edge	½"	1¼"	46½"	Oak	1
E seat	¾"	16¾"	46½"	OP	1	P back trim	¼"	1¼"	38"	Oak	2
F divider	¾"	23⅛"	35¼"	OP	1	Q front trim	¼"	1¼"	17"	Oak	2
G bottom	¾"	22"	33¾"	OP	1	R bottom trim	¼"	1¼"	20"	Oak	2
H box top and bottom	¾"	10½"	17"	OP	2	S seat side trim	¼"	1¼"	17¼"	Oak	2
I box sides	¾"	10½"	11½"	OP	2	T seat back trim	¼"	1¼"	21⅛"	Oak	2
J head support	¾"	2⅜"	45"	OP	1	U box stile trim	¼"	1¼"	13"	Oak	2
K head piece	¾"	3⅞"	46¾"	Oak	1	V box rail trim	¼"	1¼"	19½"	Oak	2

Material key: OP—oak plywood, CL—construction lumber (Douglas fir or spruce)
Hardware: 1¼-inch coarse-thread drywall screws, 1½-inch coarse-thread drywall screws, 2-inch coarse-thread drywall screws, 4d finishing nails, 1-inch brads, 30-inch piano hinge, self-balancing lid support
Supplies: Glue; 80-, 150-, and 220-grit sandpaper

A. Cutting the plywood

1 Set the tablesaw fence to 38 inches and, with a helper, crosscut 38 inches from two sheets of plywood for the back (A), the sides (B), and the box back (N) as shown in the cutting diagram on page 220. Or use a circular saw with a straightedge guide (pages 30-31).

2 Set a rip guide on the circular saw to rip 1½ inches including the kerf, and rip the edge from one of the remaining plywood pieces. The seat back (C), front (D), seat (E), and bottom (G) will have beveled edges, but first crosscut them to the rough widths shown in the cutting diagram.

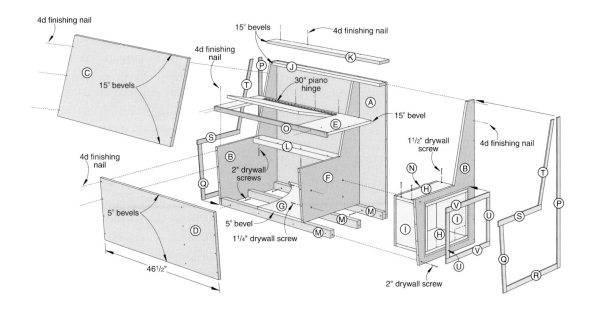

A. Cutting the plywood (continued)

3 Set the rip fence to 23⅞ inches and rip the two side pieces (B); you'll make the angled cuts and the box back (N) later. Set the fence to 35¼ inches to crosscut the divider (F) and bottom (G). Rip the divider to final width and the bottom to rough width.

4 Rip the head support (J) and head piece (K) to rough widths, then use the miter gauge with an auxiliary fence to crosscut. Set the rip fence to 10½ inches and cut four pieces for the box sides (I) and box top and bottom (H). Crosscut these pieces to length.

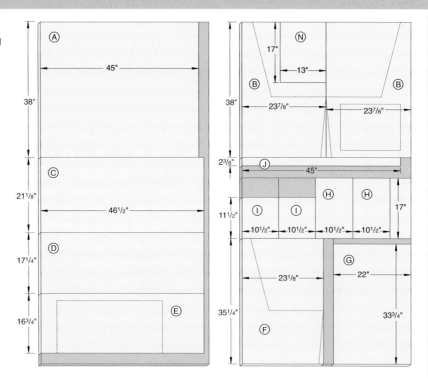

CUTTING DIAGRAM

INCLUDING THE KERF
Hook the tape over the blade

In the case above, you want to reduce the plywood sheet's width from 48 inches to 46½ inches. So the saw blade's thickness must be included in the material you remove. Hook your tape measure on the outside of the saw blade as you adjust the circular saw rip guide to 1½ inches.

B. Cutting the bevels

1 Tilt the tablesaw blade 15 degrees and, using the pieces themselves as a guide, set the rip fence to bevel one side of the head support, the head piece, the seat, and the bench back. Be sure the outside faces are up during the cuts.

2 The bench back gets beveled on both sides. The bevels are parallel to each other. Lay out the second bevel, and then place the piece on the saw. Align the tilted blade to the layout line and then adjust the fence to meet the workpiece. Cut the second bevel.

STANLEY PRO TIP: **Set your saw's angle accurately**

The tilt-angle gauge on a tablesaw or circular saw may not be precisely accurate, so it's best to use a sliding bevel gauge to set the angle. Start by drawing the angle on a piece of paper as shown at *top right*. (When you tilt a saw blade to 15 degrees, you're really tilting the blade 15 degrees from 90 degrees. On a protractor, that's 75 degrees.) Then set the angle on the bevel gauge, as shown *below right*.

LAY OUT THE SECOND BEVEL
Accurate layout with a sliding bevel gauge

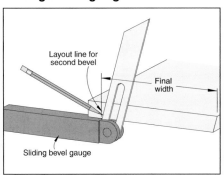

Layout line for second bevel

Final width

Sliding bevel gauge

With your sliding bevel set to the angle you need, you can use it to lay out the second bevel on the seat back and the bench front. Measuring from the long side of the first bevel, mark the final width of the pieces. Then use the bevel gauge as shown to draw a layout line for the second bevel.

B. Cutting the bevels *(continued)*

3 Set the tablesaw blade to 90 degrees. Set the fence 16¾ inches from the blade. Place the beveled side of the seat against the fence, long side of the bevel up, and rip the seat to final width. Repeat for the head support, head piece, and bench back.

4 Like the bench back, the bench front (D) has parallel bevels on its long sides. This time, the bevel is 5 degrees. Use the same process: Bevel one side first, then lay out the bevel on the piece before cutting the second bevel. Cut a 5-degree bevel on the bottom piece.

C. Cutting the bench sides

1 Lay out the outside cuts for each bench side and the divider as shown in the drawing *below*. Lay out the opening for the book box on the side that will be exposed. Score the layout lines with a sharp utility knife so the circular saw won't splinter the top veneer.

SAFETY FIRST
Remove power before adjustment

Whenever you adjust a portable power tool—whether adjusting a ripping guide on a circular saw, tilting a blade, or changing a router bit—be sure that the tool is not plugged in. Many newer saws have an extra safety switch you must press with your thumb while pulling the trigger. These switches do reduce the risk of accidentally starting the saw, but you are still much safer if there is no power to the tool. Likewise, if you have a battery-operated saw, be sure to remove the battery before adjusting the blade.

REFRESHER COURSE
Use the right blade for smooth cuts

To make smooth cuts in plywood with your circular saw, install a fine-toothed hollow-ground plywood blade.

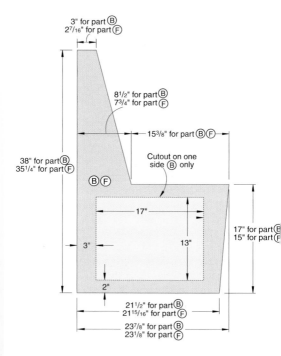

3" for part Ⓑ
2⁷⁄₁₆" for part Ⓕ

8½" for part Ⓑ
7¾" for part Ⓕ

15³⁄₈" for part Ⓑ Ⓕ

38" for part Ⓑ
35¼" for part Ⓕ

Cutout on one side Ⓑ only

Ⓑ Ⓕ

17"

13"

17" for part Ⓔ
15" for part Ⓕ

3"

2"

21½" for part Ⓑ
21¹⁵⁄₁₆" for part Ⓕ

23⁷⁄₈" for part Ⓑ
23¹⁄₈" for part Ⓕ

2 For the three side pieces, place a circular saw straightedge guide (pages 30-31) along the layout line for the bench seat. Cut until the saw blade reaches the seat back line. Then cut the seat back line using the straightedge. Finish the cuts with a handsaw. Use the straightedge to cut the seat front line.

3 To make the book box cutout, clamp the straightedge guide along a line. Position the front of the saw on the guide. Pull the saw's guard up, turn the saw on, and carefully lower the blade into the wood, checking first that the cut will start near a corner but won't overshoot.

4 Stop the cut when you reach a corner. Repeat this process for all four sides of the cutout. Then finish the cutout with vertical handsaw strokes in each corner. You can also use a jigsaw to finish the cuts.

FINISH THE CUTS WITH A HANDSAW
A few strokes make cuts meet

When you cut two lines to an intersecting point with a circular saw, the cuts won't be completed at the bottom. Finish the cuts with a jigsaw or handsaw.

OPTIONS TO CONSIDER
Make cutout with a jigsaw

Plunge-cutting with a circular saw is safer and easier than it looks, as long as you keep a firm grip on the saw and the blade is sharp. However, you may prefer to make the book box cutout with a jigsaw. To do this, first drill ¼-inch holes in each corner of the box layout. Insert the jigsaw blade in the holes to make the cuts.

D. Making the lid

1 Lay out the sides of the lid on the bench seat. (Make sure the beveled cut will be at the back.) Set a combination square to 2 inches and use it to guide a pencil as you lay out the back of the lid. Score the layout lines with a sharp utility knife.

2 Rip and crosscut a piece of solid oak for the lid trim (O). Predrill holes, then attach the trim to the front of the bench seat with glue and 4d finishing nails. Keep the piece flush with the top and keep nails away from where you'll saw out the lid.

3 Use a straightedge guide and plunge the circular saw to make the cut for the back of the lid. Then use the saw with the straightedge guide to make the side cuts. Finish the cuts with a handsaw or jigsaw.

BENCH SEAT

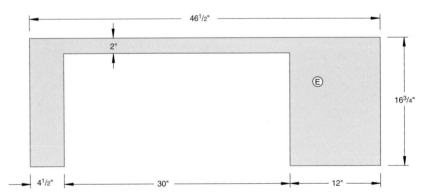

E. Building the bench

1 Rip and crosscut one of the side scraps to make the back of the book box (N). Attach the book box top and bottom (H) to the sides (I) with glue and 1½-inch drywall screws. Apply glue to the back edges of the box and screw the back into place.

2 Apply glue to the side edges of the bench back (A). Put a side piece against the back, making sure it is flush. Secure with 4d finishing nails, being careful to nail at 90 degrees. Now attach the other side. Set the nails and wipe away glue squeeze-out before it dries.

3 Apply glue to the front edges of the side pieces. Put the bench front (D) in place, making sure it is flush with the outer face, top, and bottom of each side. Secure the front with 4d finishing nails.

4 Rip 2×4 stock to 2 inches wide for the bottom supports (M) and cut the supports to length to fit between the sides. Put glue on one of the supports and place it against the inside of the back, flush with the bottom. Attach it with 2-inch drywall screws driven through the support.

5 Center another bottom support and fasten it flush to the bottom using one 2-inch drywall screw through each side. Keep the screws within 1 inch of the edge. Attach the third support flush with the bottom, meeting the bottom of the front.

6 Slide the book box into the opening in the bench side. Make sure the box edge is flush with the outer face of the side, then drive two 4d finishing nails through each side, the bottom, and the top of the box into the bench side. Set the nails.

7 Place the divider (F) inside the bench and attach it to the back of the book box with four 1¼-inch drywall screws. Extend light pencil lines up the divider and the side to help you locate the middle divider for nailing when you install the bottom.

F. Assembling the seat

1 Place the seat and lid on a work surface. Make sure the lid is flush with the front of the seat and there is an equal space at each side between the lid and the seat. Attach the 30-inch piano hinge with the screws provided.

2 Glue and nail the seat to the bench, making sure it is flush with the sides. Then cut the 2×4 seat support (L) to length. Lift the lid and attach the support under the seat with glue and 2-inch drywall screws. Make sure the support is flush with the back of the lid opening.

3 Install a self-balancing lid support to prevent the lid from slamming shut on someone's fingers or head. Attach one end to the face of the 2×4 seat support near the middle of the opening. With the lid open, attach the other end to the lid.

FINISHING THE BENCH
Solid wood needs more attention than plywood

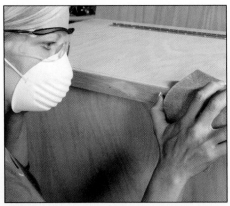

1 Remove the hinge and finish the lid separately. Fill all the nail holes with oak-colored wood filler. Then use a piece of 80-grit sandpaper to lightly round over all the solid wood edges. The top of the seat trim can be rounded more.

2 When the filler dries, sand all the solid wood parts with 80-, 150-, and finally 220-grit sandpaper. Use a random-orbit sander or a sanding block. The plywood requires just a light sanding with 180- and 220-grit sandpaper.

3 Vacuum the bench and wipe it with a damp cloth to remove all sanding dust. Apply a first coat of clear satin polyurethane finish.

G. Installing the trim

1 Rip enough ¼-inch-thick oak to 1¼ inches wide for the trim parts (P through V). It's easiest to mark the pieces to fit, then cut them as you go. Start with the back trim pieces (P), cutting one end square, and then putting the piece in place to mark the other end.

2 Attach the back trim with glue and 1-inch brads in predrilled holes. Cut a 5-degree angle on the bottom end of the front trim (Q), mark it in place for a 5-degree angle on the other side, then attach it.

4 Attach the seat back (C) to the sides with glue and 4d finishing nails. Then install the head piece (K) with glue and six or eight 4d finishing nails in predrilled holes. Make sure the front of the head piece is in the same place as the seat back. Set all nails.

3 Mark, cut, and install the bottom trim (R). Cut one end of the seat back trim (T) at 15 degrees, mark and cut the other end at 15 degrees, and install. Cut one end of the seat side trim (S) at 15 degrees and mark the other end square to the lid trim. Cut and install the trim.

4 Cut two 13-inch-long box stile trim pieces (U) and install with their inside edges flush with the inside of the box. Mark and cut the box rail trim pieces (V) to fit, then install them.

4 When the first coat cures, sand it lightly with a hand sanding block and 220-grit sandpaper. Just remove any air-bubble bumps and scuff the surface for the next coat. Apply a second coat. Lightly sand and coat again, if you want.

CORNER LINEN CABINET

Corner cupboards put often-unused space to work. This compact closet is designed to hold linens or towels. It's small enough to tuck into a hallway by the bathroom, the bathroom itself, or a corner of a bedroom. Don't be put off by those handsome doors; there's no fancy joinery involved in building them.

Materials and finishing

The face frame and doors of this cabinet are made of birch plywood and solid poplar that looks great when painted. You might choose to make these parts of oak and matching plywood or of another hardwood with a clear finish. The sides and shelves, which won't be visible with the doors closed, are made of lauan plywood, which doesn't take paint quite as smoothly as birch but still looks fine and is a bit less expensive.

PRESTART CHECKLIST

☐ **TIME**
About 16 hours to construct, plus finishing time

☐ **TOOLS**
Hammer, nail set, combination square, bar clamps, tape measure, chisel, stepladder, tablesaw, circular saw with ripping guide, power drill/driver with #6 adjustable counterbore bit and ¹⁄₁₆-inch bit (for predrilling nail holes), router with ½-inch piloted rabbeting bit, doweling jig, pocket-hole jig

☐ **SKILLS**
Accurate measuring, sawing, routing, drilling

☐ **PREP**
Assemble tools and materials, prepare a large work area, prepare installation site

MATERIALS NEEDED

Part	Finished size T	W	L	Mat.	Qty.	Part	Finished size T	W	L	Mat.	Qty.
CABINET						**UPPER DOORS**					
A side	¾"	19⁷⁄₁₆"	94"	LP	1	J rails	¾"	1½"	12¾"	PL	4
B side	¾"	18⁵⁄₈"	94"	LP	1	K stiles	¾"	1½"	34½"	PL	4
C shelf blanks	¾"	12⁵⁄₈"	25³⁄₈"	LP	7	L panels	¼"	10¾"	35½"	BP	2
D side cleats	¾"	¾"	6"	Pine	14	M center stile	¼"	1½"	34½"	PL	2
FACE FRAME						**LOWER DOORS**					
E side stiles	¾"	2½"	87"	PL	2	N rails	¾"	1½"	12¾"	PL	4
F upper center stile	¾"	1½"	36½"	PL	1	O stiles	¾"	1½"	45"	PL	4
G lower center stile	¾"	1½"	47"	PL	1	P panels	¼"	10¾"	46"	BP	2
H rails	¾"	3½"	30"	PL	2	Q center stile	¼"	1½"	45"	PL	2
I center rail	¾"	3½"	25"	PL	1	**TRIM**					
						R top trim	¼"	3½"	31½"	PL	1
						S shoe molding	¾"	¾"	31½"	Pine	1

Material key: LP—lauan plywood, BP—birch plywood, PL—poplar
Hardware: Eight semi-concealed hinges, four magnetic catches, four handles or knobs, 1¼-inch coarse-thread drywall screws, 1½-inch coarse-thread drywall screws, 4d finishing nails, 1½-inch brads, pocket-hole screws
Supplies: Edge banding veneer, glue, 80-grit sandpaper, paint, ¼-inch dowels

CORNER LINEN CABINET

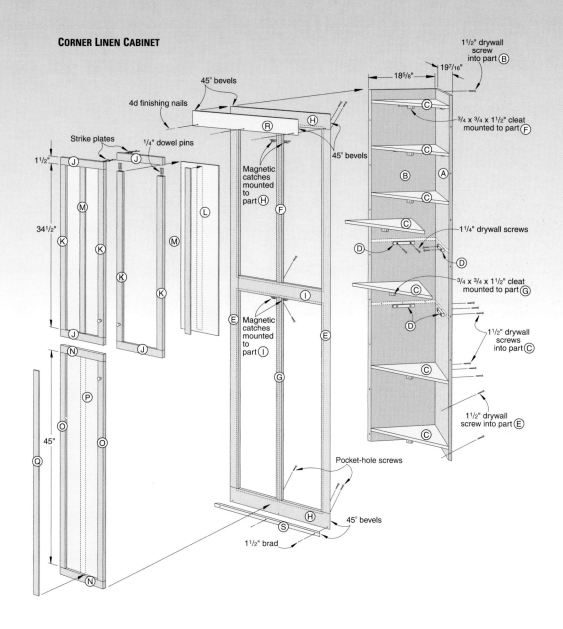

45° bevels

4d finishing nails

Strike plates

1/4" dowel pins

1 1/2"

Magnetic
catches
mounted
to
part (H)

45° bevels

Magnetic
catches
mounted
to
part (I)

34 1/2"

45"

Pocket-hole screws

1 1/2" brad

45° bevels

18 5/8"

19 7/16"

1 1/2" drywall
screw
into part (B)

3/4 x 3/4 x 1 1/2" cleat
mounted to part (F)

1 1/4" drywall screws

3/4 x 3/4 x 1 1/2" cleat
mounted to part (G)

1 1/2" drywall
screws
into part (C)

1 1/2" drywall
screw into part (E)

A. Make the cabinet

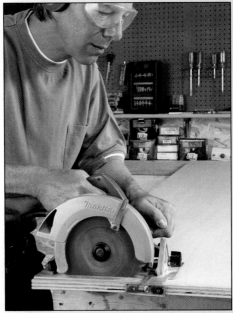

1 Set the rip guide on the circular saw to cut 2 inches wide, including the kerf (page 220). Cut off one end of a sheet of ¾-inch lauan plywood leaving you a 94-inch sheet for the sides (A and B).

2 Set your tablesaw fence to 19⁷⁄₁₆ inches and tilt the blade 45 degrees. With someone to help support the plywood, rip the sheet to make side A. You could make the cut with a circular saw set to 45 degrees and guided by a straightedge.

3 Set the blade to 90 degrees and set the fence to 18⅝ inches. Put the beveled side of the remaining piece against the fence with the bevel's point on top, then rip side B. With a circular saw and straightedge, it's better to leave the factory edge square and recut the beveled side.

CUTTING DIAGRAM

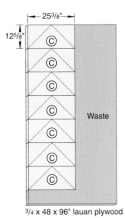

³⁄₄ x 48 x 96" lauan plywood

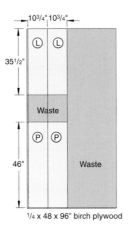

³⁄₄ x 48 x 96" lauan plywood

¼ x 48 x 96" birch plywood

BEVEL'S POINT ON TOP
Avoid dangerous kickback

Whenever you rip with a beveled edge against the fence, make sure the bevel's point is the top of the board. If the point were at the bottom it could get wedged under the rip fence, ruining the cut and possibly causing dangerous kickback.

4 Have a helper hold side B upright while you stand on a stepladder to apply glue to the long square edge. Put side A in place and make sure its edge is flush with the back of B as you join the pieces with 1½-inch drywall screws spaced about 12 inches apart.

5 Check the inside dimensions of the cabinet. Because plywood thickness can vary, you might have to slightly adjust the shelf dimensions *(below right)*. Rip a sheet of ¾-inch lauan plywood to 25⅜ inches for the shelf blanks (C). Then set the fence to 12⅝ inches to rip the blanks to width.

6 Lay out the triangular shelves on the blanks as shown in the drawing *below*. Set the miter gauge on your tablesaw to the 45-degree mark to the left of 90 degrees. Put the gauge in the slot to the right of the blade and make one cut on each blank.

WHAT IF...
You have tall ceilings?

This cabinet is 94 inches tall so you can easily maneuver it into place under an 8-foot ceiling. (A trim board covers the gap.) If your ceiling is taller, you can purchase a 10-foot-long panel of hardwood plywood for sides A and B. Depending on species, you may have to order the panels at a lumberyard. Be prepared to wait until the yard's next delivery from the supplier.

RIP THE BLANKS TO WIDTH
Start with smaller pieces

It's dangerous and awkward to make a narrow cut across a full-length plywood panel. Instead, do a little math and rough-cut the panel near the middle first with a circular saw. In this case, four shelf blanks need 50½ inches plus ½ inch for four kerfs. If you cut the sheet at 51½ inches to be safe, that leaves 44½ inches, plenty for the remaining three panels.

TRIANGULAR SHELF

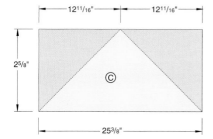

12¹¹/₁₆" 12¹¹/₁₆"

2⅝"

ⓒ

25³/₈"

A. Make the cabinet *(continued)*

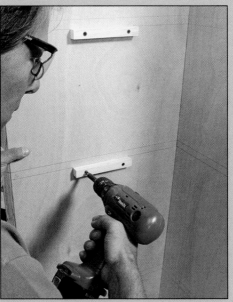

7 Reset your miter gauge to the 45-degree mark on the right side of 90 degrees. Put the gauge in the slot to the left of the blade and make the second cut to complete the shelf triangles.

8 Cover the front edges of the shelves with edge-banding veneer (page 44). Lay out the positions of the shelves on the sides as shown in the drawing *below left*. Extend the lines around the outside of the cabinet to help locate screws later when you install the shelves.

9 Rip and crosscut side cleats (D) to the dimensions listed. Predrill and countersink two holes in each cleat. With glue and 1¼-inch drywall screws, attach a side cleat under each shelf location, 6 inches from the back of the cabinet.

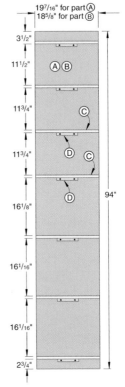

SHELF POSITION

19⁷/₁₆" for part Ⓐ
18⁵/₈" for part Ⓑ

3¹/₂"
11¹/₂"   Ⓐ Ⓑ
11³/₄"   Ⓒ
11³/₄"   Ⓓ   Ⓒ
         Ⓓ
16¹/₈"   94"
16¹/₁₆"
16¹/₁₆"
2³/₄"

STANLEY PRO TIP: **Label parts with sticky notes**

You should always label parts as you cut them. You can mark the parts in pencil, but the marks can be hard to find and you'll have to sand them off for finishing. Use sticky notes instead to label the parts. They come off easily and don't leave adhesive residue on the wood.

B. Assemble the face frame

10 Apply glue to the top of a pair of cleats and install a shelf. Drive three 1½-inch drywall screws through each cabinet side into the shelf. Install the remaining shelves the same way.

👆 **PREDRILL AND COUNTERSINK**
The right bit makes the job simple and neat

The #6 adjustable counterbore bit shown is the size you'll need to predrill and countersink drywall screws. Loosen the setscrew to set the bit 1 inch from the countersink depth to drive 1¼-inch screws flush to the surface.

Part E
Cut does not extend into front face.

1 Rip and crosscut poplar to make the face frame parts E through I. Set the tablesaw blade to 45 degrees and bevel one back edge of each side stile (E) and the ends of the rails (H). Be careful not to reduce the front face dimensions of the pieces.

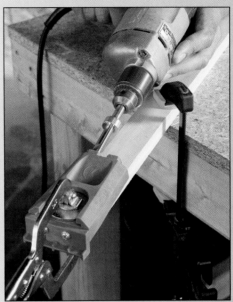

2 Use glue and pocket-hole joinery to join the parts (page 64). Use two pocket-hole screws for each joint to attach the rails (H and I) to stiles and one screw at each joint to attach the center stiles (F and G) to rails.

3 Lay the frame face down. Apply glue to the edges of the cabinet sides, top, bottom, and middle shelf. With someone to help, place the cabinet on the face frame. Make sure the stiles extend equally past both cabinet sides. Drive 1¼-inch screws every 12 inches straight into countersunk holes through the back and into the stiles.

4 Turn the cabinet on one side. Add a pocket-hole screw through the bottom of each shelf into the center stile. Drive screws into the middle of the rail for the top, bottom, and middle shelf.

C. Make the doors

1 Rip and crosscut poplar to make the door rails and stiles (J, K, M, N, O, and Q). Use glue and two ¼-inch-diameter dowels (page 59) at each joint to join the stiles to the rails. Clamp the joints with bar clamps.

3 Rip and crosscut ¼-inch birch plywood to make four door panels (L and P). Apply glue in the rabbets and press the panels in place. Turn the doors over and wipe off any glue squeeze-out.

2 Put a ½-inch piloted rabbeting bit in the router and set the depth to ¼ inch. Rout clockwise around the inside of all the rails and stiles. Square the rounded corners of the rabbets with a chisel.

4 When the glue has cured, mark each rail at the center of the door panel. Mark center points on the ends of the ¼-inch-thick center stiles (M and Q). Align the marks and glue the stiles to the panels.

D. Install the doors

1 To locate the hinges on the doors, lay out lines across the back of each left stile 2 inches from each end. Position semi-concealed hinges on the lines and screw them to the backs of the doors.

2 The doors will overlap the face frame by ½ inch on all sides. To locate the doors, set a combination square to ½ inch and draw guide lines around the opening, ½ inch from it. Have someone help align the door on the lines while you predrill hinge holes in the stiles.

E. Finish and install

1 Remove the hinges from the doors to paint the cabinet. Rip stock for the top trim (R) but leave it long for now. Smooth all the solid wood parts with 80-grit sandpaper, slightly rounding the edges. Prepaint the top trim along with about 3 feet of shoe molding.

2 If there is baseboard in the corner, carefully remove it. Put the cabinet in place. Cut the baseboard at 45 degrees to butt into the cabinet, then reinstall it.

3 Measure across the top of the cabinet and cut 45-degree angles on the top trim to fit. Remember, your measurement is for the back of the miters—the front will be 1½ inches longer. Cut the shoe molding to fit the same way.

4 Put the trim piece against the ceiling. Predrill holes and attach the trim piece to the face frame with 4d finishing nails. Attach the shoe molding with 1½-inch brads. Replace the doors and touch up the paint.

5 You can use any door pulls or knobs that suit your taste and décor. Center them across and along the stiles. Screw magnetic catches under the top for the top doors and under the shelf below the middle shelf for the bottom doors. Attach the mating metal plates to the inside of the doors.

WHAT IF...
There are gaps on the sides?

Walls often aren't plumb or perfectly flat so there may be small gaps on the sides. Cover them with a thin flexible molding—¾-inch cove molding works well.

GLOSSARY

Air-dry: Describes sawn lumber that has not been artificially seasoned; a moisture content of about 12 percent.

Arbor: A rotating metal shaft on a woodworking machine to which another rotating part, usually a bit or blade, is attached.

Banding: Solid wood trim attached to plywood edges to conceal plies.

Bevel: An angle formed along the edge or end of a piece of wood that extends from face to face.

Biscuit joint: A joint that uses wooden wafers glued into slots cut in edges of mating pieces.

Board foot: The volume measurement of hardwood lumber, calculated by multiplying length times width times thickness in inches and dividing by 144.

Bore: To drill a large hole.

Bow: A warp in which the ends of a board both curve in a direction away from the desired plane.

Brad-point: A type of drill bit with two cutting edges and a guiding centerpoint.

Break: The action of sanding wood edges to remove sharpness.

Burl: The swirling figure in wood grain caused by growths on the outside of the tree or root.

Carcase: The box-like component of a cabinet or bookcase that surrounds and encloses its doors, drawers, or shelves.

Chamfer: An angle formed along the edge or end of a board that does not extend from face to face.

Check: A small split in the end of a board; a drying defect.

Collet: A device that positions and secures a bit to the shaft in a router.

Counterbore: A screw hole deep enough to accept a wooden plug after the screw is in place.

Countersink: A drilled hole that fits the shape of a wood screw.

Crosscut: A cut across the grain that reduces material to a desired length.

Cutter: A blade or bit that cuts wood.

Dado (groove): A channel cut in wood that runs across the grain. A groove is a channel that runs with the grain.

Dowel: A cylindrical piece of wood, often a joint reinforcement.

Dry-fit: Preliminary joining of wood assemblies without glue to check fit.

Edge grain: The edge of a board that was flat (plain) sawn perpendicular to the growth rings.

End grain: The porous wood at the ends of a board.

Face frame: A four-piece wooden assembly attached to the front of a cabinet.

Face grain: The pattern of the grain on the largest surface of a board.

Featherboard: A kerfed safety device, usually of wood, that holds a board securely against a tablesaw or router table fence.

Feed: The action of moving wood into a machine, such as a tablesaw.

FHWS: Abbreviation for flathead wood screw.

Figure: The visible arrangement of wood grain in a pattern.

Forstner bit: A patented bit for drilling holes that do not fully penetrate the wood and leave a flat-bottomed hole.

Frame-and-panel: A construction technique where a wooden frame holds a floating wooden panel.

Grain direction: The direction in which the dominating, elongated fibers lie in a piece of sawn wood.

Green: Undried wood. Green wood still contains most of the moisture it had when cut and milled.

Heartwood: The usually darker, mature wood at a tree's center.

Hone: To refine and polish a cutting edge against a hard, slightly abrasive surface or material.

Jig: A device that holds a workpiece or tool in a certain way to efficiently and accurately saw or shape wood.

Joining: Permanently fastening one piece of wood to another.

Jointing: The technique of using a machine (jointer) or hand plane to create two surfaces perfectly perpendicular to each other, such as the edge of a board to its face.

Kerf: The slot left by a saw blade as it cuts through material.

Kiln-dry: Describes artificially seasoned wood with a moisture content of 6-9 percent.

Make-up: Edge-joining smaller pieces of wood to obtain wider panels.

Miter: An angle, often 45-degrees, cut across the grain on a piece of wood.

Moisture content: The percentage, by weight, of moisture in wood.

Molding: Shaped wood used as trim.

Mortise: An opening cut in a piece of wood to accept a mating piece of wood (tenon).

Nominal: The generic dimension of sawn lumber, e.g. 2×4; a nominal 2×4 actually measures less, 1½×3½ inches.

Open time: The interval between application of adhesive and when it can no longer be worked; also called working time.

Outfeed: The exit of wood from a machine, such as a tablesaw.

Pilot: A guide, such as on a router bit.

Pilot hole: A hole drilled to guide a screw into wood.

Plunge cut: Starting a saw in wood away from an edge.

Pocket-hole: A joining technique that employs screws driven into holes drilled at an angle.

Push stick: A safety device used to feed wood into a saw blade.

Rabbet: A channel sawn or formed on the edge of a board or panel.

Rail: One of the two horizontal pieces in a face frame.

Resaw: To saw a thick board into thinner ones without reducing length or width.

RHWS: Abbreviation for roundhead wood screw.

Rip-cut: To reduce a wide board by sawing with the grain; a cut along the long dimension of a sheet or panel.

Rout: Shaping or cutting wood with a router and bit.

Sapwood: The new, outermost wood in the trunk of a tree; the usually lighter-colored wood in a board.

Slot cutter: A router bit designed to cut a slot in the edge of a board.

Square: Surfaces or parts that meet at a 90-degree angle.

Squeeze-out: The thin ribbon of glue forced out of a clamped joint.

Stile: One of the two vertical pieces in a face frame.

Stop block: A piece of wood clamped in place to limit the sawn length of a board.

Stopped cut: A channel (dado, groove, or rabbet) that does not exit the wood at an edge or end.

Straightedge: A metal or wood implement clamped to the workpiece to ensure a straight cut.

Tenon: The tongue-like extension cut on the end of a piece of wood to fit into a mating mortise.

Toe-kick: The wood part that is recessed beneath a cabinet base.

Veneer: Thin sheets or strips of solid wood.

Warp: Distortion of a board due to uneven drying.

Waste: Solid wood and residue left after wood has been cut or machined.

Workpiece: A board or piece of wood being made into a project part.

INDEX

METRIC CONVERSIONS

U.S. Units to Metric Equivalents			Metric Units to U.S. Equivalents		
To convert from	Multiply by	To get	To convert from	Multiply by	To get
Inches	25.4	Millimeters	Millimeters	0.0394	Inches
Inches	2.54	Centimeters	Centimeters	0.3937	Inches
Feet	30.48	Centimeters	Centimeters	0.0328	Feet
Feet	0.3048	Meters	Meters	3.2808	Feet
Yards	0.9144	Meters	Meters	1.0936	Yards
Square inches	6.4516	Square centimeters	Square centimeters	0.1550	Square inches
Square feet	0.0929	Square meters	Square meters	10.764	Square feet
Square yards	0.8361	Square meters	Square meters	1.1960	Square yards
Acres	0.4047	Hectares	Hectares	2.4711	Acres
Cubic inches	16.387	Cubic centimeters	Cubic centimeters	0.0610	Cubic inches
Cubic feet	0.0283	Cubic meters	Cubic meters	35.315	Cubic feet
Cubic feet	28.316	Liters	Liters	0.0353	Cubic feet
Cubic yards	0.7646	Cubic meters	Cubic meters	1.308	Cubic yards
Cubic yards	764.55	Liters	Liters	0.0013	Cubic yards

To convert from degrees Fahrenheit (F) to degrees Celsius (C), first subtract 32, then multiply by ⅝.

To convert from degrees Celsius to degrees Fahrenheit, multiply by ⅝, then add 32.